Library of
Davidson College

JOURNAL FOR THE STUDY OF THE OLD TESTAMENT
SUPPLEMENT SERIES

32

Editors
David J.A. Clines
Philip R. Davies

Department of Biblical Studies
The University of Sheffield
Sheffield S10 2TN
England

THE PROPHETIC PERSONA

Jeremiah and the
Language of the Self

Timothy Polk

Journal for the Study of the Old Testament
Supplement Series 32

To my family, for holding fast,
and to the memory of my father

Copyright © 1984 JSOT Press

Published by
JSOT Press
Department of Biblical Studies
The University of Sheffield
Sheffield S10 2TN
England

Printed in Great Britain
by Redwood Burn Ltd.,
Trowbridge, Wiltshire.

British Library Cataloguing in Publication Data

Polk, Timothy
 The prophetic persona : Jeremiah and the
 language of the self.—(Journal for the
 study of the Old Testament supplement series,
 ISSN 0309-0787; 32)
 1. Bible. O.T. Jeremiah—Commentaries
 I. Title   II. Series
 224'.206   BS1525.3

ISBN 0-905774-70-1
ISBN 0-905774-71-X Pbk

CONTENTS

Chapter 1 AN INTRODUCTION
BIOGRAPHICAL INTEREST: THE PROBLEM AND
ITS APPROACHES   7

Chapter 2
THE METAPHOR OF THE HEART AND THE
LANGUAGE OF THE SELF   25

Chapter 3
THE 'HEART' IN CONTEXT: JER 4 AND THE
ENACTMENT OF IDENTITY   35

Chapter 4
THE PROPHETIC 'I' AND ITS AMBIGUITIES:
SELF-IDENTIFICATION AND THE PORTRAIT OF A
PARADIGM   58

Chapter 5
THE CONFESSIONS: THE PROPHET AS EXEMPLAR
AND METAPHOR   127

Chapter 6
SUMMARY AND CONCLUDING HERMENEUTICAL
REFLECTIONS   163

Notes   175
Bibliography   217
Indexes   227

Chapter 1

AN INTRODUCTION

BIOGRAPHICAL INTEREST:
THE PROBLEM AND ITS APPROACHES

Nothing distinguishes the book of Jeremiah from earlier works of prophecy quite so much as the attention it devotes to the person of the prophet and the prominence it accords the prophetic 'I', and few things receive more scholarly comment. The introductions typically observe that we learn more of Jeremiah's life and personality than of any other prophet's, thanks to the abundance of both third and first-person materials.[1] From the theologian's side, Gerhard von Rad, discussing the third-person narratives, speaks of a 'shift in the centre of interest from the message to the messenger', a shift which 'is in fact characteristic of the whole tradition connected with Jeremiah'; and of the first-person poetic material, von Rad observes that it forces upon us the question of 'how . . . to evaluate this remarkably large increase of the element of pure poetry'.[2] With a somewhat different emphasis Walther Eichrodt points out that in Jeremiah 'the personalism of the prophetic preaching reached its definitive form', fashioning 'a new life-relationship between the community and the individual'. He adds, in words that reflect the importance with which he regards the subject:

> How in the life [of Jeremiah] the false pretensions of personality advanced by the spiritual attitude of his times were broken, and a new personal nature awakened to life through repentance and forgiveness, can be seen supremely in his [first-person] Confessions and in the [third-person] narratives of his friend and disciple Baruch. To this great experience of the prophet, however, was added another, namely that this personal I, which was delivered up to death by God's hand, but also sustained and restored by him, was granted a new relationship with God which even the with-

drawal... of the collective guarantees of God's nearness, the national community and the Temple congregation could not destroy.[3]

The relation between the book's biographical interest and this 'personal I' of which Eichrodt speaks will be the focus of our study. More specifically, our task will be to trace the picture drawn of the prophet by the first-person poetic, so-called autobiographical, passages and to describe the function this picture performs. The approach will be intensive rather than extensive, however, and only selected passages will be subjected to a close reading. Chapters 2 and 3 will focus on Jer 4.19, Chapter 4 on Jer 8.18–9.25, 10.19-25 and 14.1–15.4, while Chapter 5 will treat two of the Confessions, 17.12-18 and 20.7-18.

The effort is required on two counts: 1. More often than not the prophet's self-portrait is described in general terms and, as it were, from a distance; rarely is it subjected to a close exegetical scrutiny and its particular lines traced in detail, at least in the manner undertaken here (to be described shortly). 2. Relatedly, and as evidenced by the scholarly comments, both the description and the assessment of the portrait can be governed by a variety of interests, few of which are entirely compatible. Theological interests invariably become entwined with questions of literary and religious history, questions even of the history of consciousness. The entwining may be quite necessary, but it must be carefully controlled, for when the different modes of discourse get mixed, category confusions frequently ensue. It is here hoped that by seeking first the intention of the text in its first-person portraiture and by pursuing the logic of the text's status as canonical scripture of Synagogue and Church, our exegesis might avoid, perhaps also disentangle, some of the confusions. Prior to the exegesis, however, the disentangling must begin with several particularly urgent conceptual and methodological clarifications. These have to do with, first, a distinction between the Jeremiah of history and the Jeremiah rendered by the text and, second, the concept 'self'.

Historical Figure vs. Literary Persona—Synchrony and Intentionality

The distinction is nothing new to Jeremiah scholarship. A product of historical-critical inquiry, it is a specific instance of what Hans Frei has described as the general breakdown in the pre-critical equation of historical reality with biblical depiction–a breakdown not incidentally

1. Biographical Interest

accompanied by a shift in how the text's meaning is conceived, i.e. from meaning conceived as 'explicative sense' (the text means what it says) to meaning as historical reference (the text means what it refers to).[4] The resulting difficulty is not so much that we have two Jeremiahs but, because the shift was extraordinarily subtle and could therefore itself escape critical reflection, that only one, the historical figure, has received adequate attention. The other, the biblically depicted Jeremiah, has been virtually forgotten.

This neglect will be chronicled throughout our study, but here it can be best illustrated in works of the 'life and times' variety that proliferated in the first part of the present century.[5] A continuation of the biographical explosion in the nineteenth century ('more notable for quantity of production than quality of workmanship'),[6] and reflecting the Carlyle—Toynbee 'great man' theory of history, such works as Rudolf Kittel's *Great Men and Movements in Israel* and Fleming James's *Personalities of the Old Testament* sought to employ the critical methods to illuminate the prophet's lasting religious significance. This significance Kittel was inclined to describe in terms like these:

> We owe this man almost more for the insight he has given us into his own soul than for all he did and said... [H]e did an immortal service to the world's literature and all people who love to meditate upon the souls of the great men of the past.[7]

The rather vague religious humanism seen here, one of the characteristic traits of the age, sometimes combined with another characteristic trait, sentimentality:

> It is touching to see how Jeremiah cannot leave God. As a lover sighs for love which makes him unhappy but without which he cannot do, so he would like to free himself from Yahweh's service but cannot. His lot with Yahweh is hard, but without him he is in danger of pining away.[8]

Both traits distort the portrait and its purpose.

James's theological interests were more explicitly defined. His work was designed to recapture the Old Testament's spiritual value, to allow it to perform its proper function, to

> speak to us so that we today may perceive God addressing us personally, searching our hearts and consciences, convicting us of sin, calling us to faith and trust, awakening in us love, inspiring us

with hope, illuminating us with insight, strengthening us for our tasks, in short, making us aware of Himself and of His profound interest in each one of us.[9]

By showing 'that it is in the personalities of the Old Testament that the truth becomes instinct with life and power', James believed he could prompt us to 'put ourselves into the various situations with inward participation', to 'recreate in our imagination vividly the scenes and experiences portrayed by... story-teller, poet, and prophet'.[10] In light of the avowed concern with scripture's spiritual intent, it is all the odder that James decides to draw his information on Jeremiah from only those classes of material, the memoirs of Baruch and the oracles of the prophet himself, deemed to be 'reliable' and 'genuine'.[11] Thus, it is not really the personality *of* the text that James wants to show but the personality *behind* it (and behind only part of it), and the 'scenes and experiences portrayed by story-teller, poet, and prophet', in which we are to participate inwardly, must first be authenticated and then rearranged.

In short, Kittel and James both recognize—and this is extremely important, however obvious—that the book of Jeremiah is religious literature, that it intends a religious function, and therefore that Jeremiah is religiously significant; but they also recognize that the book is not true biography (or autobiography) by modern standards (which require chronologically sequential depiction and historical reliability). Consequently, Kittel and James approach the text primarily as a collection of sources from which to construct their *own* biographies of the prophet, and they end up identifying his religious significance in a way that the text can only very remotely begin to regulate. It seems never to occur to them that the textual depiction is itself worth exploring or that it might have its own theo-logic and religious agenda. As indicated before, this study will attempt to redress the imbalance by attending to the prophet *as depicted in the text*. Regarding this depicted Jeremiah as to some extent a literary-theological construct, we shall, to avoid confusion, refer to him as the prophetic 'persona'.

The approach taken by Kittel and James, along with its inherent weaknesses and potential confusions, was by no means limited to the more popular works of the genre; it extended as well to the very best, namely John Skinner's *Prophecy and Religion: Studies in the Life of Jeremiah*. Skinner, too, used the text as a source for reconstructing a fuller picture of the prophet. Further, he valued it, and recognized it

1. Biographical Interest

as meaningful, to the extent that it referred to actual events, to real experiences in the life of the real Jeremiah. In this he shared in the dominant (historicist) hermeneutic of the day. At the same time he accorded the text a higher degree of referential reliability than many recent form critics would allow.[12] Skinner was fully confident, for example, that the commissioning sequence of Jer 1 reflected (referred to) the formative moments in Jeremiah's actual career, even while acknowledging the separate and later origins of the prose vision reports that make up half the chapter.[13] An excessive confidence, in other words, may have led him into the category mistake of treating as a historical report what is actually a literary construction designed by redactors 'to present an interpretative introduction to the book'.[14]

What may be even more significant than a wrong assessment of the material's historical reliability, however, is the fact that Skinner then uses this assessment as the basis for a psychological redescription—bordering on a demythologization—of the 'events' and a filled-out biographical sketch rooted no more in the text than in an idealist metaphysics and a *religionsgeschichtliche* thesis. For illustration, consider the following:

> We may now sum up the impressions which this whole narrative [Jer 1] conveys of our prophet's character and individuality. Jeremiah comes before us here in the freshness of his youth, modest and shrinking from publicity, and as one whose days have been 'bound each to each by natural piety'. He knows already something of what it means to be a prophet, and is familiar with the writings and thoughts of Hosea. He is awakening to the consciousness that the times call for another such voice to bring men to a sense of realities. A foreboding of coming doom, a conviction that all is not well between Israel and Yahweh, has taken possession of him and cut him off from the innocent gaieties and pleasures of youth. He is subject to moods of visionary abstraction, in which spiritual things take bodily shape before the inner eye. In one such hour the call of God comes to him with irresistible power; and after a momentary hesitation he yields to its constraint, and is filled with a new inflexible courage which makes him as a wall of brass against all the assaults of an unbelieving world.
>
> In all this we have already an indication of the course which his religious development was to follow. The conviction that he was predestined to be a prophet in itself suggests the consciousness of a broader and more human relation to God than is involved in the call to a special work; and the suggestion is confirmed by his

peculiar response to the divine summons. It is as if the sense of vocation appealed only to one side which cries out in protest against it . . .

. . . Of that protracted inward agony [created by the conflict between 'the natural affections of the heart and the imperative mandate of the divine word'] there are many poignant expressions in Jeremiah's later poems, and in these we shall find the key to the significance of his personality as the first great exponent of individual and universal religion.[15]

However much one may find such redescriptions heuristically helpful, or perhaps hermeneutically necessary, the important point is that Skinner's sketch of the prophet is *not* the same as the text's (especially with respect to the significance he assigns the prophet, as our ensuing chapters will demonstrate).[16] It follows that doing theology on the basis of the former can be a radically different task, and can have radically different results, from doing it on the basis of the latter. But indeed, Skinner's exegetical sketch is already a sort of theology, and not simply a preparation for it.

Skinner's study was ostensibly historical in design; that is, it proposed to describe 'the peculiar function of prophecy in the Old Testament'.[17] However, the *thesis* was supra-historical. As Skinner acknowledged, it was essentially Wellhausen's way of doing history that he adopted, a way in which a clearly formulated (theological) conclusion stands at the beginning:

> Why the perfect religion should have sprung from the bosom of a national faith is a question on which it is idle to speculate. But accepting the fact as we find it, we can see that the final mission of prophecy was to liberate the eternal truths of religion from their temporary national embodiment, and disclose their true foundation in the immutable character of God and the essential nature of man.[18]

Hence, it was only natural to discover that 'Jeremiah's specific greatness lies in the sphere of personal religion':

> The strongly marked emotionalism of his temperament is not to be regarded as a weakness or an impediment, but as the endowment of a spirit touched to fine issues, and perhaps a necessary condition of the heart to converse with God which unsealed within him the perennial fount of true piety,—the religious susceptibility of the individual soul . . .

1. Biographical Interest

> Now this discovery of individual fellowship with God which is Jeremiah's great contribution to the religious experience of the Jewish Church is also the clue to his own spiritual biography.[19]

It is a fearful symmetry, if not a vicious circularity, to which this last sentence points: Jeremiah's spiritual breakthrough into personal religion is not only seen as *the* significant datum derivable from an historical analysis of the text; it is also the *point* of the text.

It will be argued in this essay that 'piety' is indeed an important part of the text's identity description of the prophet, though scarcely in the manner Skinner imagines it to be. The analysis of the persona's first-person speech will show that 'personal religion', in the sense of 'individual fellowship with God', is *assumed* by the text, not argued or justified as something new and unheard of, and moreover that the text indicates nothing of the categorical opposition implied by Skinner between personal and corporate, or 'national', religion *per se*. Rather, the prophet's person is always depicted in terms of his vocation, which is fully corporate in orientation, and the public vocation always involves him at a level most personal. There are, in short, two wrong sides to a false issue here, and along with Skinner's we shall have occasion (Chapters 4 and 5) to confront the other side which totally disparages the personal in Jeremiah's faith and being in order to emphasize the corporate. Finally, it should be apparent that the problems which we shall have to face are here a function of Skinner's having virtually identified a *religionsgeschichtliche* issue with the subject matter of the text and then interpreting the text to illustrate his *religionsgeschichtliche* thesis. If we wish to do justice to the Jeremiah persona, a more inductive approach than Skinner's is required, one less inclined to hastily redescribe the text in terms so different from the text's own.

Also required is an exegesis less dominated by an historical interest. As indicated before, the biographical reconstructions of the 'life and times' variety are just one way that an historical interest has dominated the exegetical effort. Another, seen in those studies that attempt to reconstruct the book (i.e. to describe the course of the book's formation), will provide the dialogue partners for much of the remainder of this essay. Again, the hermeneutical bias in both enterprises is to treat meaning as reference, and to read any given passage primarily in terms of its historical referentiality, whether by asking what it tells us about the historical Jeremiah, his school, and his age, or by asking where the passage fits in the chronological and sociological scheme of the book's composition, or both. In place of this history-interested approach, which we shall refer to as 'diachronic', we propose to offer an exegesis that is 'synchronic' in orientation. The terminology merits explanation.

'Diachronic' and 'synchronic' are key terms in the structural linguistics pioneered by Ferdinand de Saussure. Saussure conceived of language as 'a system of relations and oppositions whose elements must be defined in formal, differential terms'.[20] Of our terms, one is more appropriate for such definition than the other. Jonathan Culler explains:

> The relations between individual units and their historical antecedents are irrelevant in that they do not define the units as elements of the system. The *synchronic* study of language is an attempt to reconstruct the system as a functional whole, to determine, shall we say, what is involved in knowing English at any given time; whereas the diachronic study of language is an attempt to trace the historical evolution of its elements through various stages. The two must be kept separate lest the diachronic point of view falsify one's synchronic description. For example, historically the French noun *pas* (step) and the negative adverb *pas* derive from a single source, but that relationship has no function in modern French, where they are distinct words that behave in different ways. To try to incorporate the historical identity into one's grammar would be to falsify the relational value and hence the value that each of the words has in the language as now spoken. Language is a system of interrelated items and the value and identity of these items is defined by their place in the system rather than by their history.[21]

It is immediately evident that the structuralist perspective described here would place limits on the validity of, say, the comparative philological method. In fact, James Barr has criticized this method in terms quite similar to Culler's. Barr observes that the comparative philologist's predilection to think of meaning in terms of cognates 'has often tended to confuse the field of semantics' and that this predilection together with a heavy emphasis on etymology has frequently obscured the fact that 'the meaning of a word is its meaning in its own language, not its meaning in some other'.[22] These strictures should help to explain, among other things, the method chosen in Chapter 3 below for analyzing the terms *lēb*, 'heart', and *mēʿîm*, 'bowels', of Jer 4.19.

It may not be quite so evident how the structural linguistic

1. Biographical Interest

perspective relates to the analysis of whole texts. Clearly, application of the diachronic-synchronic distinction to matters of literary interpretation involves a metaphoric extension of its use.[23] In particular, to adopt a synchronic approach in the manner we propose is to view the Bible as a *literary* work. The Bible is more than that, to be sure, but it is at least that. As a literary work, it constructs its own world, which of course may not be one of total harmony and perfect congruity, but then few worlds are, literary or otherwise.[24] As such, as a work having a world whose parts share at minimum a family resemblance, the Bible is like a language—a 'system of relations', a 'functional whole'. Accordingly, the meaning of any of its parts depends on that part's relation to the whole more than 1. upon some datum of intention that is supposed to have existed in an author's mind at the time of composition, or 2. upon a reconstructed historical reference to something outside the world of the text, or 3. upon the part's function and meaning at a stage prior to the work's final shape. Each of these alternatives may be thought of as forms of etymologizing the text.[25] They also constitute the bulk of the category mistakes of which we have spoken: to the extent that a theological exegesis ought to illuminate the explicative sense of the text, the mistakes occur when, in Culler's terms, the diachronic point of view gets mixed with and consequently falsifies the synchronic description.

Certain other features in our exegesis follow from the synchronic orientation. If we view the text as in some sense a present, simultaneous whole, this is not to say that all modes of temporality are irrelevant to its analysis and understanding. Two in fact are especially important. The first is the temporal scheme delineated by the text itself, that which belongs to the world the text constructs. Consequently, we shall avoid replacing the text's chronology, to the extent that it provides any, with a 'corrected' one, for it is in the former that the prophetic persona lives, not the latter. The second is the temporality of the reading process, the temporality implicit in the very concept 'book' (or 'scroll'), the normative logic of which entails a sequential reading—front toward back, beginning toward end, one verse (and chapter) after another. Hence, we shall not avoid reading juxtaposed materials sequentially even though they may be generically and genetically different. It bears remembering that the meaning that tends to accrue from, say, two expressions which are ten verses apart can be quite different from that which accrues by thinking of them as being ten decades apart.

The synchronic orientation proposed here thus requires a broad shift in emphasis from the writing process and the period of composition onto the work itself and the reading process. A concern with the 'work itself' has of course become increasingly familiar in biblical studies;[26] the interest in the reading process somewhat less so.[27] However, the importance of the latter cannot be overestimated. Against any effort to equate meaning simply with an author's intention, or to locate it as residing *in* the text, we want to maintain that meaning only transpires when the *articulated* thought of one person is *heard* by another.[28] It is a process, in other words, something that happens *between* text and reader, and is incomplete in either an intention or a text taken by itself. We shall argue our case further in the last chapter. In the meantime our exegesis will attempt to take note of the conventions, expectations, and competencies that must be in place in the reader for the text to make sense in any given way. (And it might be noted at the outset that one of the things the text does *qua* religious literature is to fashion and train reader expectations and competences in particular ways.)

It is also a function of our synchronic approach that there will be (and has been already) occasional reference to the 'intention of the text'. For instance, we shall be explicating the identity of Jeremiah as 'intended by the text', not as reconstructed according to the modern canons of historiography. Or, we shall consider effects 'the text intends' to have upon its readers, e.g. the capacities it seeks to develop in the believer. This may well seem an odd locution, inappropriately anthropomorphic on the one hand, while on the other inconsistent with our refusal to equate intention with meaning and locate the latter *in* the text.

Certainly, 'the text intends' is an anthropomorphism; it is a metaphor and is used in all deliberateness as such. To be sure, texts are not people, and most of the things that people do texts do not— like feel sick, will improvement in their table manners, think about what to do tomorrow, walk, sleep, and suffer headaches. Still, they do *express* (sometimes we might even say 'entertain') willings, feelings, and thoughts. In this respect texts come very close to people, close enough in fact that we frequently allow ourselves the liberty of saying that a text *speaks*, that is *says* and *means* something (though of course only as it is read or 'heard'). When it comes to verbal communication, the similarities (and not just the causal relations) between texts and people spawn lots of metaphors, including those of intentionality.

1. Biographical Interest

But this is not to say that talking about a *text* intending something is the same as, or is reducible to, talking about its *author(s)* intending something. Again, the expression is a metaphor, constructed from discourse about people, but now used of texts, and so should not be viewed in any way as a disguised version of the intentional fallacy.[29] Indeed, it is designed to help shift the exegetical focus away from questions of authorship (where in biblical studies it has been too rigidly fixed too long) onto the text itself, and of course onto the reading process.

Now it is an important fact that a text can adopt or exhibit a disposition toward its subject matter, attain a voice, and effect through its structure, diction, and theme a meaning beyond what an author may have envisioned.[30] This is all the truer of a composite text like the Bible which has been centuries in the making at the hands of countless authors, editors, and the like, and when the issues are so relentlessly those of life and death, when deep calleth unto deep.[31] It is a case of the result being more than the sum of its parts, though that is too simple a formulation. To make guarded use of a New-Critical dictum, the finished text has a certain, not absolute, autonomy vis-à-vis its authors. To attend to the relation between various ingredients (like tone, diction, theme, and structure) and the resultant meaning is, in texts as in people, to explore intention. Talking about intention is a way of talking about the patterned production of meaning.

Even still, the anthropomorphism might be unacceptably odd *if* it were the case that 'intention' referred to something in the head, to a mental process or datum of consciousness, as if it were always and only locatable in conscious cogitation prior to an action, as if having an intention required having an awareness of it. Obviously, texts are not conscious of their intentions the way people can be. The important point is that people are not always conscious of their intentions either. The anthropomorphism might also be unusable *if* it were the case that intentions, (wrongly) conceived as 'something in the head', *caused* the actions that are their objects. But this notion is false too. Once we break the misleading, and pervasive, habit of thought that connects intention with consciousness and causality, the concept's applicability to texts turns out to be less ludicrous than one might at first have thought, depending on the circumstances.[32]

These circumstances should be specified. This will also provide an opportunity to demonstrate a kind of analysis in use throughout this study. In the 'ordinary language' philosophy associated with Ludwig Wittgenstein and his students, one tries to identify the mode of discourse, or 'language game', in which an expression functions; one describes the sort of activity in which it is most at home. The game governing 'the text intends' is that of exegeting passages whose meanings are in question. In particular, the phrase is most at home in situations of interpretive dispute where the question 'What is the text's point?' might be raised with some urgency. As part of the response to that question, the expression 'the text intends' represents a perspective that views the literature, again, synchronically, i.e. as a relatively coherent whole whose meaning is primarily a function of the internal relations among its parts, over against the diachronic perspective that regards meaning as adhering only to the text's (hypothetically reconstructed) independent parts, as bound to the (supposed) time of its composition, and as grounded in the (inferred) intentions of its (mostly anonymous) authors, while ignoring, dismissing as illegitimate, and/or leaving to homiletics the question of an overall coherence of the text in its completed form.

In sum, 'the text intends' is a shorthand way of saying that one reading is to be preferred to another on the basis of what is perceived as the text's comprehensive structure, thematic concerns, point(s) of view, tone, diction, and whatever other internal, literary features are deemed as relevant and recognized as impelling text and reader to 'the point'. In the present case the point is a depiction of the prophet that evokes a set of insights into God's purpose and a set of responses to his call.

Genre, the Concept 'Self', and the Pronoun 'I'

Common to the 'life and times' studies in Jeremiah scholarship was a certain indifference to matters of literary genre. Kittel, James, and Skinner were all, methodologically if not chronologically, pre-form-critical; although their investigations proceeded from the recognition that the book was not biographical in any strict sense, that recognition was, as we have said, an intuitive one unsupported by a direct generic scrutiny of the material. What one finds when genre does become an object of attention is that Jeremiah's personhood, including his quality as a self, also becomes an issue. At bottom, naturally, is what it means to be a self; several levels above that is the issue of what the scholarly discussion may have implied, inadvertently or otherwise,

1. Biographical Interest

about the appropriateness of using the concept 'self' in talking about Jeremiah.[33]

The correlation between a concern with genre and the issue of 'person'-related concepts is seen at once in Mowinckel, who no sooner raised the question of the book's biographical status than he concluded it in the negative. It is his explanation, however, that is interesting:

> A 'life of Jeremiah', a biography, he [the author/redactor] could not and would not write, simply because he lacked the conceptual condition for this, the concept of the *Bios*. The concept of a life as something produced out of a unitary development or borne by a unified character was lacking generally in the ancient orient. This concept cannot arise out of the fabric of purely mythic thought since in such climate what pertains is not the ruled nature of personality but magic and divine decree. Instead of the concept of the *Bios* there is the scheme of the heroic legend (e.g. Sargon, Moses).[34]

Apart from questioning the loose attribution to the ancient orient of 'purely mythic thought', we might wonder about the direction Mowinckel's thought actually took. Did he conclude that the book of Jeremiah is not biographical because the conceptual conditions were not right? Or did he rather conclude that the conceptual conditions were not right on the basis of having first recognized that the book was not (strictly) biographical? The latter procedure would be somewhat more problematic than the former, and we shall return to comment on this later. In the meantime we need only note that implicit in Mowinckel's terms for the conditions requisite to the concept of a life—i.e. the terms 'development', 'character', and 'ruled nature of personality'—are notions ingredient in the concept 'self': respectively, the notions of identity as an achievement, of the person as moral agent, and of behaviour as something internally ordered (neither random or externally compelled). Mowinckel, in other words, implies that Jeremiah's culture lacked the concept 'self'. We hope to show him wrong.

Mowinckel's negative assessment of the book's biographical status went largely uncontested until Klaus Baltzer's impressive form-critical study, *Die Biographie der Propheten*.[35] Baltzer's purpose was the same as characterized most of the preceding form-critical investigations of prophecy: he wanted to isolate that particular *Gattung* which most closely connected with prophetic tradition and in which

Israel's understanding of the prophet found its clearest and most direct expression: the quintessential prophetic genre.[36] He found it in what he termed the 'ideal biography', a form supposedly developed on the model of the installation reports and career biographies of the Egyptian viziers. Focusing on the public life of its subject, the ideal biography typically began with a report of the subject's installation into office, proceeded to an episode (or Holy War motif) confirming the installation and demonstrating the subject's charisma and fitness for the task, and went on to show him performing administrative, judicial, and cultic functions. Often it concluded with a notice about the subject's successor and sometimes his death.

Baltzer believes that the *Gattung* was current in pre-monarchic Israel, although the biographies of the early figures—Moses, Joshua, Gideon, Deborah, and Samuel—are in their present form thoroughly reworked and elaborated specimens.[37] However, this literary development is most significant for the shape of the prophetic corpus, for ultimately Baltzer's claim is that 'the greater unity of a prophetic book... is to be understood literarily as ideal biography'.[38] If it is the case, as I believe it to be, that both the general thesis and this specific claim are flawed, perhaps fatally, nevertheless, they come closest to hitting the mark with the book of Jeremiah.[39] At the very least, Baltzer's analysis successfully highlights (synchronic) literary features that run throughout the book, establish a conceptual coherence, and without question evince the biographical interest, if not exactly *Gattung*, that is central to the book's design.[40]

For the present, however, our main interest is how in Baltzer, as in Mowinckel, thinking about genre converges with thinking about selves. For example, at the very outset Baltzer qualifies the concept 'biography' by pointing out that the contemporary notion may not be applicable to the ancient situation wherein private life and the development of personal identity were of far less importance than one's public life and the performance of a social role or 'office'. Individual destiny would have been of less interest than the fact that one had contributed to the public good—though it would hardly have occurred to anyone in antiquity to make such a distinction, much less the comparison. The propensity to concentrate attention on public behavior inclined the ancient biographer to emphasize, however unwittingly, a subject's typicality, his quality as a type or model, at the expense of his particularity. Hence, in the oldest and purest example of the genre in the OT, 'the last words of David' in 2 Sam

1. Biographical Interest

23.1-7, historical particularity is almost completely subordinated to the stylized vision of an office and its proper execution. But as the genre developed over time, and the force of historical circumstance and the uniqueness of personal identity made themselves felt, such stylization yielded more and more to a particularizing depiction. Nevertheless, the former remained dominant: throughout the era the figure in Israelite biography was assimilated to the office or function he was called upon to perform, and was to that extent idealized. Naturally, chronology and sequential depiction were of little relevance to this conception of identity. The narrative mode was rather the illustrative vignette, the non-causal and atemporal juxtaposition of scenes portraying the figure's proper execution of the various aspects of his office. Such scenes can be thought of as the 'little stones with which one pieces together a mosaic'.[41]

Before all else we should acknowledge the importance of Baltzer's initial qualification. Judiciously put, and thoroughly insightful, it clearly exposes to criticism any views by which modern preferences in biographical approach are thought to adequately delimit the genre for all periods of history. Such views must in fact be met since they continue to muddle the problem in numerous ways.

Characterized by the notion that the 'pure' form of the genre explores a subject's particularity rather than his typicality, reveals character instead of describing action, and prefers interiority to mere externals—these views can be roughly identified as constituting a 'man-in-himself' school of biography, and as suffering two obvious and fundamental defects.[42] The first, which applies in some measure to Baltzer himself, is that (auto)biography, in either antiquity or the present, seems to be incorrigibly hybrid in nature, resistant to any strict and prescriptive definition in terms of form, dominant interest, or purpose.[43] In that a biographical 'interest' or autobiographical 'force' can be found within other well-established literary genres (e.g. Osborne's drama *Luther*), it becomes a good question how one tells at what point such interest or force achieves status as independent genre. Moses Hadas suggests, in appropriately broad and flexible terms, that it is simply when the personage comes to overshadow the story in which he figures.[44] A more objective criterion seems unlikely to emerge. In any case, under such conditions it makes little sense to speak of generic purity.

The second problem with the 'man-in-himself' definition is the presumption (or simply the half-conscious expectation) that the subject *can* be presented 'in himself', as if a certain unrelatedness between the private self and the public self were not only common, but normative for personhood, and as if character and action did not require reciprocal delineation.[45] But the concept 'self' entails a world which is constituted, at the very least, by a network of relations rooted in the self. The self can thus not be described apart from its world.[46] As Martin Kessler has observed, 'Not even modern writers can write "lives" in isolation, much less the ancient authors'.[47] The subject of biography is invariably a self in some capacity, and the motivation for the writing of a person's life is that he is deemed significant *as* something.[48] Luther, for example, is presented *as* son, *as* monk, *as* reformer.[49] Certainly, if in Jeremiah's identity his public role looms uncommonly large, if his personhood cannot be grasped apart from his vocation, that does not separate him qualitatively from many a more recent biographical subject.

In effect, Baltzer's qualification of the concept 'biography' is a corrective to a position based on an unbalanced, distinctly romantic (and restricted) notion of what is 'personal' about people. However, there is a danger that Baltzer's view of ancient personages can be misleading as well. In Mowinckel, for instance, it was exaggerated to an extraordinary degree. The fact is that the view is common to, and perhaps inherent in, the form-critical method—a method which takes as axiomatic a fundamental dichotomy between the ancient and modern world, and axioms can be overworked. Gunkel stated the position quite succinctly when he remarked that 'in ancient Israel personality, even in the case of an author, was far less developed... This is due to the fact that in antiquity the power of custom was far greater than it is in the modern world.'[50] The emphasis upon the convention-laden quality of ancient life and a consequent underdevelopment of personality has been maintained by recent form critics as well, such as Klaus Koch:

> In the ancient world the spoken and the written word kept far more closely to the established literary types than is usual today. Not only in pre-Christian Israel but throughout the whole pre-Christian world... the inclinations of the individual were much more controlled than they are in the West today. His entire life, from birth until death, was strictly regulated by custom and practice.

Koch adds, quoting Gunkel, 'In those days the individual was far more bound by custom and did not have the distinction he has today'.[51]

1. Biographical Interest

The measure of truth in these remarks is of great importance. The danger arises when the insight into the historically and culturally conditioned character of human thought is raised to the level of natural law and metaphysical principle so that diachrony utterly forecloses on synchrony. Then the various, oft-cited distinctions between ancient and modern people are transformed into a monolithic singular. Again, no one would dispute that there are many, but *specific*, modes of thought with which certain of the ancients were at home but which are alien to us, just as there are numerous questions of vital import to us that never would have occurred to them. Neither can anyone discount the impact of Enlightenment, Technology, and World War, or the profound influence of a Luther, Marx, Darwin, Freud, Einstein, *et alii*, on aspects of the mentality of our age. The crucial point is that the picture should not be falsified by imagining the cleft between old and new to be everywhere the same in depth and width, everywhere a virtual chasm, and by ignoring that there are places where in fact the cleft disappears because the structure of certain features of existence then and now is the same.

A major task of this essay, therefore, will be to chart several of those places where the cleft is not so great as both our critical methods and our uncritical habits of thought might lead us to believe. In particular, in the uses to which Jeremiah puts the first-person singular pronoun, we shall find evidence for that fundamentally similar structure of experience referred to above, evidence that would necessitate re-evaluating the remarks of even as sensitive and cautious a scholar as von Rad:

> The 'I' of which the prophets became conscious because Jahweh spoke to them differed both from the 'I' used by the oriental rulers of the period and, to an even greater degree, from the 'I' used by present-day Western man, the meaning of which has been so influenced by idealist philosophy and the romantic movement.[52]

What von Rad has overlooked is that present-day Western man has, as did his ancient counterpart, not just one 'I' but many, or rather an 'I' with a *variety* of uses, some of which have a primitive (in the sense of fundamental and pre-theoretical) logic and remain quite untouched by *any* philosophy or movement.[53] These uses are primitive in the sense that we do not so much learn them by virtue of the culture as we become members of the culture by virtue of learning them. Further, the primitive uses of 'I' may not always have an institutional, literary and theological expression within a culture, but they nevertheless attest a concept of the self. It would be a mistake to think that there is no concept just because there is no definition (or formal genre) for it. Thus, to return to our question about the direction of Mowinckel's thinking, we may note that while a concept of the self is indeed a prerequisite for telling one's life, telling one's life, (auto)biography, is not a condition for having a concept of the self.

Principal among the uses of 'I' in Jeremiah, it will be seen, is the expression of emotion. Attesting a self, Jeremiah's emotion-language will also be seen to attest a notable degree of interiority and particularity, a fact which should counteract any too-hasty or overdrawn generalizations about the corporate nature of personality in ancient Israel (see Chapters 2 and 4 below). Given the 'primitive' logic behind Jeremiah's 'I', not even the modestly-stated view of Baltzer—that particularity in depiction is but a function of the transformation of the ideal biography, or more broadly, a development in the history of consciousness—is adequate to describe the picture of a self that emerges in the book. In Chapter 5, as we observe how the Confessions render Jeremiah in a complex pattern of typicality and particularity, we shall seek to identify the interests and purposes that we feel *do* govern that picture.

Finally, we shall be arguing throughout the essay that emotion language not only attests a self, it is constitutive of the self. People become selves as they use such language, for using the language is essential to the exercise and development of the capacities for feeling, thought, and action which give the self definition and substance. These facts will have their point against certain conclusions that might be drawn (and in effect have been drawn) from the remarks of Gunkel and Koch above. It is a given that genre and convention must play an important role in the interpretation of biblical texts. It is much less clear that genre and convention reflect a restricted status of the concept 'self' in ancient Israel.[54] Accordingly, we shall take frequent note of the way conventional language can be used to express authentic emotion, and thereby constitute as well as reveal the prophetic persona's self.

Chapter 2

THE METAPHOR OF THE HEART
AND THE LANGUAGE OF THE SELF

The concern in the following pages is with the language that expresses a concept of the self. Three points may be summarized at the outset: 1. certain uses of language demonstrate that the user has a working concept of the self; 2. such a concept is itself formed in and by just such uses; and 3. such uses have a primary logical status (i.e. are independent of, or prior to, theory and metaphysical 'systems') in thinking and talking about people and who people are. In other words, it will be argued that for the purposes of explaining a particular range of behavior this language has a synchronic validity and irreducibility.

The discipline of Old Testament anthropology has traditionally been concerned with the language of the self and has provided many valuable studies, especially of the Hebrew concept 'heart', which H.W. Wolff calls 'the most important word in the vocabulary of Old Testament anthropology'.[1] This word, particularly as it occurs in Jeremiah, will occupy our attention presently. At the same time the orientation of its treatment in selected studies will be critically evaluated, especially with regard to its status as a metaphor.

Johannes Pedersen's monumental work, *Israel: Its Life and Culture*, provides a suitable starting point. This work has already been thoroughly critiqued by James Barr, who finds that it entails a highly suspect methodology. By Barr's analysis Pedersen begins from a psychological orientation, presupposing the distinctiveness of the Hebrew mentality and assuming that this 'must somehow be manifested in the linguistic phenomena'.[2] Pedersen thus explains certain linguistic peculiarities as reflections of that distinctive mentality, yet without considering other linguistic features that point in a different direction.³ To be sure, this strategy is reflected in Pedersen's notion of 'totality', which he thinks characterizes all Hebrew thought and in particular the Hebrew concept of the individual as simply an instantiation of 'the predominant type'.⁴

Despite the dubious generalization, however, Pedersen is surely right about the concept 'heart' (*lēb, lēbāb*) when he describes it as that which in summary fashion characterizes the basic shape and direction of a person's life. He speaks of it as designating 'the whole of the essence and character', as for instance when he describes Samson's heart as 'the whole of his peculiar stamp and essence, his strength and the conditions thereof—in short his being a Nazirite'.⁵ Pedersen is right, but not in virtue of something peculiar in the Hebrew mentality, rather because that is the way the term operates in certain modes of discourse, then as now. With this qualification, Pedersen seems to recognize 'heart' as a metaphor and to treat it in the particular way that we should like to construe 'metaphor': that is, as a highly compact expression for gathering up and magnifying a host of considerations (in the case of 'heart', specific feelings, emotions, passions, motives, intentions, and related capacities and competences) that have no other way of being meaningfully centered.⁶

Similar to Pedersen's notion of 'totality', but given a more systematic and, for the purposes of analyzing 'heart', misleading turn are the correlated concepts 'corporate personality' and 'diffusion of consciousness' which appear in the work of H. Wheeler Robinson⁷ and L.H. Brockington.⁸ By 'corporate personality' is meant 'the idea of a close relation, and for some purposes, an identity of the individual and the group to which he belongs'.⁹ Robinson wisely cautions against sharpening the corporate emphasis into an antithesis with individual identity.¹⁰ Modestly stated as such, and when viewed in the context of explicating, say, the nature of Hebrew law or the representative function of psalms couched in the first-person singular, there is no denying the force and value of this idea. However, to the extent that 'corporate personality' is treated as a *primitive* conception out of which a sense of the independence and unity of the individual only gradually emerged,¹¹ it suggests a picture of the historical development of the concept of selfhood that is incompatible with the logic of certain kinds of self-referential language.¹² It is this picture that must be rejected or at the very least suspended for want of proof, though what would constitute proof—a society in which no one

2. The Metaphor of the Heart

spoke in the first-person singular—is virtually unimaginable and certainly not to be found among the ancient Hebrews. As Aubrey Johnson says, to entertain this picture 'is to overlook the existence from the first of the personal pronouns in the rich variety of their independent, prefixed, affixed, and suffixed forms'.[13] In any case, even Brockington admits that the word 'heart' conveys 'the sense of self-hood and individuality'.[14]

The theory of the diffusion of consciousness represents a belief in 'the independent functioning of organs and limbs, which goes hand in hand with the non-recognition of a central unifying organ...' The theory has it that 'each several organ or limb should be pictured as self-operative and capable of psychical as well as physical function'.[15] Like the idea of a corporate personality, this notion is tied in with the conception of consciousness as developing from a primitive to a modern status.[16] It too must be called into question, however, if the textual expressions on which it is based (such as the eye's being said to be unsatisfied, expectant, asking, desiring, etc.[17]) are actually instances of synecdoche, as Aubrey Johnson has shown them to be.[18]

Synecdoche as it occurs in the biblical language of personal description/expression is a figure of speech 'whereby in certain circumstances an important part of one's... person acquires a heightened significance, and so may be used picturesquely and graphically with reference to the individual *as a whole*'.[19] Johnson finds that the synecdochal uses of 'heart' are among the most frequent in the OT, and not surprisingly, 'because the heart in all its wide range of emotional, intellectual, and volitional activity is obviously found to be of supreme importance to the *ego* or unit of consciousness (*'ănî* or *'ānōkî*) as an organ of self-expression'.[20] Johnson's insights thus cut against any tendency the diffusion-of-consciousness theory might have to distort the logic of the Hebrew use of 'heart' by literalizing it and thereby devaluing its autobiographical and biographical force, i.e. its potential for revealing and rendering character. And indeed, the tendency toward a literalizing distortion is evident in the following remark of Robinson:

> A point... to remember [in considering the diffusion of consciousness] is the fact that the distinction between science and imagination, fact and metaphor, is a comparatively modern one. We still use the term 'heart', for example, in a popular psychical sense, but every educated man knows that he is using it metaphorically. What the educated man frequently does not know, or, at any rate, forgets, is

the fact that such a usage is *not* metaphor in the Bible, but represents the extent of current scientific knowledge. This non-metaphorical point of view underlies the use of every physiological term for psychical activities... Even though we grant that the psychical activity, not the physical organ, is primarily in view in most cases, the source of the terminology and the implicit standpoint involved will remain; together they contribute an important element in the peculiar and characteristic atmosphere of such ancient literature as the Old Testament.[21]

It must first be asked whether the modern distinction Robinson cites (and note the syntactic equation of 'science' with 'fact', 'imagination' with 'metaphor') is valid and then whether his manner of treating it does not result in skewing his conclusion about *ancient Israel's* supposedly non-metaphorical point of view.

Much of the recent work in the philosophy of science issues in a clear rejection of the validity of the science–imagination distinction.[22] As for that distinction when it is conceived in terms of fact and metaphor, when we say of someone who has lost his commitment to his work or his enthusiasm for a task that his heart is no longer in it, our assessment is no less factual for being metaphorical. There are many different kinds of facts,[23] and it well may be that one has access to some of these *only* through metaphor. As Philip Wheelwright says, arguing against the position he labels 'semantic positivism': 'It is needful to recognize, then, that there are kinds of truth to which the criterion of maximum exactitude is not applicable, and which can perhaps be referred to only vaguely, indirectly, and in soft focus', i.e. metaphorically.[24] Paul Holmer makes much the same point with respect to the concept 'heart' (and with a helpful qualification of Wheelwright's phrase 'vaguely, indirectly, and in soft focus'):

But 'heart' as an abridgement is not proposed to satisfy a cognitive interest as is a generalization about a biological or botanical range of specimens. People seldom fit such psychological generalizations anyway, at least when we discuss their feelings and emotions. For the lineaments and features of human nature are not quite fixed, nor are they wildly random either. Surely they do not permit quite the precision of a universal nor the exactness of science. The difficulty is not that the facts are too difficult to master or the variables too many. It is rather that the complexities and diffusion do not reduce any further, and the application of law-like concepts and too great a precision is plainly logically wrong as well as empirically infeasible.

2. *The Metaphor of the Heart*

But there is a kind of order nonetheless. The logic of the metaphor 'heart' is such that it fits people as they are.[25]

That is, it fits the 'facts', facts of the sort that Robinson seems to have overlooked.

Now, if the science–imagination/fact–metaphor distinction is invalid even for the *modern* era (Robinson already having ruled out its applicability to Hebrew antiquity), then certainly it makes no sense for him to think that the OT's supposedly non-metaphorical use of 'heart' presupposes some theoretical underpinning to guarantee its facticity, or in his words, 'represents the extent of current scientific thought'—any more than the fact that our use of the term 'in a popular psychical sense' requires a scientific or theoretical basis for its intelligibility and justification.[26] In any case, as will be shown in the discussion of Wolff's work, there is simply no evidence for any such body of scientific thought, no textual support for the 'implicit standpoint' that Robinson attributes to the OT.

A final step remains to be taken in our dissection of the Robinson quotation. It involves the concept 'literal' which is clearly implied by the words 'non-metaphorical point of view' and which, equally clearly, is conceived as standing in a genetic relationship to 'metaphorical'. Owen Barfield has addressed this matter directly in an article titled 'The Meaning of the Word "Literal"'.[27] Adopting I.A. Richards' terms 'vehicle' and 'tenor'[28] to describe, respectively, 'the literal or surface meaning of an expression ... and any other meaning which it properly conveys', [29] Barfield analyzes the widely held view that the tenor, which typically is thought to have an immaterial sense (such as a moral quality or any phenomenon not accessible to sense-observation), is a product of the historical development of the literal sense, its vehicle, which is thought always to refer to material, physical reality. He quotes Jeremy Bentham, who gave this view succinct formulation: 'to every word that has an immaterial import, there belongs, or at least did belong, a material one'.[30] The statement implies that at a final stage of development the original, 'material' meaning (Barfield calls this the 'born literal' sense) may have fallen out of use so that the tenorial, immaterial sense now becomes the sole meaning, or in other words, has an 'achieved' literalness. This in turn 'raises the whole question of what a literal word of immaterial import *does* mean',[31] or to what, by this view, abstract nouns *refer*. This, in capsule form, is the notion of language that words *name things*, refer to 'entities', real or fictitious, the notion against which the later Wittgenstein so strongly inveighed and which he and his students sought to lay decisively to rest.[32] Barfield's essay would drive a final nail in the coffin.

The more immediate question, however, is how in the historical development presumed by this view an immaterial (metaphorical) sense ever found expression in the first place, i.e. in a world of purely literal (material) meanings. 'What we are trying to imagine now is the first metaphor in a wholly literal world.'[33] That we cannot do so means simply that such a 'wholly literal world' must never have existed. It cannot be that all words began their life with purely material meanings. Many must in fact have begun and long continued in a state where material and immaterial senses coexisted, a state in which vehicle and tenor participated indistinguishably in an inchoate union. The possibility of such union is grounded in the fact that 'consciousness and symbolization are simultaneous and correlative'.[34] For human consciousness, in other words, there are affinities given in the nature of things between the so-called material and immaterial worlds. Barfield cites Freud's observation 'that many images have a bodily significance', noting that along with this should go the corollary that 'the body has an imagined significance'.[35]

Now, Robinson's assertion about the inapplicability of the fact (read 'literal')-metaphor distinction to the ancient Hebrews in their use of 'heart' would seem to be congruent with Barfield's suggestion that many words may have from the first combined material and immaterial senses inextricably. Accordingly, he might be expected to agree with Barfield when the latter writes, explicating the concept of 'achieved literalness': 'That which the physiologist takes to be the literal meaning of the word *heart*, for example, is no less "achieved" than that which the theologian takes to be the literal meaning of the word spirit'.[36] But agreement does not follow, and Robinson misses the logic of this position with his conclusion that the physiological term *underlies* the psychical sense, is its 'source'. It may well be that Robinson's confusion only lays bare something potentially, if not inherently, misleading in the vehicle-tenor description of metaphor.[37] For no matter how emphatically one points out the frequent inability to separate vehicle from tenor in the resultant meaning of a metaphor (or the plain wrong-headedness of identifying the metaphor with the tenorial sense alone),[38] this description invites a view of metaphor as parasitic upon a supposed literal sense and, in the case of 'heart', a search for some direct relation between physical and psychical uses.

2. The Metaphor of the Heart

In H.W. Wolff's *Anthropology of the Old Testament*, which he conceives as a 'language primer of biblical anthropology', the author would appear to be trying to avoid just the sort of trap in which we found Robinson ensnared.[39] Wolff's use of the twin concepts 'stereometry of expression', i.e. the multiple employment of synecdoche for the purpose of 'circumscribing man as a whole', and 'synthetic thinking', in which a 'member [of the body] and its efficacious action are synthesized',[40] seems designed to characterize the holistic picture ancient Israel had of man as, in A.R. Johnson's words, a 'psychophysical organism'[41] without prejudice to either half of the expression. Nevertheless, prejudice is bound to emerge if the psychical and physical aspects are pulled apart and analyzed separately, as if to show that the Hebrews did have after all a physiological view of man distinguishable from the psychological. And this pulling apart is precisely what Wolff intends, as evidenced by this statement at the beginning of his investigation of 'heart': 'For our analytical understanding of the synthetic way of thinking, it is again advisable to start from the question, what ideas about the *l.* [*lēb*] as a physical organ are to be found in the Old Testament?'[42] The statement suggests not just that such ideas are there to be found but that they would constitute a literal grounding of the term, which would in turn illuminate its sense in metaphorical usage. Ultimately, Robinson's trap ensnares Wolff as well, and the resultant search often ends in a torturous literalizing of the text.

At best Wolff is only able to show that the Old Testament writers knew of the heart's beating, under normal conditions, or throbbing, in situations of distress, and that it is located in the chest.[43] Yet it is only the latter, the heart's anatomical *position*—not its *function*, as would be required by definition of 'synthetic thinking'—that appears to have any significance for its metaphorical employment: 'The heart is always recognized as being an inaccessible, hidden organ inside the body... In all these cases, therefore, the heart stands for the inaccessibly inexplorable—for anything that is quite simply impenetrably hidden.'[44] But even this insight is vitiated by the fact that other organs such as the liver and kidneys are also internal, hidden, protected; yet rarely do they bear the metaphorical freight the heart does. Thus, what ideas the biblical writers had about the heart as a physical organ are both meagre in number and detail (and certainly of no interest to the writers themselves) and singularly devoid of illuminating power for its use as a metaphor.

All of this remains quite unaltered by Wolff's analysis of Jer 4.19, a passage he regards as crucial to his case and one of direct relevance to our topic. Wolff writes,

> A further contribution to the anatomy of the heart is offered solely by Jeremiah, when he speaks on one occasion about 'the walls of the heart...' The context tells that the prophet becomes aware of an approaching cry of war. Its purpose is to announce a coming catastrophe. He is then struck down by a heart attack. For there is no other way of interpreting the words which he groans:
>
> > My innards, my innards! I writhe in pain!
> > Oh, the walls of my heart!
> > My heart is beating wildly;
> > I cannot keep still.
>
> Apparently violent pain or constriction in the region of the heart is here producing a suffocating sense of fear. This is the way that the paroxysm is described which is one of the symptoms of angina pectoris. Perhaps, therefore, 'the walls' of the wildly beating heart are a reference, not so much to the chest as to the pericardium 'inside' the body, which feels as if it is going to burst when the heart is beating wildly with fear. In view of the more than 800 mentions of the human heart in the Old Testament, it is surprising that no more than the passages mentioned contribute anything to its anatomy.[45]

For all of Wolff's deep sensitivity as an exegete elsewhere, this is an instance of literalizing reductionism in the extreme. Certainly, the reason for his surprise should not be sought in some *oddness* in the silence of the OT but in his own approach—in his wrenching these words and sentences out of the language game in which they are at home, that is, out of their ordinary employment for expressing and exercising certain emotions and capacities, and forcibly transposing them into an alien mode, here the language of physiology and anatomy.[46] Accordingly, there *is* another, and much preferable, way of interpreting Jeremiah's words than as the report of a heart attack and a description of the anatomy of the thorax. The point of the words is not their physical referentiality but, as will be demonstrated, the prophetic compulsion to speak and the anguish that is attendant upon that compulsion, indeed, that is attendant upon the whole complex and unique situation of one specifically commissioned to be God's prophet, to stand between God and his people and to suffer with and speak for both.

2. The Metaphor of the Heart

To miss the point of the words is of course to miss what is really significant about their subject matter. Hence, Wolff's physically referential reading of Jer 4.19 fails to do justice to the emotion content of the term 'heart', to the way emotion concepts work in general and in this passage in particular, and therefore to the picture the text intends to portray of the figure of Jeremiah.[47] To illustrate briefly, consider the assumption that 'pain... is here producing... fear'. Granting for the sake of argument that the pain is in fact that of a heart attack, the direction of the presumed causal connection (from pain to fear) is skewed, for the context would suggest that it is just the reverse, namely that the fear of the approaching enemy has induced the heart attack and its consequent pain. But more fundamentally, one must wonder how Wolff so easily arrives at the idea of fear (it is not explicit in the text), unless he has assumed a direct and singular relation between pain and fear, between physical sensation and emotion, such that the latter can be virtually deduced from the former. This assumption must be disavowed, however, in light of the fact that different emotions may be accompanied by the same sensation (e.g. goose-flesh for both negative and positive anticipation, a lump in the throat for both joy and grief, the blush of embarrassment and the flush of rage) while the presence of one sensation that typically accompanies a given emotion does not guarantee the presence of that emotion (e.g. one's goose-flesh does not necessarily reflect anticipation, it may merely indicate chilliness). The point is not that fear plays no role in Jeremiah's expression but rather that it does not follow directly, cannot be simply extrapolated, from the pain. To speak as if it does and can be is, very subtly, to reduce the emotion to the sensation and thus to disguise the real complexity and particularity of Jeremiah's experience.

At a yet more fundamental level it is the idea of a *causal* connection between physical pain and fear that obfuscates matters. In general, the language of causality can obscure the relations between emotions, their objects, and their grounds, assimilating what are (*often* with respect to 'objects', *always* in the case of 'grounds') only *thoughts* about events, states of affairs, and things to the actual events, states of affairs, and things themselves.[48] In particular, Wolff's use of causal language ('pain produces fear') belongs to a mechanical model for explaining emotion behavior. Emotions like fear, however—unlike more-or-less objectless states, such as manic depression and free-floating anxiety—are not satisfactorily accounted for in terms of physiological mechanisms. Ordinarily, when people ask about causes of emotions, they are actually asking about *reasons* and have in mind cognitive matters on which the emotions are grounded, i.e. beliefs, evaluations, conjectures, doubts, and other sorts of thoughts.[49] Thus, one might fear a gun because he knows or thinks it is loaded and wielded by a psychopath. Jeremiah may have feared the advancing enemy because, among other factors, he knew it to be the instrument of God's judgment and therefore invincible.

But finally, Wolff's principal confusion is that the pain Jeremiah suffers is, at bottom, physical. It is hard to imagine that he would have arrived at this reading had he not come to the passage specifically seeking to abstract from it various ideas about the physical heart in the first place and, in the second place, had he paid more attention to the context. With a more contextual study of the passage the physical heart and the notion of a physical pain will fall out of prominence, if not altogether out of view, and a different sense of the words will become plain; indeed a literal sense will emerge in which a subject, a self, is being shaped in and by the process of entertaining and exercising a rich network of emotions through the metaphorical language of the heart.

Chapter 3

THE 'HEART' IN CONTEXT:
JER 4 AND THE ENACTMENT OF IDENTITY

One can go about determining the context of a given passage in different ways. One way is to treat the text diachronically by sorting out the various layers of material and arranging them according to the order in which they may be supposed to have been originally composed, delivered, or interpolated into the text. This has been the traditional approach of Jeremiah scholarship from the mid-nineteenth century to the present.[1] Without denying the value this approach may hold for particular purposes, we nevertheless follow a more synchronic tack, taking the (Masoretic) text in its present shape and supposing that this shape has a logic and organization in its own right which it is the task of the exegete to discover and elucidate. This is largely an inductive enterprise requiring a close reading of the text and employing basic literary techniques (which indeed may also play a major role in the historical methods of source, form, and redaction criticism and has special prominence in rhetorical criticism)— specifically for the identification of the significant terms, motifs, themes, and formal literary patterns that cluster in a batch of material and allow it to be seen as a unit.

Whereas most diachronic studies situate 4.19 in a context beginning with 4.5, William L. Holladay's rhetorical analysis leads him to take 4.1 as the starting point. 4.1-4, Holladay contends, is the prelude to a 'foe cycle' (4.1–6.30; 8.4-10a, 13) which is distinguishable on several grounds from a 'harlotry cycle' that precedes it.[2] In fact, whatever the evaluation from a diachronic perspective, the four verses at issue, 4.1-4, are intimately (but differently) connected with *both* the preceding and succeeding material.[3] Synchronically, they are transitional, at once a concluding response to 3.21ff. and an introduction to 4.5ff. Therefore, and prompted by practical necessity, we take 4.1-4 as a suitable starting point for a contextual analysis of Jer 4.19. Although Holladay's rhetorical criticism can help in establishing a fitting context, it often focuses on verbal structures virtually without regard to their semantic value, identifying patterns almost solely on the basis of the shape and sounds of the words. By contrast, and for formal observations to have interpretive value, our interest must be in the conceptual significance this prelude has for the material it introduces. As a prelude, in other words, Jer 4.1-4 invites the exegete to explore and chart the network of semantic relations between it and the material that follows. If it *is* a prelude, such a network will be manifest. To chart this network is thus also to chart the logic of the passage, to trace the denotative, connotative, and metonymic sphere which the language circumscribes and in which the language has its home.

1   'im-tāšûb yiśrā'ēl n^e'um-Yhwh
     'ēlay tāšûb
     w^e'im-tāsîr šiqquṣêkā mippānay
     w^elō' tānûd

2   w^enišba'tā ḥay-Yhwh
     $be^{\ae}met$ b^emišpāṭ ûbiṣdāqâ
     w^ehitbār^{e}kû bô gôyim
     ûbô yithallālû

3   kî-kōh 'āmar Yhwh
     l^e'îš y^ehûdâ w^elîrušālaim
     nîrû lākem nîr
     w^e'al-tizrē'û 'el-qōṣîm

4   himmōlû laYhwh
     w^ehāsirû 'orlôt l^ebabkam
     'îš y^ehûdâ w^eyōš^{e}bê y^erûšālāim
     pen-tēṣē' kā'ēš ḥāmātî
     ûbā'ărâ w^e'ên m^ekabbeh
     mipp^{e}nê rōa' ma'al^{e}lêkem

1   If you turn, O Israel—the utterance of Yhwh—
     to me you should return,
   And if you remove your detestable things from my presence,
     and do not waver,

2   And [if] you swear 'as Yhwh lives!'
     in faith, in justice, and in righteousness,

3. The 'Heart' in Context

   Then nations shall bless themselves in him,
    and in him shall they boast.
3 Thus indeed says Yhwh
   to the man of Judah, to the inhabitants of Jerusalem,
  Till afresh fallow ground,
   and sow not among thorns!
4 Circumcise yourselves to Yhwh;
   remove the foreskins of your heart,
    O man of Judah, O inhabitants of Jerusalem,
  Lest my wrath issue forth like fire
   and burn with none to quench it,
    because of your evil doings.[4]

This is intensely personal language. Through his prophet God speaks to his people in a highly impassioned way. One index of the passion is the variety of speech forms. Here are pleading, promising, commanding, and threatening—different language games but all bearing a family resemblance that permits their being gathered into a coherent effort of argument and persuasion. One musters impassioned argument (one combines plea, promise, command, and threat) when something of utmost value and importance is at stake. What is at stake, it will become evident, is the 'self', the self of Jeremiah, the many selves of Judah and Jerusalem, and ultimately the selves of the book's readers.

'im tāšûb in v. 1 strikes the keynote of the passage, indeed sounds a principal leitmotif of the entire book.[5] The motif *šwb* in fact relates the Jeremianic voice with the voice of the deuteronomic literature in general.[6] As Holladay has observed, the Jeremianic voice is characterized by the frequent paronomastic use of the root *šwb* in both verbal and nominal forms, playing off and coordinating its sense of physical motion and its religious sense as either 'repent' or 'be apostate', a paramount example being 8.4-5.[7] So in 4.1 *tāšûb*, along with the other verbs of motion, *tāsîr (swr)* and *tānûd (nwd)*, works metaphorically, its physical sense intersected by a religious signification.

Holladay's insight can be sharpened, however, and the force of the word-play enhanced, by an important if apparently minor adjustment in his terminology. To speak of *šûb* and *nûd* as 'verbs of motion' as Holladay does is accurate only to an extent, for it is a minimal expression that leaves people undistinguished from physical objects in general.[8] It is of course specifically people who are being addressed here, and people—unlike rocks, trees, stars, and atoms—do not merely move; they *act*. It would be more precise therefore to speak of *šûb* and *nûd* as verbs of action.

To speak of action is to speak of movement towards a goal. Action entails intentionality, and intentionality, by implication and metonymy, brings into view a broad range of similar notions like motives, purposes, desires, and wishes—notions indispensable for understanding a vast sphere of human behavior. Further, if we wanted to explain people's actions with some precision, we would in the weightier cases have to consider such things as their likes and dislikes, loves and hates, fears and confidences, loyalties and disloyalties, and similar highly cathectic emotions. It is no small thing to observe that it is people's nature as *intentional agents* that defines in a fundamental way their personhood, while making them the inscrutably complex, interesting, and creative creatures they are, or can be. People come to be who they are through their actions, and by their actions they are known—to the extent that these actions can be understood.[9] To affirm that people's actions are indispensable to their identity is to acknowledge that there is a teleological component to the self. As Ronald Hustwit writes in explicating Kierkegaard's and Wittgenstein's views of the soul, 'having a self entails having a telos. And there is no teleological suspension, unless it is in favor of some higher telos, *without a loss of the self*.'[10]

Hustwit's remark points up the immense pathos of Jeremiah's use of the 'action' verb *šûb*, and its parallel *sûr*, especially in view of their being couched in the conditional mode (*'im*), i.e. in that a choice is required. The people's turning (back to, away from) and turning aside (hiphil: 'remove') are a goal-directed activity, and everything depends on what goal (telos) they choose. This activity involves an orientation of the self, an orientation all-important for what the self is and will be. It is a question, as Holladay correctly observes, of the people's ultimate loyalty, and on this loyalty depends their ultimate identity.[11] '"If you turn, O Israel", it is Yhwh who speaks, "return to *me*!"' The ultimacy of matters, posed here summarily and with stark economy, is fully elaborated in earlier passages. The choice is between the nation's glory and that which is lacking in all benefit (2.11), between the 'fountain of living waters' and 'broken cisterns that can hold no water' (2.13). On the one side is Yhwh, father-husband, a merciful healer; on the other, a 'delusion', fealty to which guarantees the self's dissolution in divine 'anger', human 'shame' and 'dishonor' (3.12, 14, 19, 22-23, 25). The final colon of 4.1, 'and do not wander' ($w^e lō' tānûd$), rules out a third option people have, vacillation. The verb suggests a 'wandering' between motion and action, indicating a confusion about one's telos, an indecisiveness which precludes clear action and in which the self thereby forfeits definition and is truncated.

Grammatically, v. 2a may easily be read as a continuation of the conditional clause in v. 1 and therefore as a continuation of the first verse's teleological perspective. At the same time it develops that perspective by referring to a speech activity that vividly attests the dimension of goal-directedness ingredient in an ordinary, non-theoretical conception of the self. The formula 'as Yhwh lives' ($ḥay$-$Yhwh$) belongs to the language game of oath-taking, an activity in which people pledge themselves by publicly ratifying commitments and attesting the veracity of statements or the genuineness of behavior. Naturally, its normative use is only on the lips of Yhwh worshippers, for whom it virtually constitutes a confession in him.[12] As such it is mentioned as a requirement by Deut 6.13 and 10.20. Again, to use the expression is to adopt for oneself an ultimate telos (or to affirm having already done so) and thereby to define oneself in an essential manner, to give one's life a particular shape, presumably of harmony and congruence between one's thoughts, words, and deeds on the one hand and on the other the nature and requirements of that to which one's loyalty is professed.[13]

Of course, an oath can misfire and fail to perform its normative function, whether by failure of the will and ability of the oath-taker so that the intended ratification is annulled, or by rank hypocrisy that subverts the oath at the outset and, with repeated use, eviscerates it of all meaning. In these cases too the self achieves definition, but of a negative sort, and one's life-shape is formed, though especially in the case of hypocrisy we might more accurately say *de*formed. Surely, it is in this context of the possibility of, and human proclivity for, the oath's misfiring that the commandment against vain swearing in Yhwh's name (Exod 20.7; Deut 5.11) has its theological basis: as a general prescription the third commandment stands *for* the preservation of meaning and *against* the deformation of individual and community life. Jer 4.2 gives the general prescription a specific focus and determination by addressing the empirical actuality of Israel's hypocritical use of the oath (see 5.2). It is this specific misuse of the oath that warrants the three-fold qualification *be'ĕmet b^emišpāṭ* ûbiṣ^edāqâ and gives it special poignancy. The relational quality of each of these three words is well known,[14] and the force of the bicola might be summarily rendered, 'If you swear "as Yhwh lives" in the manner befitting the covenantal relation in which you stand to God, and for once without the glib carelessness that is your custom, then nations . . .' The qualifiers thus emphasize the loyalty which had been conspicuously absent from the people's oath-swearing behavior. Hence, the terms also highlight and flesh out the teleological dimension implicit in such behavior.

The apodosis to the conditional clause ('If you turn, remove, swear . . .') follows in v. 2b ('then nations shall bless, . . . boast'), invoking the promise to the patriarchs. The corollary to the teleology of self is the teleology of history. The correlation constitutes a fundamental theme in the Old Testament and finds its paradigmatic formulations in Gen 12.1-3, 22.18, 26.4-5, and 28.14. The conformity of language in our verse to the paradigms is not insignificant. As with the identity of Abraham, whose obedience was the definitive manifestation of his telos, so the identity of Jeremiah's audience (whose obedience is precisely what is at issue) is here grammatically and conceptually connected with the overarching purpose of God in history. To have Yhwh as one's telos is to adopt his purpose as one's own, and to gain one's identity thereby.

As with v. 2, the meaningfulness of v. 3 does not turn on settling questions as to the authenticity, original placement, or independence of the verse in its entirety or in its various parts, since it is perfectly intelligible as it stands.[15] Along with v. 4 it builds cogently and persuasively on the argument of vv. 1-2 and further attests a teleological understanding of the self. From the synchronic perspective the messenger formula *kōh 'āmar Yhwh*, rather than setting off the following speech from the preceding one and thus indicating a disjunction, *connects* the two sets of statements by attributing to the latter set the same authority as divine word that was conferred on the former by the phrase *n^e'um-Yhwh*.[16] The *kî* functions asseveratively, since the relation between vv. 1-2 and 3-4 is not causal (explanatory) but elaborative.[17] As with the messenger formula, the function of the address *l^e'îš y^ehûdâ w^elîrûšālayim* is not dissociative but associative: the word spoken to the 'North' (3.12), 'Israel' (4.1), is equally applicable to the South. In effect, the concept 'Israel' has become—at the level of a synchronic reading—inclusive of Judah-Jerusalem.[18] The switch from the conditional to the imperative mode of the verbs

3. The 'Heart' in Context

heightens the argument. Pleading gives way to commanding (vv. 3-4a), which issues not in a promise (v. 2b) but a threat (v. 4b). Nevertheless, an element of promise is implicit in the command, particularly that of v. 3, for out of the fresh tilling and careful planting—this effort to make a new beginning of life—one may naturally expect to reap a rich harvest, that is, a quality of life marked by the blessing that comes with being in a right relation to God. This is to speak once again of the possibility of a certain construction of the self.

The fact that Jeremiah employs the same expression, *nîrû lākem nîr*, as found in Hos 10.12 is of considerable significance for our interpretation, although any question of borrowing, at either the oral or literary stage, is not to the point. Neither is it to be answered here whether C.H. Dodd's thesis regarding NT quotations from or allusions to the OT works within the OT itself (namely, the thesis that such quotations were intended to invoke a whole context surrounding the material specifically cited or alluded to).[19] But given the synchronic approach that attends to the reading process, it may certainly be said that the co-incidence of significant, identical expressions in different passages, or even of similar verbal patterns, can in fact and in certain instances *should* trigger in the reader an associative process leading to a semantic transaction between the passages, a transaction involving not just the specific words or patterns shared but their contexts as well.[20] With any attentive reading, in other words, the passages will naturally tend to bear upon, influence, and color one another. Accordingly, we observe that in Hos 10.12, which like the Jeremiah passage is an appeal to repentance, the notion of 'quality of life' is *explicitly* connected with the metaphor of breaking new ground:

> Sow for yourselves according to righteousness,
>   reap according to the fruit of covenant love.
> Till afresh fallow ground;
>   it is time to seek Yhwh,
> That he may come
>   and rain down righteousness upon you.

H.W. Wolff comments on this verse: 'He who "sows" according to this order [i.e. $ṣ^e dāqâ$, the 'saving sphere'] will harvest "according to loyalty" and will therefore experience the goodness of the covenantal God through what he "harvests" in life'.[21] What is explicit in Hosea, we would argue, confirms what we have said is implicit in the

Jeremiah passage (namely, the promissory element of a blessed life), and, by the transaction between the two verses that is prompted by their use of the same phrase, Hosea's sense insinuates itself into Jeremiah's words.

With its radical metaphor of the circumcised heart, v. 4 supplies the capstone to the argument of the prelude. As observed by various of the commentators, imagery of the soil (v. 3) gives way to imagery taken from the cult,[22] and in the process the theological specificity implicit in the former is bodied forth by the latter. The new planting and sowing means a new beginning for the self that is offered, dedicated, fully committed from its center out, to Yhwh. From the standpoint of a sequential reading of the OT in its final shape, this is not the first time the idea of the circumcised heart is encountered. It has already appeared in Deut 10.16 and 30.6. There is a difference in the formulations of Deut and Jer, however, that bears noting. Deut's expressions are more compact: 'Circumcise therefore the foreskin of your heart...' and 'the Lord your God will circumcise your heart...'. Jeremiah employs poetic bi-cola with two verbs in parallel, 'circumcise yourselves' (*himmōlû*) and 'remove' (*hāsirû*); only the latter has the independent object 'the foreskin of your heart', the former being a self-contained predicate. The grammatically more elaborate second colon is also the patently more metaphorical one. The effect of the first colon is to keep the actual cultic rite of circumcision firmly in view and thereby to sound again the theme of covenant. The fact of a covenantal significance in circumcision was established for the reader by Gen 17.10-14 ('and it shall be a sign of the covenant between me and you', v. 11). The purpose of v. 4, as throughout the passage and the surrounding context, is to emphasize the fundamental importance of strict fidelity in Judah–Israel's relationship with God.

Still, if circumcision is a *sign* of the covenant and thus an expression of fidelity, then the rite itself has a metaphorical quality which carries over into Jeremiah's reference to it. Accordingly, the relation of the first colon to the second is not simply that of a purely literal statement to a patently metaphorical one; nor are their senses to be contrasted in terms of an outward-physical vs. an inward-spiritual action. Rather, the second colon stands in synonymous parallelism with the first and serves to explicate it, cashing out its implicit value as a demand for the reorientation of the total self. Curiously, the more obviously metaphorical statement makes plain

3. The 'Heart' in Context

what the ostensibly less metaphorical statement entails (and in the process tells what 'circumcision' means).

To speak of the 'patently metaphorical' quality of the second colon is to make a remark that is simultaneously empirical and logical. None of the commentators has misconstrued Jeremiah's meaning by thinking he intends a surgical removal of an anatomical appendage from the physical heart, since the foreskin belongs not to the heart but the penis; the logical incongruity, the absurdity, of such an operation is self-evident. The point of belaboring the obvious is that Jeremiah's use of the word 'heart' in 4.4 epitomizes his heart-talk throughout the passage, not least in 4.19. The use of 'heart' here in 4.4 focuses attention on the moral agency of human subjects. It is a way of addressing or representing people in their capacity as creatures profoundly responsible for what they do and who they are, and what they make of themselves. This is to bring to the fore yet again the teleological aspect of selfhood. Now indeed, Jeremiah's command presupposes that what the audience have made of themselves is somehow skewed or not enough: they stand in need of a radical operation, but 'operation' of the sort appropriate to moral agents, not simply physical objects, one of the sort that will restore moral powers and capacities and bring them into proper working order, removing any blockages in the way.

The nature of such powers and capacities can be specified more closely by looking at a similar remark of Jeremiah's about 'uncircumcised ears' in 6.10:

> To whom shall I speak and give warning
> > that they may hear?
> Behold, their ears are uncircumcised,
> > they cannot listen.
> Behold, the word of the Lord is to them an object of scorn;
> > they take no pleasure in it.

'Uncircumcised ears' is said of people on whom words of warning are lost (i.e. who lack the capacity to take instruction), who fail to acknowledge in the word of Yhwh the authority proper to it (who lack the capacity to recognize and submit the self to legitimate authority), and for whom the word holds no power of enhancement (who lack the ability to take pleasure in what is most profoundly true and real).

Another relevant passage is Jer 5.20-28, particularly vv. 21 and 23:

21 Here now this,
       O people foolish and without heart,
    Who have eyes but do not see,
       ears but do not hear...

23 But this people has a stubborn and rebellious heart;
       they have turned aside and gone away.

Lacking heart (v. 21) or having a stubborn heart (v. 23) is a form of folly whereby people neglect inherent powers of understanding or refuse to learn new ones. References to eyes and ears, sight and hearing, in the same context with 'heart', as we have here, are frequent in the OT (e.g. Deut 4.9-14; 29.4; 1 Kgs 3.9; Isa 6.9-10; Ezek 40.4; Prov 2.1-10; 22.17; 23.12). In these passages 'eyes', 'ears', and 'heart' function as correlative concepts; they bespeak faculties of perception, but obviously not perception of the ordinary sort, rather a perception-in-depth. For more is involved here than a physiological registration of sensory impressions. H.W. Wolff draws attention to the role of the intellect in this sort of perception by describing it as a 'perceptive reason'.[23] But the understanding that these concepts entail also involves more than the intellect and is hardly to be ascribed, as Wolff does, simply to 'the head and the brain'.[24] We should want to say that this understanding—as Jer 5.22 and 24 suggest ('Do you not fear me? says Yhwh' and 'They do not say in their hearts, Let us fear Yhwh...')—comes in a *doing* that includes thinking but goes beyond it. It entails obedience (e.g. 5.28) which issues necessarily out of the proper fear of God, and such obedience is a matter of the whole person. It is a catena of emotions, attitudes, thoughts, purposes, and concrete actions, all of which are things people 'do' and in which the psycho-physical unity of the human being remains indissoluble. Yet while this obedient understanding (seeing, hearing, and having heart) are activities people can do, they are also, as suggested above, things they can avoid doing. In other words, they are capacities that must either be exercised and developed or neglected and allowed to atrophy.

In sum, and as illuminated by the other passages discussed above, the metaphor of the circumcised heart in Jer 4.4 is used in an effort to impress upon listeners and readers the need for a resuscitation of a host of faculties, powers, and capacities that constitute people as responsible selves. It occurs at the pivotal point of the passage's argument for the ultimate urgency of this resuscitation: either the people return to Yhwh, genuinely pledge themselves to him, make a fresh beginning with him as their telos, and thereby participate in his purpose and promise, or they leave their hearts unaltered, permitting their humanity to wither and losing themselves in divine judgment.

With this explication of 4.1-4 we have attempted to identify the language game—the mode of discourse and the sort of subject matter—in which Jeremiah's use of the term 'heart' has its natural home. The succeeding verses and the recurrences of 'heart' within them are to be viewed in the light of this prelude and to some extent as determined by it. Accordingly, we proceed by observing that the threat of judgment in 4.4 leads directly into a series of prophetic visions in which the threatened judgment is seen as a present reality. The semantic force of the visions is left untouched by speculations as to the precise identity of the invaders, who at most are said to be 'evil from the north' (v. 6), 'besiegers from a distant land' (v. 16). For the rest there are only images and metaphors expressive of their irresistibility and ferocity. The lack of specificity effects a sense of something uncanny, sinister, and terrifying afoot. Ultimately, it serves to emphasize the fact that it is Yhwh himself who is the force and agent at work in Judah–Jerusalem's destruction.[25] In addition, the oracles focus attention on the condition and response of the people who must suffer this judgment of destruction. Relatedly, there is the paradox that at the same time as the judgment is depicted as inexorably in progress, it is implied that it can also be averted, or at least prove not to be the final word, depending on the response it seeks to elicit (see especially v. 14). The response is sought from various strata of the society. Thus the visions include commands, questions, and accusations directed to the populace at large (vv. 8, 14, 18, and 30), a narrative description of the reaction of king and courtiers, priests and prophets (v. 9), and, not least, first-person responses of Jeremiah himself (vv. 10, 19-21). The relation between what is said to and of the populace and their leaders and what the prophet says in response is of utmost significance.

In v. 8 the people are instructed, 'gird you with sackcloth, lament, and wail, for the fierce anger of the Lord has not turned back from us'. Such grief behavior would be natural and appropriate in the face of disaster. Indeed, it is so natural, or its absence so odd when the whole land lies desolate, that the prophet can attribute it even to the non-human sphere of creation, without the pathetic fallacy's seeming fallacious:

> For this the earth shall mourn,
> and the heavens above be black ... (v. 28 RSV)

If the grief behavior is so natural, does not the directive to the people to lament then become a superfluous ornamentation or, at best, merely a way of emphasizing the certainty of destruction? Not if the people are so obtuse as not to recognize disaster when they see it. Verse 30 makes it clear that this is precisely the case:

> And you, O desolate one,
> what do you mean that you dress in scarlet,
> that you deck yourself with ornaments of gold,
> That you enlarge your eyes with paint?
> In vain you beautify yourself. (RSV)

Like the absence of shame (6.15; 8.12), the failure to lament appropriately can provoke wonder and reproach. It is a moral obtuseness, an incapacity that bespeaks a deficiency in the make-up of the self, a virtual degradation of human nature. Jeremiah's instruction can be seen then as a summons to begin to be human by acting humanly. The implication is that if grief can be practiced, new life is still possible.

It may be asked what significance there is in the fact that, while the verbs summoning the people to grieve are in the second-person plural, the prepositional phrase *mimmenû* in the explanatory *kî* clause is couched in the *first*-person plural? Evidently, the prophet is identifying himself with the people he addresses; he ranges himself alongside them under the same divine judgment.[26] What threatens them threatens him. It belongs to his identity that this should be so, for the identification of the prophet with his people is ingredient in the very nature of intermediation and in the prophet's intercessory role in particular.[27] But this intermediation entails an identification-with-a-difference. The prophet cannot share entirely his people's limitations and incapacities, or their failure to exercise these endangered capacities, for he must speak and do for them in relation to God what they cannot speak and do for themselves.[28]

It may be proposed, then, that the lamentation which the people are called upon to make in v. 8, but are incapable of making, Jeremiah, in expressing his own grief in v. 19, makes for them there.[29] He *makes* lamentation. His words do not only *say*, they *do*. They do not describe a condition so much as enact one. They do not refer to, render an account of, offer a theory on, or speak discursively about (among other things) a physical human heart or the historical personage who owned it. Rather, the words are *of* and belong to a man's lamentation. Actualizing the human capacity for grief and *being* the grief behavior itself, the words actualize the self who speaks them. They constitute the speaker as a grieving self. Jeremiah makes lamentation *for them*. He grieves for his people as well as for himself. As a prophet who mediates between God and humans, he must do this.[30] He stands in their place before God and renders to God what is fitting and natural for them to say and do, even though, and precisely because, they cannot say and do so for themselves. In the process he shows them what is fitting and natural for them to *be*, to be as human beings, full subjects of Yhwh, even in the midst of Yhwh's judgment.[31] In this sense his words constitute him as a profoundly sympathetic self.

It may be observed here that the text, in rendering these words in just this way, is at once rendering an identity description (that is, characterizing the persona Jeremiah) while showing how identity happens, how a self comes to be, achieves form and definition, indeed constitutes itself. Specifically, it shows the self to be the achievement of the responsible, first-person use of the language of the heart.

In v. 9 attention shifts from the general populace to their leaders.

> And it shall be in that day—the utterance of Yhwh—
> The heart of the king shall vanish
>   and the heart of the princes;
> The priests shall be appalled,
>   and the prophets dumbfounded.

The temporal phrase *bayyôm-hahû'* indicates that the frame of reference remains eschatological; we are dealing here with the leadership's response to the catastrophe that is upon them. As in v. 4 the use of 'heart' in the first bi-cola is patently metaphorical. The gist of the phrase about the loss or failure of heart is that the king and princes lack the resources to enact a significant response, i.e. to perform the function proper to their office. The RSV's rendering of *lēb* as 'courage' is quite to the point. The next line is parallel in thought to the first. The religious authorities are likewise incapacitated.

But if the establishment prophets are 'dumbfounded' (*tmy*), quite literally, Jeremiah proves in v. 10 that he is not, though he is indeed perplexed. Perplexity is precisely the name of the game in which the expression operates, *wā'ōmar 'ăhāh 'ădōnāy Yhwh*.[32] The word *'ăhāh* is itself a particle of lamentation (see Jer 22.18), and *'ăhāh* is conjoined with *'ădōnāy Yhwh* at the beginning of Jeremiah's prayer concerning the command to buy the plot in Anathoth (32.16-25), a prayer that ends by remarking on the seeming incongruity between the command and the readily apparent facts of the matter: 'the city is given into the hands of the Chaldeans'. *Wā'ōmar* is of course a narrative element, and the paradigmatic instance of the formula complete with *wā'ōmar* is in the protest sequence of the opening 'call narrative'.[33] There the prophet expresses wonder and apprehension that he who is too young to know how to speak should be appointed to so awesome a task as has been given him (1.6). Then in 14.13 the formula recurs as Jeremiah puzzles over Yhwh's demand not to 'pray for the welfare of this people', a demand grounded in Yhwh's determination to 'consume them'.[34]

This last passage is directly relevant to ours, for what troubles Jeremiah is the fact that the prophets had been telling the people that Yhwh 'will give you assured peace in this place'. Similarly, the clear implication of 4.10 is that it was through what were ostensibly *his* prophets (not Baal's, cf. 2.8, 26-27) that Yhwh had been saying 'Peace shall be yours'. By no means did Jeremiah regard such words or the prophets who spoke them as *a priori* inauthentic. Quite to the contrary, he accorded them respect, perhaps even belief, unless and until events and a word of Yhwh, directed specifically to him, proved them false. Thus in response to Hananiah's salvation oracles in 28.2-5, 9-11, Jeremiah pronounced *'āmēn* and 'went on his way' (28.6, 11), returning only after receiving the counter-word from Yhwh himself (28.12-16). In 14.13-16 Jeremiah's confusion is dispelled by Yhwh's telling him that 'the prophets are prophesying lies in my name. I did not send them ...' Accordingly, Jeremiah has taken in all seriousness the salvation word which he quotes in 4.10, so seriously that he can accuse Yhwh of deception since now, instead of peace, 'the sword is laid at their throat'.

The point is this: taking seriously the previous word of the prophets, he now in a sense takes their part. Indeed, his words are his own 'spontaneous and impassioned outcry' manifesting his personal perplexity, anger and grief.[35] But in articulating these emotions, he does what the prophets should be expected to do but cannot. In this he identifies himself both with them and over against them. They are perplexed and so is he. But they lack heart; he does not. Thus he can take his and their perplexity, articulate it, and direct it back to God. And even if his speech takes the form of harsh accusation, by

3. The 'Heart' in Context

speaking it he maintains, even heightens, the self-relatedness to God which vv. 1-4 passionately urged. Thereby he fulfils the prophetic office. Thereby he also helps mark himself as the *true* prophet.

To summarize the discussion up to this point, it has been argued that 4.1-4, *qua* prelude, establishes themes and concerns central to the following material. In summoning the people to return to Yahweh and reorient their lives, these verses attest the teleological component in the concept 'self'. They treat the self as a function of vital faculties and capacities which may be either exercised and developed or ignored and allowed to atrophy. Many of these capacities are brought into focus through the use of the metaphor 'heart' in 4.4. By exercising and having heart, i.e. by exercising a range of human capacities, one actualizes and defines the self, giving it shape and substance. By ignoring the heart and its resident powers, the self remains amorphous, undirected, and in danger of dissolution.

In the ensuing verses it was seen how the prelude's concern with the self's reorientation and reconstruction in God-relatedness was advanced specifically with regard to the capacity for grief, expressed (linguistically exercised) in lamentation and protest over God's judgment. The explication of v. 19 was begun at this point by observing that there Jeremiah performs the lamentation and enacts the grief appropriate to the people as a whole and demanded of them in v. 8. Further, it was shown that by performing his own lamentation, thereby constituting himself as a grieving self, and by performing it also in behalf of the people, Jeremiah enacts his prophetic identity as intercessor between people and God. Similarly, vv. 9-10 were viewed in terms of a dynamic between Jeremiah and the royal and religious authorities, the prophets in particular. Jeremiah's ability to speak his perplexity and protest in circumstances where other prophets are rendered speechless is another instance of the actualization of the self and the realization of his authentic prophetic identity.

Again, the role of the metaphor 'heart' in all this merits emphasis. In vv. 4 and 9 'heart' is used in addressing and characterizing people as moral agents responsible for what they make of themselves through their exercise or neglect of the capacities proper to and constitutive of human subjects. This use of 'heart' in relation to the moral agency of selfhood is likewise illustrated by v. 14—'O Jerusalem, wash your heart from wickedness'—again an obviously metaphorical expression. Out of this pattern of metaphorical usage emerges the 'plain sense' of the passage as a whole, i.e. a literal sense not equatable with physical reference but rather dependent upon a normal metaphorical usage. The use of 'heart' in v. 19 will prove to conform and contribute to this pattern.

Still, evaluation of the contextual evidence is not complete without consideration of v. 18, the penultimate moment in the sequence 4.1-19 which we have been tracing. In the light of this verse the metaphorical reading of 'heart' in v. 19 becomes utterly unavoidable.

> Your way and your doings
>   have brought these upon you.
> This is your doom/wickedness—how bitter!
>   How it has reached your very heart![36]

It may be observed at the outset that there is a structural connection between vv. 18 and 19 centered on the word 'heart'. The connection suggests that the latter verse be interpreted in direct relation to the former. Note the parallel positions of *lēb*:

> *zō't rā'ātēk kî mār*
>   *kî nāga' 'ad-libbēk*
> *mē'ay mē'ay 'whwlh*
>   *qîrôt libbî*

'Your [Jerusalem's] heart' is counterposed to 'my [Jeremiah's] heart'. The poetic structure seems to reflect the dynamic we have traced between the prophet's self-constituting words and his enacted identity on the one hand and the unrealized selfhood of the people and their leaders on the other.

The final clause of v. 18b—*kî nāga' 'ad-libbēk*—figures in another structural-rhetorical feature that influences the reading of v. 19. With slight modifications it recapitulates the last colon of v. 10: *w^{e}nāg^e'â hereb 'ad-hannāpeš*. As a whole v. 18 is Jeremiah's summary evaluation of his battle visions (vv. 5-8, 13-17). It is his explanation to the people of the battle's meaning.[37] The effect of the recapitulation is to intensify the sense of the crisis's ultimacy and to bring the preceding discourse in its entirety to a climax. Everything that has gone before is distilled in this final statement. Thematically, everything is focused on the metaphorical heart. A physically referential reading of v. 19 would distort this focus.

Also noteworthy in v. 18 is a series of ambiguities on which the recapitulation observed above has a bearing. It is not immediately obvious, for example, what the antecedents are for the relative

3. The 'Heart' in Context

pronouns *'ēlleh* and *zō't*. Nor is it clear whether *rā'ātēk* should be interpreted as 'doom', i.e. 'evil' in the sense of 'calamity', or as 'wickedness', i.e. evil in an ethical sense. Finally, what is the subject of *nāgaʿ*?

Perhaps the least ambiguous element is *'ēlleh*, which most likely refers to 'besiegers' in v. 16 (note the plural), the enemies encircling Jerusalem like 'keepers of a field' (v. 17). Determining the antecedent for *zō't* (singular), however, as well as the subject of *nāgaʿ*, turns on how *rā'ātēk* is to be construed. The recapitulation warrants taking *rā'ātēk* in the sense of 'calamity', for 'sword' (v. 10) is clearly a martial image representing the national military disaster depicted in the battle visions. Accordingly, *zō't* functions as a collective resumptive of *'ēlleh* and means 'this disaster', and the nominal sentence *zō't rā'ātēk*, taken as 'This [national calamity] (is) your doom', is the implied subject of *nāgaʿ*.

It follows from this reading that Jeremiah's personal lamentation in v. 19 has this 'doom' as its motivation, as has already been argued in the discussion of v. 8. Further confirmation comes with the explanatory *kî* clause in the final bi-cola of v. 19 along with the ensuing statement:

19b   For I have heard the sound of the trumpet,
         my soul the alarm of war.
20   Disaster follows hard upon disaster...

It is in the face of this disaster, which besieges Jeremiah's heart as well as that of the people with whom he identifies, that the prophet must speak, or in his words 'cannot keep silent'.

Now, the ambiguities observed in v. 18 permit a different, though not necessarily antithetical, resolution from the one just described. While the rhetorical play between vv. 10 and 18 promotes reading *rā'ātēk* as 'doom' (and along with this we should note the similar use of *rā'â* in v. 6), v. 14 has employed the term in its ethical sense of 'wickedness'—a wickedness located in the heart no less, from which it must be washed. This sense too is present in *rā'ātēk* in v. 18, in which case the nominal sentence *zō't rā'ātēk* can refer to the first colon, 'Your way and your doings'. The latter expression has in turn picked up on the explanation given in the previous verse for the siege against Jerusalem: 'because she has rebelled against me, says the Lord'. 'Your way and your doings', the reader must conclude, are purely and simply a matter of rebellion. It does not seem unlikely in this regard that *kî mār* in v. 18b is a word-play on *kî-'ōtî mārātâ* in v. 17: Jerusalem's rebellion, her ways and doings, in short her *rā'â*, is bitter. The subject of *nāga'*, then, is still the nominal sentence *zō't rā'ātēk* but now in its ethical sense. Telescoping the syntax, we may paraphrase the final bi-cola as, 'This your most bitter wickedness has reached your very heart'. This is to say of the people that rebellion has stamped their whole being and infected their vital powers. They too have enacted an identity of sorts. They have become what they have done, and have been limited by what they have done.[38]

From this perspective Jeremiah's lamentation is a response to the people's self-attenuation through evil-doing. The infection of their heart afflicts his. Yet in this his unique status as prophet who stands not just with them but over against them is underscored, for the deep consternation at the core of his being (i.e. in his 'groaning heart') belongs to the compulsion that he speak Yhwh's condemnation upon them (see also v. 12). It is quite to this point that suddenly in v. 22 Yhwh's voice breaks through the prophet's in exclamation upon the people's willful ignorance:

> How foolish my people are![39]
>   They know me not.
> Stupid children are they
>   and void of understanding.
> They are wise in doing evil,
>   but of doing good they know nothing.

This verse helps throw into relief the contrasting situations of people and prophet. Jeremiah's heart-talk stems from a knowledge of Yhwh, an understanding of Yhwh's pathos and will, fatally absent from the people's heart. This knowledge for better *and* worse, i.e. to his 'delight' (15.16) and to his grief, distinguishes his heart from theirs.

It was suggested above that the two different resolutions of the ambiguities in v. 18 are not necessarily antithetical. That must be affirmed by maintaining first that it is in the nature of poetic discourse, as of metaphor itself, to generate multiple and simultaneous meanings; and second, that while such multiple meanings may frequently coexist in tension, or may even be starkly opposed, this is not so in the present case. Indeed, *rā'ātēk* means *both* 'your doom' and 'your wickedness'. Jeremiah's lamentation is doubly motivated: he laments the disaster that is overtaking the nation of which he is a part and whose fate he must share, and he laments the wickedness that brings about the disaster. For the purpose of thus analyzing the

3. The 'Heart' in Context

different aspects of the lament's motivation, the two meanings are distinguishable though still intimately related. And the distinction is useful for seeing how vv. 19c-21 relate to v. 22. But apart from these purposes the meanings remain coterminous: they are *rā'â*.

Much has already been said of v. 19 in the course of the contextual analysis, which is now complete. It remains only to confirm and elaborate these views by an internal analysis of the verse. The opening words, a double exclamation, *mē'ay mē'ay* ('my innards! my innards!'), attest the depth of the emotions that grip the prophet. They attest as well the peculiar resemblances (and the potential confusion) between the language game of emotion behavior and that of physiological sensation or malady. One may indeed 'feel' emotions, some of which one feels as pain (*'āḥûlâ*, 'I writhe in pain') and, further, as pain in the guts (*mē'îm*). However, that one does not normally feel such pain in the shoulder, neck, or foot may be as much a matter of learned linguistic conventions as of bio-chemical processes. In any case it would surely be inadequate to explain the pain as a stomach-ache, the result of acid indigestion, or by some more sophisticated physiological terminology.

Certainly, within the OT there is a linguistic convention for emotion behavior in which *mē'îm*, 'innards', has a well established place. Two important points should be noted in the examples that follow: the first is the frequent occurrence of 'heart' in the same context as 'innards'; second is the association of the emotions that affect or are entertained in the *mē'îm* with the *expression* of those emotions, in several cases as if the emotions were expressed *by* the *mē'îm*. To put it another way, the emotions to which the *mē'îm* play host are of such a compelling sort that to *have* them is to *manifest*, i.e. enact, them.

1. Ps 40.8f. The worshipper's avowal that he delights in doing the will of God, God's *Tôrâ* having been implanted *bᵉtôk mē'ay*, immediately issues in the report of his having 'told the glad news of deliverance in the great congregation', of his not hiding 'your saving help *bᵉtôk libbî*'.

2. Job 30.27. Job complains that, confronted with 'days of affliction', 'my bowels have been made to boil and cannot keep silent' (*mē'ay rūttᵉḥû wᵉlō' dāmmû*), a condition summarized four verses later as 'my lyre is turned to mourning'. That is, the emotion is expressed.

3. Lam 1.20-21. A personified Jerusalem cries,

See, O Yhwh, how distressed I am:
My innards [*mēʿay*] are in ferment,
My heart [*libbî*] turns over within me,
because I have been so rebellious...
They heard [LXX, Hear] how I groan...

4. Isa 63.15. In a supplicatory lament 'the murmuring of your innards' is a metaphorical corollary of Yhwh's mercies:

*hămôn mēʿêkā weraḥămêkā
ʾēlay hitʾappāqû*

The murmuring of your innards and your mercies
are withheld from me.

5. Isa 16.11; Jer 48.36. Each verse is part of an oracle on Moab. The first lines are strikingly similar, but where Isaiah has the 'innards' groaning, Jeremiah has the 'heart':

*ʿal-kēn mēʿay lemôʾāb
kakkinnôr yēhĕmû*

Therefore my innards for Moab
moan like the lyre.

*ʿal-kēn libbî lemôʾāb
kaḥălilîm yehĕmeh*

Therefore my heart for Moab
moans like the flute.

6. Jer 31.20. In the final bi-cola of this salvation oracle Yhwh's innards are said to groan or murmur with compassion for Ephraim:

*ʿal-kēn hāmû mēʿay lô
raḥēm ʾăraḥămennû neʾum-Yhwh*

Therefore my innards moan for him;
Surely, I will have mercy on him, says the Lord.

The examples demonstrate a normal employment of the term *mēʿîm* in talking about or giving expression to deep emotions, which may be as different as grief, delight, and compassion. They attest in other words a convention, or language game, the rules of which Jer 4.19 also seems to follow closely. The parallel use of 'heart' with 'innards'—

*mēʿay mēʿay ʾāḥûlâ
qîrôt libbî*

—much as in items 1, 3, and 5 above, shows 'heart' to be part of the same convention. The phrase *hōmeh-lî libbî* corresponds to the emotion-manifestation, or the having-enacting, pattern that characterizes the convention. In particular, the same verb *hmy* appears here as in items 5 and 6 (the derived noun *hāmôn* being employed in 4). In light of this correspondence, the stricter translation 'My heart groans to me' is to be preferred to the looser 'My heart is beating wildly' of the RSV, Wolff, and others, as the latter reflects a physically referential reading which proceeds from, or may lead to, a misconstrual of the language game operative here.[40] Again, the point is that the prophet is in the grip of emotion so deep and compelling that it *must* find expression; his heart groans with it, that is, as if the heart itself were speaking the emotion. Bright and Wolff's rendering of the next colon (*lō' 'aḥărîš*) as 'I cannot keep *still*' is to be rejected for the same reason.[41] The more specific 'I cannot keep *silent*' better suits both the convention and the context.

Lō' 'aḥărîš spoken by the prophet marks the intersection of the phenomenon of prophetic compulsion with the ordinary linguistic convention of emotion-manifestation.[42] As indicated by the examples listed above, the fact that having deep and powerful emotions entails expressing them is not in itself extraordinary; it belongs to the nature of such emotions, it is part of their enduring logic, that they be expressed. The expression *is* the emotion. However, that in the present case Jeremiah has and enacts the emotions at all *is* extraordinary. How he comes to do so calls for explanation.

Jeremiah's heart-talk stems from and presupposes a privileged knowledge of Yhwh; indeed, it is Yhwh's self-revelation through his word that marks Jeremiah's initiation as a prophet. It is because Yhwh's own words have been put in his mouth (1.9) and ingested (15.16) so as to become part of the fabric of his being that the prophet knows the severity of the people's situation and, knowing that, can lament—indeed, is compelled to lament—the impending 'doom' (*rā'â*), grieving both for himself and for the people. At the same time, it is because he has received Yhwh's words with all their burning irresistibility such that they cannot be held in (6.11; 20.9), and because he has been overpowered by Yhwh and so possessed by him as to suffer personally the same scorn, reproach, and mockery which the people display toward Yhwh's word (6.10; 15.15; 20.7-8)—it is because of all this that the prophet knows and is compelled to lament the nation's 'wickedness' (*rā'â*). In this respect his grieving is a grieving with God. Jeremiah's knowledge of God, in other words, means a sharing of God's emotions. As regards our interest in the self-constituting quality of his grieving, it can be seen that Jeremiah's words constitute him and enact his prophetic identity as one in sympathy with God. And as one in sympathy with God, he cannot keep from speaking God's response to 'wickedness'.[43]

It is evident that the emotion structure of 4.19 is complex, combining as it does elements of the human and divine pathos. Part of its complexity is its fact-presupposing quality. The grief presupposes several sets of facts having to do with the life of the people and the pathos and purpose of God. Further, as remarked before, the grief is multiply motivated with different grounds and objects, e.g. the coming disaster and the national corruption. The grief, therefore, is not a simple and singular quality but a composite phenomenon colored with other emotions. On the human side the anguish of the innards, the writhing pain, and the murmuring of the heart suggest fear, fear at the sound of the trumpet and the battle alarm, i.e. fear of the coming judgment. On the divine side the lamentation suggests anger, a suggestion informed and substantiated by other passages where Jeremiah speaks of being 'full of the wrath of Yhwh' (6.11) or of Yhwh's having 'filled me with indignation' (15.17). To see God's anger as a component of Jeremiah's grief makes it fully intelligible that the remark 'I cannot keep silent', taken as an expression of the prophetic compulsion, should issue in Yhwh's indignant statement on the people's ignorance and obduracy in v. 22, a statement which, as always, comes through the mouth of the prophet.

Summary

This exegesis has attempted many things. It has sought to provide and justify a metaphorical reading of the word 'heart' against Wolff's physically referential reading (or against any assumption of a simple genetic relation between the two). This required an explication of the metaphor in terms of the language games, the linguistic activities and conventions, in which it has its normal placement. By analyzing the conventions we gained insight into the emotion entailments, or emotion structure, of the text (4.1ff.), and especially of Jeremiah's first-person utterances (vv. 8, 10, 19-21). At the same time we were led to explore a dimension of selfhood that these conventions, and within them the metaphor 'heart', brought into focus. While the

3. The 'Heart' in Context

biblical text does not as a rule speak discursively or theoretically about the concept 'self', by delineating a range of behavior regarded as essential to a proper relation to God, it illustrates what it means to have a self. A basic ingredient in having a self, the text leads us to conclude, is using the *language* of the self, which Jeremiah does with notable skill.

That the historical Jeremiah, or the text's redactors, or the literary-theological persona of the prophet had a *concept* of the self— which surely they did/do, if the criterion for having at least a practical concept of something is the proper and intelligent use of that something (in this case the language of the self)—does not finally seem to be a significant point for understanding the design and intention of the text. What is significant is that the text seems intent on showing a self-in-progress, though it does not present the progress in a systematically chronological way. The text is concerned with rendering a unique identity, indeed a uniquely prophetic identity, and with depicting Jeremiah's enactment of this identity by his self-constituting language and the exercise of essential human faculties and capacities. It remains to be seen to what extent this identity and the mode of its depiction function as an interpretive device for the book as a whole.

Chapter 4

THE PROPHETIC 'I' AND ITS AMBIGUITIES: SELF-IDENTIFICATION AND THE PORTRAIT OF A PARADIGM*

In the last chapter it was observed how the first-person language of Jer 4.1-22 articulated the prophet's sympathetic self-identification with both God and people. This identification and the mode of its enactment are not unique to that passage. Nor are they an accidental element in the text's characterization of the prophet. An investigation of three other blocks of material in which first-person language figures prominently will show them to be a carefully patterned theme at the very center of the portrait drawn by the text. The three passages are, in order of presentation, 10.17ff., 14.1–15.4, and 8.4–9.25.

The immediate difficulty raised by these texts is the ambiguities they present as to who the first-person speaker is at any given point, whether Jeremiah, Yhwh, the people, or some combination of the three. Scholarly opinion is sharply divided. Martin Buber represents one end of the spectrum of opinion when he writes (specifically with respect to differentiating between prophet and people),

> But no word of Jeremiah is simply personal... His 'I' is so deeply set in the 'I' of the people that his life cannot be regarded as that of an individual. In general those who tend to distinguish precisely in Scripture between the collective and the individual 'I' are mistaken. The 'I' of the individual remains transparent into the 'I' of the community. It is no metaphor when Jeremiah speaks of the people of Israel not only as 'we' but also as 'I'...[1]

At the other end of the spectrum stands William L. Holladay who is confident that rhetorical analysis resolves the ambiguities into a clean separation of voices. Referring in particular to the versions of Buber's position represented by Rudolph and Heschel, Holladay observes that

4. The Prophetic 'I' & its Ambiguities

... earlier commentators, faced with the confusing changes of speaker, have often resorted to theories of the *blending of voices*— where the 'I' of God and the 'I' of Jeremiah are identified, or even where God and the people are identified. But I have found it best to keep the voices quite distinct; we shall find, I think, that the rhetorical patterns can be understood satisfactorily without resort to any theory of blending.[2]

Our course will steer between these two poles. To the extent that we find significant signposts in the text indicating the prophet's own voice, there we shall have reason to believe, contra Buber, that Jeremiah's 'I' has an individuality that the text does not wish utterly dissolved at the outset into the 'we' of the community. On the other hand, to the extent that at certain points the finished text allows its ambiguities to stand in such a way as to 'blend' the voices of its personae, we shall accept this blending as a datum of literary and theological relevance and reject Holladay's efforts to keep the voices consistently distinct by recourse to a rhetorical reconstruction of the text in a form prior to that of its completion.

I. *Jeremiah 10.17ff.*

Of the three units to be analyzed, this is the most hotly contested, the crux being vv. 19-20 in particular:

19 'ôy lî 'al-šibrî
    naḥlâ makkātî
  wa'ănî 'āmartî
  'ak zeh ḥŏlî
    w^e'eśśā'ennû
20 'ohŏlî šuddād w^ekol-mêtāray nittāqû
    bānay y^eṣā'ūnî w^e'ênām
  'ên-nōṭeh 'ôd 'ohŏlî
    ûmēqîm y^erî'ôtay

19 Woe is me because of my hurt.
     My wound is grievous.
   But I said,
   'Truly this is an affliction,
     and I must bear it.'
20 My tent is destroyed and all my cords are broken;
     my children have gone from me, and they are not;
   There is no one to spread my tent again
     and to set up my curtains. (RSV)

It appears self-evident to the commentators only that whoever the speaker is here, it is not Yhwh. Is it then Jeremiah, as some believe on the basis of the linguistic parallels between v. 20 and 4.20? Or is it the personified city/land (i.e. the people), as others maintain? Further, does *wa'ănî 'āmartî* ('And/Then/But I said') in v. 19b signal a shift in speaker, and if so, does the second voice end in 19b (note the RSV's closed quotation marks) or extend through v. 20? Or again, is there a blend of voices, and at what point(s)?

Textual emendation has been one route to a coherent reading. By moving *wa'ănî* from 19b to the beginning of the verse and reading a *wāw*-consecutive *wa'eśśā'ennû* in place of simple *wāw* plus imperfect (thus, 'But as for me, woe is me... I have said, Surely this is my pain and I *have borne* it'), B. Duhm was able to say, 'Only the terrified complaint speaks throughout. Indeed, no third party complains (say, the people), rather Jeremiah himself, which the kinship of this poem with 4.19-21 clearly shows.'[3] Volz worked to achieve consistency of speaker also, but from a different starting point and with opposite results. Having identified the people as the speaker in 4.19, he radically emended 10.19b to read 'bitter schrecklich ist meine Krankheit, ich kann's "nicht" tragen'.[4]

For a synchronic approach emendation is the least satisfactory means of solving the problem, since often it proposes either to know what the text wants to say better than the text itself, or to reconstruct it in an earlier, supposedly purer form. Still, the implication of both Duhm and Volz's 'solutions' is interesting. Both seem concerned to counter an impression created by the present text that a different voice (Duhm's 'third party') is speaking in 19b. This is an impression we shall seek to substantiate.

Duhm's emendations in v. 20 are equally interesting. Here he substitutes the LXX reading 'my sheep' for the admittedly difficult MT *y^{e}ṣā'unî* and deletes *bānay* as an editorial interpretation 'which has been influenced by Isa 54.1ff. and proceeds from the notion that Israel or Zion is speaking here'.[5] Again, this is a notion that will be later confirmed. The point is, that in adducing (rightly or wrongly) how the material was heard by a redactor and how it was further shaped to enhance that hearing, Duhm ironically witnesses to the effect of the final shape of the text.

W. Baumgartner in his landmark form-critical study *Die Klagegedichte des Jeremia* also resorts to emendation to maintain consistency of speaker. He cuts the Gordian knot by deleting the offensive *wa'ănî*

4. The Prophetic 'I' & its Ambiguities 61

'ămartî as an explanatory gloss. As we shall see, there is form-critical evidence that militates against this move. Baumgartner then attributes the complaint all to Jeremiah, observing that 'the words *šbr*, *mkh*, and *ḥly* pertain originally to bodily suffering and have been taken from the lamentation song...'[6] H. Wildberger follows suit, arguing against Volz that the unit is *not* a complaint of the land since 'the image of sickness belongs to the lamentation of the individual'.[7] Once again, it will be shown that the evidence on *šbr* in particular is more ambiguous than Baumgartner and Wildberger admit, and further that there is evidence internal to the book of Jeremiah for associating this language with the personified city or land. In the meantime, suffice it to say that the *original* locus of a term does not in general preclude its expanded use in later contexts (and that here in particular the form-critical categories are employed by these scholars more as straitjackets than guides).

Against Duhm, Baumgartner, and Wildberger, most commentators side with Volz in attributing vv. 19-20 to the people/city/land. Representing the majority position, H. Lamparter comments:

> The answer to this frightening threat [vv. 17-18] is the wail of the people who, like a mother bereft of her sons (v. 20), like some homeless nomad deprived of his tent, complain of their terrible plight... The burden of the text lies in v. 19: Now, since they have been led into exile, it becomes painfully clear to the people that the 'wound' which they suffered is 'incurable'; the stroke received is fatal. The hope that the period of oppression would be brief, their manifest self-consolation that things would not come to their worst, has proved delusive.[8]

Crucial for our interpretation is the connection Lamparter sees between vv. 17-18 and the following verses. This will be treated later in greater detail. For the moment we may note his handling of v. 19b which he renders with the past perfect of *denken*, 'Und ich hatte gedacht...', thereby creating the effect of speaker continuity with 19a. And the form in which he casts the following quotation ('Nur eine Krankheit ist's, die ich ertragen kann') suggests that it is indeed the people speaking here as they recall their expectation that their troubles would pass more or less harmlessly away.[9] Identical in thrust with the other interpretations that view the people as speaking uninterruptedly through vv. 19-20,[10] this reading of 19b has in its favor simplicity, logical clarity, and a tolerable compatibility with the

Hebrew. Though we may ultimately prefer a different construal, this one cannot be definitively ruled out.

It would appear to be only a minor qualification of Lamparter's position when some commentators note that it is the prophet speaking 'for' or 'as' the people in these verses.[11] Here is the 'blending of voices' theory mentioned above, a theory which Heschel illustrates in radical form with the statement, 'The prophet who had served as a voice castigating the people was now, in sorrow, the voice *of* the people'.[12] However, the qualification takes on profound significance for the prophet's identity when viewed, say, in the context of Heschel's 'theology of pathos'[13] or in terms of a possible cultic *Sitz-im-Leben*. The latter idea was applied to our passage by Weiser, who saw here a 'traditional schema, the cultic lamentation ceremony',[14] and even more vigorously by H. Graf von Reventlow, for whom the passage *is* the cultic liturgy itself, with Jeremiah the liturgist, his 'I' entirely a representative 'I', or in Buber's words, thoroughly 'transparent to the "I" of the community'.[15] Without denying that an earlier cultic *Sitz-im-Leben* may be a relevant factor in the passage's interpretation, I would want to question Reventlow's assumption that the path from cult to text is so direct as not to permit a substantial transformation of the transmitted material. This and other questions pertaining to Reventlow's thesis will be taken up in the next section. For now we shall only observe that the blending theory, as formulated by any of the scholars cited above, makes an important contribution to the interpretation of the passage; nevertheless, it is still too imprecise to do justice to the subtle dynamics of the text.

An alternative position to those maintaining consistency of speaker in vv. 19-20—whether that speaker is regarded as Jeremiah, the people, or Jeremiah *qua* people—is offered solely by S.R. Hopper in the exposition portion of the IB. Noting the dialogical flavor of the unit 17-22, Hopper writes:

> The reply of the people is deep and moving. The woe and hurt which they express carries within it the overtones of Jeremiah's own deep wound. Metaphors of the collapsed tent and its broken cords are reminiscent of Jeremiah's earlier use of this figure (4:20). It is the land which has been destroyed, the children (sheep) have been dispersed, and there is no adequate leadership to restore the country's well-being...
>
> The depth of the personal tone in vs. 19, with the undeniable realism of its cry—

4. The Prophetic 'I' & its Ambiguities

> Truly this is an affliction,
> and I must bear it—

persuades Skinner that Jeremiah is speaking here within the context of 'an experience of which he himself is the subject.' The similarity of this passage in tone to the depth-penetrations of the confessional poems makes it impossible not to share in this recognition, however the question as to the allegorical character of the passage is resolved.[16]

Hopper's remarks are more profitably viewed in relation to his earlier discussion of the double-pointedness of the imagery in 4.20:

> The tents are undoubtedly the tents of the people... No more pathetic image of rout and defeat could be chosen than that of the collapsed tents with their colorful curtains dishevelled and torn. But the recurrence of this image in 10:19-22 suggests that it is not merely the tents of the personified Judah that are ruined, but something in Jeremiah too is fallen or collapsed. The reader... is made to feel at once the inner consternation and panic in conjunction with the outer confusion of the enemy pouring through the walls...[17]

Now, it was Skinner who raised the question of the 'allegorical character' of 10.19-20, suggesting that to read the passage as the 'personified nation' was to read it allegorically. He dismissed this option on the basis of the 'personal' quality of 19b, and was thereby 'driven to interpret it after the analogy of 4.20', which he had read as the personal speech of Jeremiah.[18]

Skinner's opposition 'allegorical' vs. 'personal' is a false one that has no bearing on either the reading which hears the personified nation speaking throughout or on Hopper's that hears Jeremiah's own voice in 19b, although Hopper apparently senses a threat that it might. In effect, Hopper's own exegesis of the double-pointed imagery quite precludes any such threat. He explicates Jeremiah's 'inner consternation' in analogy with the tent image taken as a whole, resisting the urge to tie every feature of the depiction of the tent to a feature of Jeremiah's inner life, i.e. as if the broken cords, the lost children, the lack of anyone to spread the tent again or erect the curtains each made specific reference to a different aspect of the prophet's distress. Such would be the path taken by allegory, and in this case, as typically in the OT, there is no textual warrant for it.

What textual warrants are there for a reading like Hopper's which posits first the people, then the prophet speaking in 10.19? First, we would want to insist with many others that vv. 19f. be seen in context with vv. 17-18.[19] Whatever the original use of these two units, whether they once circulated independently or not, their present juxtaposition in the larger literary context invites the reader to probe for the connections between them that make their juxtaposition intelligible.[20] Certainly, the connections are more direct than those between 17-18 and the preceding argument against the idols with its hymnic elements of praise to the Creator (10.1-16). The command to prepare for deportation and the announcement of Yhwh's judgment in 17-18 represent a quite different order of discourse from what precedes it; the language game is one in which a response of anguished complaint would be at home.

The significant fact about the command is that it is couched in the second feminine singular:

17 *'ispî mē'ereṣ kin'ātēk*
  yōšebety[21] *bammāṣôr*

> Gather up your bundle from the ground,
>   O you who dwell under siege! (RSV)

The second feminine singular address occurs elsewhere in Jeremiah, most notably in 4.14, 4.30-31, and 6.8, in each of which the addressee is explicitly identified as Jerusalem (or 'daughter of Zion', 4.31). The identification is implicit in 5.7 ('How can I pardon you [*lāk*]? Your sons [*bānayik*] have abandoned me...') by virtue of the mention of 'Jerusalem' in 5.1. We are compelled to conclude that it is this same personified city that is addressed in 10.17.

It is equally compelling to conclude that the one who responds to the judgment oracle is the one who was addressed by it. Analysis of the language in 19a provides substantiation. First, an exclamation of woe (*'ôy lî*, 'Woe is me'), placed in the mouth of the city, or less metaphorically its citizens, is not uncommon to Jeremiah.[22] Indeed, in 15.10 and 45.3 *'ôy lî/'ôy-nā' lî* is spoken by individuals, Jeremiah and Baruch respectively. But in the same contexts as three of the four passages cited above in which Jerusalem is addressed, the 'woe' belongs to her and/or her people. In 4.13 Jeremiah's depiction of Yhwh's approaching judgment is punctuated by *'ôy lānû kî šuddādᵉnû*.[23] Immediately following is the address to Jerusalem to cleanse her heart of wickedness 'that you may be saved (*tiwwāšē'î*)', i.e. from the ruin that calls forth the 'woe'. In 4.31 the prophet reports overhearing 'the cry of the daughter of Zion' (i.e. the 'desolate

4. The Prophetic 'I' & its Ambiguities 65

one' who was informed in the preceding verse that 'your lovers... seek your life') as she exclaims, *'ôy-nā' lî* 'for I am fainting before murderers'. Finally, in the battle scene of ch. 6 in which Yhwh announces his intention to destroy 'the daughter of Zion' (v. 2) and later addresses her with 'Be warned, O Jerusalem' (v. 8), the city is heard responding to the adversaries' battle plans, *'ôy lānû* 'for the day declines, for the shadows of evening lengthen' (v. 4b).[24] It should be noted that in each of the passages just adduced the *'ôy lî/lānû* comes in response to some form of an announcement of judgment upon Jerusalem, just as in 10.19.

The 'distress' (10.18) coming upon the city is felt as a 'wound': *'ôy lî 'al-šibrî*. Baumgartner and Wildberger had argued that *šeber* along with *makkâ* and *ḥolî* were originally terms for bodily suffering and belonged to the lamentation of the individual and that the speaker here in 19a must therefore be Jeremiah. However, to treat *šeber* and *makkâ* on the same plane as *ḥolî* is quite misleading, *ḥolî* being considerably more literal in this context than the other two terms.

The use of *šeber* in particular is metaphorical, its sense as 'wound' or 'hurt' being an extension of its more generalized meaning as 'break'. Proverbs 17.19b offers a good illustration of the metaphorical play of the word: 'he who makes high his door seeks destruction (*šāber*)', i.e. 'a breaking'. The idea of personal ruin (coming upon the man most intent on averting it) clearly trades on the picture of the impregnable door being *broken* down. The illustration demonstrates what in fact is a very ordinary application of the term to purely physical objects, such as doors, jars (Isa 30.14), and, indeed, city walls. Note, for instance, Ps 60.4: 'thou hast rent it open: repair its breaches (*šĕbārêhû*) for it totters'.

Similar instances can be found in Jeremiah. Jer 14.17 for example—

kî šeber gādôl nišbᵉrâ bᵉtûlat bat 'ammî
makkâ naḥlâ mᵉ'ōd

—is easily rendered 'For a great breach has been broken in the virgin daughter of my people [i.e. Jerusalem], a very grievous blow'. In the same vein, for *šeber 'al-šeber niqrā'* in Jer 4.20 Peake suggests 'breach meeteth breach', which is perfectly suited to the passage's imagery of military devastation.[25]

To be sure, passages like the two above entail an interpenetration of meanings, of *šeber*'s general sense as 'breakage'/'destruction', in which it is eminently applicable to the city as fortress, and its more specialized, personal sense as 'wound', where it applies to people, individually or collectively. Nowhere is this interpenetration more explicit than in the word-play of 8.21: *'al-šeber bat-'ammî hošbārtî,* 'For the *destruction* of the daughter of my people I am *wounded*'.

The same dynamic between *šeber*'s general and personal senses, between city and prophet, is at work in our passage. The immediate point, however, is that Baumgartner's argument proves no obstacle to hearing *šeber* as spoken by the personified city. And certainly, such usage is much less a matter of a form-critical development or adaptation of the individual-lament *Gattung* than it is a matter of the particular term's established range of uses.

As for *makkâ* ('smiting', 'blow', 'wound'), it is *only* in Jer 15.18 that it is used in reference to the prophet as an individual. Elsewhere within the book, as in the prophetic literature as a whole, it occurs overwhelmingly in relation to a corporate entity—the people, nation, or city.[26] Significantly, in Jer 6.7, which addresses Jerusalem as 'the city which must be punished' (v. 6), *makkâ* is paired with *ḥolî*:

ḥāmās wāšōd yiššāma' bāh
'al-pānay tāmîd ḥolî ûmakkâ

Violence and destruction are heard within her;
before me continually are sickness and smiting.

And in 14.17, already cited as an instance of *šeber*'s application to Jerusalem, *makkâ* occurs with the adjective *naḥlâ*, the same as in 10.19, in apposition with *šeber*.

All this is more significant yet when seen in relation to the 'Book of Consolation'. Here the theme of judgment that dominates the rest of Jeremiah is turned on its head in a series of proclamations of restoration and reversal of fortunes. Just as the root *šwb*—which was used as a leitmotif in the judgment oracles and here figures prominently in 30.3, 18, 23; 32.44; 33.7, 11, and 26—poetically signals the reversal theme on the grand scale, so in a detailed way specific motifs and formulations from the earlier materials are taken up and artfully ordered to underscore this new theme. In particular 30.12-17 takes up the earlier depictions of Jerusalem as the adulterous woman who was spurned and assaulted by the foes she had once solicited as lovers (e.g. 4.30-31, 8.21-22, and 13.20-27) in order now to proclaim judgment upon the lover-foes and to promise healing for her once incurable wounds. Especially noteworthy is the parallel use of *šeber* and *makkâ naḥlâ* in v. 12, similar to 10.19 and 14.17 but now, not incidentally, in the second feminine singular. It follows that when

4. The Prophetic 'I' & its Ambiguities

in 30.15 we read 'Why do you cry out over your hurt?' (again, *šibrēk*) and are thereby induced to recall concrete instances of Jerusalem's pained outcries, 10.19 comes readily to mind as a primary example. In short, 30.12-17 functions as a reprise of Jerusalem's earlier exclamations of distress with vv. 12 and 15a in particular alluding to 10.19a.

The evidence thus appears overwhelming that the speaker of 10.19a is meant to be heard as the personified Jerusalem. The same is true for v. 20:

'ohŏlî šuddād wᵉkol-mêtāray nittāqû
  bānay yᵉṣā'ṣûnî wᵉ'ênām

'ên-nōṭeh 'ôd 'ohŏlî
  ûmēqîm yᵉrî'ôtāy

To be sure, the imagery of a fallen tent can serve as a metaphor for individual death (Isa 22.24; 38.12; Job 4.21; 30.11) such that one might imagine it to be Jeremiah speaking of himself here. And recalling Hopper's remark that 'something in Jeremiah too is fallen or collapsed', we want to say that it *is* Jeremiah, after a fashion. However, the imagery is more directly applicable to a city (the single tent-abode being a constitutive part of the city) than to the human body; the latter would require a greater extension in metaphoric reach.

The tent imagery is applied to the city in Isa 33.20, though in a positive context, i.e. in a guarantee that the tent will *not* fall: 'Look upon Zion...! Your eyes will see Jerusalem, a quiet habitation, an immovable tent (*'ōhel*), whose tent stakes will never be plucked up, nor will any of its cords (*ḥăbālāyw*) be broken'. Again, in Isa 54.2 Zion is addressed under the synecdoche of the tent:

harḥîbî mᵉqôm 'ohŏlēk
  wîrî'ôt miškᵉnôtayik yaṭṭû
  'al-taḥśōkî
ha'ărîkî mêtārayik
  witēdōtayik ḥazzeqî

Enlarge the place of your tent
  and let the curtains of your habitations be stretched out;
  hold not back.
Lengthen your cords
  and strengthen your stakes. (RSV)

With the inclusion of *yᵉrî'ôt* and *mêtārayik*, this verse closely approximates Jer 10.20 in its terminology. Accordingly, we may note that these two terms are most frequently used (the latter almost exclusively so) in P material dealing with the tent/tabernacle traditions.[27] In Jer 10.20 it is quite likely that in speaking of '*my* tent' with just this language Jerusalem is in fact speaking of *the* tent, i.e. the Temple, which is not only the theological heart of Jersualem but a theological synecdoche for it, the symbol of the city itself. Stated inductively, whoever within the corpus of the OT speaks of 'my tent' in just this language is bound to sound like Jerusalem, that is to say, most probably *is* Jerusalem.

The data on *bānay*, 'my sons', leads to the same conclusion. Verse 20 *cannot* be read as a strictly literal, autobiographical statement of Jeremiah since in 16.2 Jeremiah is prohibited from taking a wife or having children 'in this place'. And nowhere in the book is Jeremiah's relation to his people even metaphorically represented as a paternal one. This is reserved for Yhwh (so 3.14, 21-22; 4.22; and 31.20) and, more idiomatically, the eponymous ancestors—Israel, Benjamin, and Judah (e.g. *bᵉnê yiśrā'ēl*).[28] Otherwise, the passages most relevant to ours are 5.7 and 31.15. In the first Yhwh addresses Jerusalem in the second feminine singular as a mother of apostate sons: *bānayik 'āzābûnî* ('Your sons have deserted me'). In the second the land is personified as the ancestress Rachel who weeps at the loss of sons:

rāḥēl mᵉbakkâ 'al-bānêhā
   mē'ănâ lᵉhinnāḥēm
'al-bānêhā kî 'ênennû

Rachel is weeping for her sons,
   refusing to be comforted
for her sons—for they are not.

The abandoned-mother/lost-sons motif, together with the use of the negative particle *'ên* plus suffix, is clearly reminiscent of 10.20—a fact in keeping with the character of the 'Book of Consolation' as a reprise of earlier themes and motifs reworked in the context of salvation.

To repeat the main point, the use of *bānay* points toward Jerusalem, the city personified as mother, as the principal speaker. Thus, our conclusions are consistent throughout: both the evidence from context (the second feminine singular address in v. 17) and from language (*'ôy lî, šibrî, naḥlâ makkātî*, the tent imagery, *bānay*, and *'ênām*) require that the voice of Jerusalem be heard in 10.19a, 20.

4. *The Prophetic 'I' & its Ambiguities* 69

It might be asked to what extent this conclusion is consistent with the reading offered in the last chapter that treated 4.19-20 as Jeremiah's speech, given the similarity in language between 4.20 and 10.20. Apart from the fact that the element of personification is more elaborate in the latter, and tighter by virtue of *bānay*, it must be remembered that 4.19-20 was in fact evaluated as expressing in part Jeremiah's identification with his people's plight, an identification grounded in his prophetic vocation. Thus, when he speaks of 'the walls of my heart' in 4.19 and employs the tent imagery in v. 20, it is not too fanciful that we should hear Jerusalem's voice resonating in his own or that his persona has, as it were, blended into and fused with the persona of Jerusalem.[29]

The same identification of the prophet with his people is also at work in 10.19-20 such that now Jeremiah's voice is heard behind, blended with, or coming through Jerusalem's. There is no inconsistency with the way we read 4.19-20, for the literary configuration is slightly altered. The personae have switched positions, Jerusalem from background to foreground, and Jeremiah from foreground to, if not precisely the background, at least to a parallel position. The difference is that here the identification is overtly stated. Jeremiah directly affirms it in 19b, identifying Jerusalem's 'affliction' as his own:

> *wa'ănî 'āmartî 'ak zeh ḥolî wᵉ'eśśā'ennû*

The question, of course, is whether this statement in 19b can and should be heard as Jeremiah's. Is it possible, much less compelling, to read it as Jeremiah's own self-conscious (and self-constituting) reflection upon his relation to his people's grief, a reflection breaking in upon Jerusalem's complaint and momentarily separating his voice from hers precisely for the sake of avowing that his formal identification with her is also a deeply felt and personal one?

At first glance the form-critical evidence would seem to be quite negative. Certainly, the self-quotation formula 'And I said', regardless of its grammatical construction (i.e. whether in the simple perfect, converted perfect, converted imperfect, and with or without the independent personal pronoun), does not in itself signal a shift in speaker. In fact, when it occurs within the 'descriptions of distress' in the lamentation and thanksgiving psalms, a shift in speaker is not only *not* required but quite inappropriate, since there the formula only marks the psalmist's recollection of a state of mind that reflects, sometimes ironically, the plight from which he was or hopes to be delivered.[30] The apparent congruence between such passages and ours might suggest that 19b is a continuous part of Jerusalem's complaint and should be read as having an ironic force, i.e. as the recollection of an earlier statement which from a later perspective proved foolish and/or false, much like Ps 30.7: 'As for me, I said in my prosperity, "I shall never be moved"'. Translating 19b accordingly, we would read, 'But as for me, I had said, "This is merely an affliction, and I can (shall) bear it"'[31]—an attitude clearly unwarranted by the gravity of the situation and indeed one proved delusive by later events.

However, certain literary factors disrupt the form-critical analogy. When such irony occurs in the psalmic material, it is an irony of which the speaker himself is conscious. He is himself speaking from that perspective from which the folly of the quoted statement is evident. Not so Jerusalem in Jer 10.19-20. Her persona as constructed by the book is of someone incapable of this sort of irony. That is precisely the pathos of her (and her people's) situation: unable to make the connection between her grief and her guilt (6.15; 8.12; 9.11-13; 13.22-27), her laments fall short of genuine confession (4.13-14, 31; 6.4; 14.7-9), and what ostensible repentance she makes is judged a 'pretense' (3.10; 5.2; 14.10; 34.15-17).[32] The kind of radical self-knowledge upon which self-irony depends is totally lacking. If one still insists on reading 10.19b as an ironic statement by Jerusalem, it is to see her as the unwitting *victim* of the irony, not its self-conscious author. But such a reading is no longer in strict form-critical analogy to the supposed parallels. The book's literary depiction of the Jerusalem persona has intervened to qualify the interpretive situation.

Should 19b then be read non-ironically but still as part of Jerusalem's lament? This would be to hear it as her own straightforward acceptance of her plight: 'But/And as for me, I say, "Surely, this is an affliction and I shall bear it"'. Nothing absolutely precludes this reading, but neither is it form-critically required. Comparison shows just how neutral the quoted statement really is: It is not really a confession of sin *to* Yhwh, like Ps 32.5, nor is it a confession *in* him, like Pss 31.15, 140.17, and 142.6. Neither is it a petition (Ps 41.5), or a remark to or about enemies (Pss 38.17; 75.5). Finally, the verb $nś'$ adds nothing to the description of distress, except the speaker's avowed owning of it. Thus, nowhere do the 'I said' statements of the psalms (including the prayers of Hezekiah and Jonah) function in quite the way this one does. In essence a redundancy with respect to

4. The Prophetic 'I' & its Ambiguities

its preceding bi-cola, v. 19b is unique with respect to the statements with which it might be compared.

In sum, the use of the self-quotation formula in Jer 10.19b is not so stereotypic or so rigidly fixed in the pattern of the complaint/thanksgiving psalms that it can only be heard as spoken by the same voice that speaks in vv. 19a, 20. In fact, it is sufficiently peculiar that a different voice seems likely. The redundancy ceases to be a redundancy *only* when someone else is speaking it.

Now there are within the prophetic literature numerous instances of the self-quotation formula used by the prophet himself, although most of these occur within a larger context of narrated dialogue. On several occasions, however, the formula is used to introduce the prophet's personal response to the conduct or plight of his people as this is depicted in an immediate context which is not otherwise marked as dialogue. For instance, in Isa 22.4, after Jerusalem has been accusingly interrogated—

> What do you mean that you have gone up,
> > all of you to the housetops,
> you who are full of shoutings,
> > tumultuous city,
> > exultant town?—

the prophet comes forward to say,

> Therefore I said (*'al-kēn 'āmartî*),
> 'Look away from me,
> > let me weep bitter tears;
> do not labor to comfort me
> > for the destruction of the daughter of my people'. (RSV)

In Isa 24.16, with a tone that contrasts sharply with the joyful clamor surrounding him, the prophet separates his voice from the crowd's with the self-quotation formula (*wā'ōmar*, 'But I said') and cries, *rāzî-lî rāzî-lî 'ôy lî*:

> I pine away, I pine away, woe is me! The treacherous deal
> > treacherously,
> > the treacherous deal very treacherously! (RSV)

In both cases the prophet's response is a grieving over his people.[33] Similarly, Jer 5.4 employs the self-quotation formula to introduce the prophet's internal reflection upon the people's refusal to feel 'anguish', take 'correction', and 'repent' (5.3):

Then I said (*wa'ănî 'āmartî*),
'These are only the poor,
    they have no sense;
for they do not know the way of the Lord,
    the law of their God'. (RSV)

These instances make it feasible to hear Jer 10.19b as the prophet's personal commentary upon Jerusalem's unhappy condition. The feasibility of such a reading is substantially heightened by the fact that the identification which is the substance of Jeremiah's commentary has been anticipated by 4.19-21 and even more pointedly by 8.21. The latter was previously cited as the most explicit example of the interpenetration of *šeber*'s personal and general senses. Now we should note that it is in fact identical in thrust with our passage. What needs explaining is not how 10.19b could be heard as Jeremiah's voice, but how, after hearing him connect Jersualem's *šeber* with his own in 8.21, we could hear it as anyone else's.

One final element of literary and linguistic logic leads to the same point; in fact it underlies the whole argument. At issue is the fundmental logic of the narrative context implied by the first-person singular verb *'āmartî*.[34] Now, in oral discourse there can be no question as to the owner of the 'I' in 'I said'; the speaker is present and manifest. However, in a literary work where an antecedent for the 'I' must be located just as it must for 'you', 'she', etc., various overlapping conventions must serve to approximate the self-evident conditions of the oral situation so as to enable us to do the locating. Often the text supplies the name of the 'I' in the immediate context. Such is the case with most dialogues and with, say, the speech of Yhwh in Jer 3.6ff. In circumstances where the name of the 'I' has *not* been immediately supplied, we rely on the text's characterization of its personae to match the content of the 'I said' statement with the persona for whom such a statement is in character. This was in part the procedure followed in analyzing the proposed form-critical analogy between 10.19b and the complaint psalms.[35] Seeing that 19b could not be spoken by Jerusalem, we are then thrown upon a convention so basic that it is only in extraordinary circumstances that one would think to mention it at all. That is, we move to a larger context, that of the work as a whole, identifying the 'I' with the persona whose perspective dominates the piece. For instance, the 'I said' of the psalms is attributed to the speaker of the entire prayer, whom we refer to generically as 'the psalmist' in the absence of a specific name.[36]

When a name *is* supplied in the psalm's superscription and we accordingly designate 'the psalmist' as, say, David—however fictitious our historical criticism may show the superscription to be—it becomes evident that the convention at work is in fact the same that is at the heart of all autobiographical genres, pure and mixed. The convention is one in which the title of the work itself bears the name of the principal persona, a persona whose first-person *perspective*, once again, dominates the work as a whole.[37] It is by this convention that we identify the frequent 'I said' statements in Qoheleth as belonging to Qoheleth. So it is in the books of Isaiah (6.5ff.; 22.4; 24.16), Ezekiel (4.14; etc.), Amos (7.2-5), and Micah (3.1). So it must also be in Jeremiah 10.19b (as also in 1.6ff.; 4.10; 5.4; 11.5; 14.13; 20.9; and 24.3). The voice intruding upon Jerusalem's complaint is Jeremiah's own.

By way of summary it remains only to fill out our reading of the passage and assess its function as part of the book's characterization of the prophet. Accordingly, we read v. 17 as a command addressed to a feminine singular subject to prepare for exile. The command is grounded in Yhwh's announced intention to 'sling out the inhabitants of the land' and 'bring distress upon them' (v. 18). The addressee, Jerusalem, personified as a mother, responds in 19a with an exclamation of woe upon her 'hurt' and 'grievous wound'. In the next bi-cola the self-quotation formula *wa'ănî 'āmartî* marks the intrusion of the prophet's voice in reflection upon the city's plight. The formula thereby serves to individuate the prophet. As one who *can* report 'But I said', Jeremiah shows that he has his own voice which can be heard separately from the community's. This can only mean that his 'I' has an integrity of its own and that we cannot, as if by some *a priori*, deductive logic, automatically equate it with, reduce and dissolve it into the 'I/we' of the corporate entity. If an equation *is* to be made, Jeremiah must make it. Of course, as the content of his reflection shows, this is exactly what he does. Affirming Jerusalem's affliction to be his own, he constitutes himself as her co-complainant and enacts his identity in terms of an identification with her. Indeed, it is precisely because of what Jeremiah does with his 'I', it is because of what he says in 19b, that we now hear v. 20 as a blend of the two voices, Jerusalem's *and* Jeremiah's. In fact, it seems doubtful that without Jeremiah's presence here Jerusalem would have any voice at all. For is it not the case, as the dynamic we observed in ch. 4 would suggest and as the one we shall trace in ch. 14 will confirm, that Jeremiah is speaking not just with but *for* Jerusalem and that without the prophet's acceptance of his intercessory role this obtuse and insentient Jerusalem would have to remain mute? Otherwise the complaint would appear more like an ideal projection of what a properly responsive Jerusalem would say when chastised, an eschatological, post-judgment Jerusalem similar to the Ephraim of 31.9, 18-19. For the complaint to be heard as the words of the actual Jerusalem who presently stands under threat of judgment, it seems likely that the prophet would have to be speaking it for her.

In any event, the effect of the blending in v. 20 is profound. The language of the complaint, already metaphoric by virtue of the personification, achieves a special density and depth by being referred to a specific person. Not only does the language direct us to picture a people speaking collectively as a city, and further to picture the city in the image of a tent—unstrung, collapsed, abandoned—and yet further (but still via the tent), to picture the city in the image of its ruined Temple; it also directs us to conceive the city's woe in terms of the personal distress of a single individual. The result is a mutual illumination of the condition of each: Jeremiah's anguish reveals the severity of Jerusalem's plight, and the depiction of the ransacked city reveals the dimension and quality of Jeremiah's anguish. The theological significance of this literary rendering is that the prophet's life is used to interpret his message.[38]

Finally, we should observe that the effect of the complex interplay of voices and personae in vv. 19-20 carries over into the first-person speech of vv. 23-25. This prayer has an ambiguous tone and enormous potential for irony when taken by itself. Both the ambiguity and irony, however, are alleviated by the prayer's close juxtaposition with the preceding complaint. For certainly, the quality of an expression depends upon who is speaking it. The penetrating insight of v. 23 that 'the way of man is not in himself, that it is not in man who walks to direct his steps' (cf. Prov 16.9), were it to come only from the mouth of the Jerusalem whose people 'have stubbornly followed their own hearts' (Jer 9.14), would be reduced to a self-serving platitude. Similarly, the supplicatory confession of v. 24 would be just a pious cant, and the request for Yhwh's self-vindication in v. 25 merely a case of vengeful hypocrisy. But in the mouth of the obedient prophet, the one who could preach Yhwh's word in 10.1-16 against the 'way of the nations', a way that seeks security in one's own works, the proverbial maxim is restored to its proper integrity. And when spoken by the prophet who ascribes all righteousness to Yhwh when he complains (12.1), by the one who bears reproach in God's service (15.15) and has committed his cause to God (20.12), the confession and request attain to something quite other than narrow self-righteousness. In sum, given the prophet's enlistment of his own voice in Jerusalem's behalf in vv. 19-20, we hear his 'I' here too; hence, the prayer of vv. 23-25 transcends in force and character what Jerusalem could muster on her own. Reciprocally, and lastly, the prayer as performed by Jeremiah represents his self-constitution as the wise, obedient, and humble servant of both his God and people.[39]

Two questions relevant to our discussion have not as yet been addressed, although their answer has been presupposed. They are, first, to what extent is it the point of the passage's (and book's) characterization of the prophet to render him as a genius of private religious spirituality, the innate possessor of extraordinary powers of sympathy? Second, and antithetically to the first, to what extent is the prophet's 'I' eviscerated of all personal, biographical significance by virtue of being a representative 'I'? These questions will be dealt with directly in the following section.

II. *Jeremiah 14.1–15.4*

Nowhere in the book of Jeremiah is the intercessory function of the prophet's office better attested than here. The concept 'intercession' was an implicit, albeit crucial, factor in the passages previously investigated. Here it rises to the surface of the text to become an explicit theme. On this point contemporary scholarship is virtually unanimous, as an inspection of three recent works will show.

In his brilliant study on the social functions of Israelite prophecy, Robert Wilson uses 14.1–15.4 to illustrate Jeremiah's rootedness in Ephraimite prophetic tradition. Unlike its Judean counterpart, this tradition regarded intercession as an indispensable ingredient in the prophet's task.[40] Intercession being essentially dialogical in structure, Wilson notes the dialogical form of the passage at hand. It consists of a description of a drought (vv. 2-6), a prayer of repentance by the people (vv. 7-9), an oracular response (v. 10) which has been expanded by a dialogue between Yhwh and Jeremiah (vv. 11-16), then a lament by the prophet (vv. 17-18), another communal confession (vv. 19-22), and again an oracular response (15.1-4).

The significant fact is that both responses to the people's prayers are negative. Instead of receiving the expected assurance of pardon and deliverance, the people are given a judgment oracle and the prophet is prohibited from interceding in their behalf, the prohibitions connecting our passage with 7.16-17 and 11.14-17. The juxtaposition of the prayers with the prohibitions leads Wilson to conclude, rightly, that the people did not address God directly but 'channeled their requests through Jeremiah, the Mosaic prophet'.[41] In other words, the first-person plural complaints of vv. 7-9 and 19-22 are to be read as intercessory prayer offered by Jeremiah standing in the people's place before God. This analysis will be substantiated and filled out by the detailed reading to follow.

But first we should take note of the rationale Wilson posits for the inclusion of the prohibitions against intercession. It appears to him to have been a matter of religious politics, of defending Jeremiah against charges of false prophecy:

> As a Mosaic prophet Jeremiah delivered oracles that inevitably came to pass, and certainly the truth of his judgment oracles was confirmed when Jerusalem fell to the Babylonians. However, as a Mosaic prophet Jeremiah should also have interceded with Yhwh for the salvation of the city. Yet, the fact that the city fell implied that the prophet's intercession had not been effective, and this in turn cast doubts on his status as a Mosaic prophet. Thus, after the fall of Jerusalem, Jeremiah's supporters, and perhaps Jeremiah himself, faced the problem of explaining the apparent ineffectiveness of his attempts at intercession. The solution to the problem was found in the notion that Yahweh had forbidden Jeremiah to exercise the Mosaic prophet's intercessory function. The prophet's oracles were thus arranged to suggest that the ban on intercession and God's refusal to listen were both part of the judgment brought about by the people's past refusal to listen to the warnings that God had delivered through the prophets.[42]

I am not convinced that Jeremiah's legitimacy was the issue, at least with respect to the effectiveness or ineffectiveness of his intercession. Certainly, the rest of the book gives no indication that he was attacked on this score. Rather, it was because he 'pronounced evil' that 'they devised schemes' against him (11.17, 19). It was because whenever he spoke he shouted 'violence and destruction' (20.8; cf. 26.11; 28.8), or because the word of Yhwh which he was entrusted to deliver, against his own wishes, did not immediately come to pass (17.16), or because of what was perceived as treasonous behavior (29.24-28; 37.11-15) that people challenged his legitimacy, and this not specifically as a Mosaic intercessor but as a true prophet in general.[43] At least that is the impression allowed to stand by the book's final editors.

Of course, the motivations behind the shaping of a text, which is what Wilson's (not in itself implausible) scenario wants to account for, and the effects of that shaping need not be the same. But to the extent that they sometimes are and that usually we have only the effects to go on for reconstructing the motivations, it seems to me that the effect of our passage points to a different rationale behind the prohibitions, one less political and more theological. Specifically, as the text itself asserts and as Wilson elsewhere observes, the prohibitions serve to underscore the people's incorrigibility.[44] But much more broadly, they belong to a comprehensive effort at illuminating God's purposes with Israel at a critical moment in her history, a moment which, in keeping with the logic of scripture, was seen and rendered as somehow epitomizing life under the divine economy of judgment and salvation. This illumination was to be achieved through the depiction of the complex inter-relationships among people, prophet, and God. In this depiction the prophet occupies the pivotal position. From the theological perspective, the point of the passage is less a parochial defense of Jeremiah than his representation as a paradigm, both in his frailty as a member of an apostate people and in the peculiar strength granted him to speak God's word and share his pathos. As a paradigm, Jeremiah's life, what he says and does and what is said and done to him, is used to reflect and interpret the experience of Israel as a whole.

Naturally, such a proposal about the design and intention of the text is not self-validating but must be demonstrated exegetically. Erhard Gerstenberger's essay 'Jeremiah's Complaints: Observations on Jer 15.10-21' takes an important step in this direction. Gerstenberger was not the first to see in 14.1–15.4 the imitation of a liturgical style (or in his words that here 'the writer of Jer adopts and reconstructs the well known form of a complaint liturgy').[45] But he makes a singular contribution in recognizing that chs. 14-15, headed by the revelation formula in 14.1 which next recurs in 16.1, belong together as an interpretive unit and further that 15.10-21 is 'exactly modeled after the repentance liturgy in 14.1–15.4', both having 'the same twofold cycle of complaint and answer'.[46] The point of the parallelism, Gerstenberger maintains, is to draw the prophet's personal fate and suffering into the picture of the terrible doom announced in 14.1–15.4.

> More than that, the prophet's life is brought into relation with the people's sin and punishment. Their rebellion against Yahweh is the immediate cause of his distress. The prophet's suffering is representative of God's own suffering. So the complaint- and answer-liturgy in 14:7ff. and the complaint and oracle of 15:10. mark opposite but corresponding roles in one drama.[47]

Yet while Jeremiah's complaints in ch. 15 show him deeply involved in the controversy between Yhwh and the people, but on *Yhwh's* side (cf. 14.11f.), they also cast him in *opposition* to Yhwh (v. 18): 'In a sense he remains a member of these people who lament, confess their sins—and are rejected (14.2f.). Therefore even the prophet has to be admonished to "turn back" (v. 19a; cf. 4.1f.).'[48] Still, the final significance of the juxtaposition of the two chapters, and of the tension in Jeremiah's dual representative status, does not emerge in his rebuke by Yhwh but in the promise that follows. Gerstenberger explains:

> The deuteronomist does not confine himself to presenting to his reader a divine office and a prophet struggling to fill it. The ultimate concern of our final editor rests with the people. He wrestled with the problem of their election and rejection in 14:2–15:9. Historical events had demonstrated that the incomprehensible could happen: God had put Israel out of his sight (15:1). Prophetic intervention had been useless (14:11ff.). Was this the absolute end for Yahweh's people? The deuteronomist answers 'no', because the prophet himself, as a member of this weak and unreliable Israel, *becomes a paradigmatic figure of salvation.* ' . . . I am with you to save and deliver you . . . ' (v. 20b) is the final pronouncement over the prophet. Thus Jer 14. ends on a more hopeful note. One man has found grace with Yahweh. This is a ray of light which shines out in the darkness of the unconditional doom expressed in 14:2–15:9.[49]

It is evident that Gerstenberger's analysis has immediate relevance for our task. The picture of the prophet as paradigm, emerging in clarity at the end of the composite unit chs. 14-15, cannot help but draw our attention to the features within 14.1–15.4 that contribute to the end product. Reciprocally, to the extent that we find such features, specifically those that express the prophet's representative status and reflect his own self-constituting behavior, the validity of this picture will be enhanced.

The third work to be considered here, and one that will occupy our attention throughout the exegesis, is Reventlow's exhaustive treatment of the passage in his *Liturgie und prophetisches Ich bei Jeremia*.[50] It is interesting that as negatively as Reventlow's overall thesis has been received, the exegetical focus of criticism has been on his handling of the prophet's individual confessions while little or no attention has been paid to the communal laments.[51] One reason for this may well be that Reventlow is on much firmer footing with the latter material, 14.1–15.4 in particular. The thesis as it relates to our passage is this: 14.2–15.4 (14.1 is stricken as redactional) is a collective lamentation liturgy, a ritual of intercession carried out in the context of a cultic fast, with Jeremiah as the official cultic intercessor. As such, and because employing the thoroughly stereotypic language of the cult, Jeremiah's 'I' is completely void of personal content and individuality and serves only as a cipher for the community's 'we'.[52]

Certainly, previous criticisms of the general thesis pertain here. In particular, and as we have already had occasion to suggest, the assumption that forms of address must remain anchored to the institutions in which they have their original setting is highly dubious. As John Bright says, 'We are certainly not required in advance to understand Jeremiah's complaints, because they are cast in a cultic form . . . , as liturgical pieces uttered in the context of the cult'.[53] The same stricture applies equally well to the communal laments. The problem is not just the historical-empirical one of whether in fact the prophets always used materials in *unaltered* form and in an official institutional capacity or, and this seems more likely, imitated and adapted a variety of genres for their own specific purposes. It is also the logical problem of whether the given form, in this case the complaint liturgy, *can* be a liturgy *per se* when situated in a larger literary context. A liturgy is a liturgy when it is performed in the cult. Placed in the book of Jeremiah it becomes something else, for the text is not the cult.[54]

As regards the quality of the prophet's 'I', the issue should not be whether Jeremiah's first-person utterances, in this passage or others, are 'authentic' or relate to specific experiences in his own life. However long a scholarly preoccupation,[55] the reconstructed 'Jeremiah of history' is once again not our concern. Our interest is in the persona rendered in and by the text. Certainly, and as Gerstenberger's analysis would imply, the function and meaning of this persona, of the depicted Jeremiah, depends heavily on the nature of his prophetic 'I'. By evacuating this 'I' of all personal significance, Reventlow challenges us to inquire into the nature of the intercession the prophet performs and the function of the liturgical language he employs. In my opinion Reventlow's understanding of both is faulty.

We begin the inquiry by noting that there are at least two very different ways of viewing the process of intercession, or more precisely the concept 'representative' which intercession entails. The difference between these two views is essentially that between a sign, something more or less arbitrarily chosen to point to something else 'with which it has no inner relationship', and symbol, which 'participates in the reality which is symbolized', 'represents the power and meaning of what is symbolized through participation', and does so because it is intuitively felt to bear an 'inner relationship' with that to which it points.[56] Reventlow seems to think of 'representative' in the sense of 'sign'. Thus, for him a representative 'I' is of no significance in its own right but is merely regarded as the 'we' it represents. It follows that a representative self would have to be temporarily suspended so as to become the perfectly clear surface on which other selves are mirrored. This self's 'participation' in the others would be nominal at best. In the 'symbol'-sense of 'representative', however, there can be no suspension of the self. One stands for others precisely as *oneself*. One's own self in its full range of aspects and qualities must remain in place in order to stand in for other selves; only in this fullness and presence does it become available as the instantiation of the community of selves, a community in which it fully participates. It follows that one must own the 'I' one speaks in order for it even to begin to be representative. Thus the representative 'I' requires and trades on the individual 'I' for its intelligibility. The latter is present whenever the former occurs.

Now, the 'sign'-sense of 'representative' is well known in the world of mathematics, but rarely is it encountered in interpersonal matters of consequence.[57] Not surprisingly, it is the 'symbol'-sense that predominates in the biblical literature, which deals with nothing if not interpersonal matters of consequence. The patriarchal ancestors in Genesis, for instance, are not simply characters drawn on the flat, stick figures artificially constructed in order to illustrate but a few salient qualities of a later entity. On the contrary, the eponymous (hence 'representative') Jacob *is* 'Israel' in all the roundness, and in all the bewildering admixture of transparency and opacity, of the actual people we meet in daily life.[58] And indeed, it is this same sense of 'representative' that comes to view in many of the materials relating to prophetic activity, especially the prophets' symbolic actions which, *qua* symbol, are to be regarded as participating in the events they symbolize, creatively prefiguring these events and setting into motion their realization.[59] Significantly, some of these actions entail the personal participation, at more than a perfunctory level, of the prophets themselves (e.g. Hos 1; Isa 20; Jer 32), and have deep personal ramifications in sacrifice and suffering (e.g. Jer 16; Ezek 24.15-18), to the point where sometimes the prophet himself, his entire life, is to be seen as an 'ôt (read 'symbol', e.g. Isa 8.18; Ezek 12.6, 11; 24.24, 27).[60]

The case is no different with prophetic intercession. In Gen 20 Abraham is shown to be a full participant in the events surrounding the intercession he makes for Abimelech. Himself responsible for the divine threat of death against the king, it is hard to imagine how Abraham's self could be factored out of the prayer he offers on the king's behalf. Samuel's self-involvement in his intercessory activity is attested both by the passion he manifests over Saul's rejection by Yhwh ('And Samuel was angry, and he cried to the Lord all night', 1 Sam 15.11) and by the fact that, by his own view, a failure to intercede for the people would be a matter of personal sin ('Moreover as for me, far be it from me that I should sin against Yhwh by ceasing to pray for you', 1 Sam 12.23). Moses, the prophet *par excellence* (Deut 34.10-12), provides the best illustration of how much is at stake for the interceding prophetic self. In his attempt to 'make atonement' for the people's sin, he addresses Yhwh, 'Alas, this people have sinned a great sin; they have made for themselves gods of gold. But now, if thou wilt forgive their sins—and if not, blot me, I pray thee, out of thy book which thou hast written' (Exod 32.31-32). That is to say, *qua* intercessor, Moses offers *himself* as a substitute for others.[61]

In sum, the evidence indicates that the concept 'representative' which operates in the biblical literature, not least in the materials dealing with intercession, is the symbolic sort whereby the self undergoes no suspension but remains fully engaged in the representative task. To say as much is also to say that when Jeremiah employs stereotypic, cultically stamped language to perform his intercession, it *cannot* be the case that such language has, necessarily and *a priori*, *no* bearing on himself and *no* personal significance. This point will be elaborated in the close reading of 14.1–15.4, to which we now turn.

The passage begins with the revelation formula (*'ăšer hāyâ dᵉbar-Yhwh 'el-yirmᵉyāhû*), which, as Gerstenberger observed, marks chs. 14-15 as a redactional unit. Consisting essentially of the verb *hyh* and the noun *dbr*, the formula occurs forty-one times in the book, forty-five times if those instances are included which substitute the piel *dibbēr* for *hyh* (45.1; 46.13; 50.1; 51.59). However, the present form which places an *'ăšer* at the beginning is relatively rare, occurring only here and in 1.2, 46.1, 47.1, and 49.34. The problem is that there appears to be no antecedent for the *'ăšer*. 1.1-2 seems to offer a solution, for here the *'ăšer* refers in all probability to *dibrê-yirmᵉyāhû* in v. 1, thereby equating 'the words of Jeremiah' with 'the word of Yhwh'. The parallel form, especially given the paradigmatic status of 1.2 as part of the book's superscription, suggests that *dibrê-yirmᵉyāhû* in 1.1 is to be understood as the antecedent for the other passages as well. Thus, we would take 14.1 to mean, '(The words of Jeremiah) being the word of Yhwh to Jerusalem concerning the drought'.[62]

The connection between 14.1 and the superscription has more than a translational view. Commenting on the superscription in Hosea, H.W. Wolff writes, 'Here *dᵉbar Yhwh* no longer means the individual prophetic utterances; rather, this refers to the prophet's total experience...'[63] By analogy, the *dibrê-yirmᵉyāhû* in Jer 1.1 can be construed as indicating that 'total experience' of the prophet which is then equated with 'the word of Yhwh', so to serve as a theological characterization of the book as a whole. This would be entirely consistent with the frequent use of *dibrê* to mean 'deeds', 'acts', or even 'history'.[64] Hence, the revelation formula in 14.1, already dependent syntactically upon 1.1-2, resonates with the expanded sense *dibrê-yirmᵉyāhû* receives in that opening passage. Accordingly, the effect of 14.1 on the material it introduces is not only to cast it as the word of God, moreover, a word of God given to the prophet such that we hear it as a distinctly *prophetic* word which has Jeremiah as its speaker, but also to characterize it as somehow rooted in and bearing upon the prophet's life, as if what Jeremiah says and who he is were related. The effect, in other words, is to prevent a wedge from being driven between the prophet's self and his words.[65]

4. The Prophetic 'I' & its Ambiguities

Of course, all this is lost on Reventlow when he dismisses 14.1 as a redactional addition. Not least to suffer on this account is his treatment of vv. 2-6. These verses clearly serve to describe the hardship brought about by a severe drought, but do they do so already as a part of the communal complaint (vv. 7-9), or as a form of prophetic proclamation *prior* to the complaint? To choose the latter would be to construe vv. 7-9 as a response to vv. 2-6, but, as Reventlow indicated by his separation of 10.17-18 from the complaint in 10.19f., this violates the form of the 'liturgy' as he understands it, since this form has the people's complaint coming only before, not after, a word of Yhwh.[66] Thus treating 2-6 as part of the lament, and therefore as spoken by Jeremiah in his capacity as intercessor, Reventlow must then explain why 2-6 lack linguistic and thematic parallels to the descriptions of distress in the communal laments of the psalter. This he does by observing that the latter are 'almost exclusively of a political nature' while the occasion for our passage is a *natural* catastrophe.[67] He is therefore forced to turn away from the psalms, where a cultic *Sitz-im-Leben* is a well established fact, and seek parallels among prophetic texts, where it is not. In my opinion, the descriptions of distress in the texts he adduces (Joel 1; Isa 15-16; and 24.4f.) provide no more evidence of being intercessory laments situated in a cultic fast over natural disaster than does Jer 14.2-6. Similar terminology and motifs may indeed by present, along with elements from the Baal cult, but this by no means proves, or even makes likely, a liturgical setting.[68]

As suggested above, vv. 2-6 must be evaluated in the light of 14.1, which is to say, in light of the final shape of the text. Given the overwhelming number of cases where the revelation formula immediately precedes a divine word to be delivered by the prophet, we are induced to read vv. 2-6 as a form of prophetic proclamation. To be sure, the subsequent intercessory prayer, and indeed chs. 14-15 as a whole, are also governed by the revelation formula so that they too function as 'the word of Yhwh', but in the extended sense of that concept. However, the unobstructed juxtaposition of 14.1 and 2, the similarity between 2-6 and other straightforward, prophetic depictions of judgment (e.g. the 'battle visions'), and the lack of logical oddities which would require the reader to move to other levels of meaning to maintain the text's intelligibility all commend reading vv. 2-6 as 'word of Yhwh' in the literal sense.[69] Thus, Jeremiah speaks here but not yet as intercessor, rather from Yhwh's perspective and, as it were, on Yhwh's side with the implication that the situation he describes represents Yhwh's judgment upon the land.

As the introduction and grounding for the lament that follows, Jeremiah's words in vv. 2-6 serve to identify the 'we' in vv. 7-9. Verse 2 explicitly anticipates the lament which is its objective instantiation:

> Judah mourns,
>   her cities pine,
> lie prostrate in grief,
>   while Jerusalem's cry goes up.[70]

Verse 7 begins the lament itself, the inhabitants of Judah/Jerusalem being the complainants:

> 'im-'ăwōnênû 'ānû bānû
> Yhwh 'ăśēh l°ma'an š°mekā
> kî-rabbû m°šûbōtênû
> l°kā ḥāṭā'nû
>
> Though our iniquities testify against us,
>   act, O Lord, for thy name's sake;
> for our backslidings are many,
>   we have sinned against thee. (RSV)

These opening words support our understanding of vv. 2-6 as a prophetic attestation of divine judgment. Clearly confessional, they presuppose that the condition afflicting the land is the result of human sin. The drought is the arid fruition of the 'iniquities' which are said to 'testify against us'.

Reventlow comments on the confession in v. 7 that it is 'but a constituent part of an established formulary', while Skinner in a similar vein had observed that the prayer as a whole 'contains nothing which rises above the popular religion of the time'.[71] Their remarks are correct but minimal in the extreme, to the point of distortion. To correct the distortion, and to understand the prayer's function in its present context, it is important to sketch the normative logic of the prayer and note several of its more salient features.

The request that God act for the sake of his name, a common feature in the psalms and particularly frequent in the context of confession, brings into view the covenantal relation between the people and Yhwh.[72] In the request the petitioners appeal to God's nature as 'merciful and gracious, slow to anger and abounding in steadfast love and faithfulness, keeping steadfast love for thousands, forgiving iniquity and transgression and sin . . . ' (Exod 34.6-7). For it

4. The Prophetic 'I' & its Ambiguities

is precisely this nature that is, at least in part, the meaning of the divine name, name and nature both being the unitary content of the revelation at Sinai and the basis of the covenant established there.[73] Thus, the appeal represents a request for the forgiveness promised by the covenant God. As such, it anticipates the confidence-motif of v. 9b. However, to the extent that this implicit confidence is selectively based on just *one* aspect of the divine nature, then the appeal conceals a deep potential irony. The possibility that in order to act for his name's sake Yhwh might have to *reject* the petition, that to do his name justice he 'will by no means clear the guilty, visiting the iniquity of the fathers upon the children and the children's children, to the third and fourth generations' (Exod 34.7), bodes ill for any whose repentance is belied by their conduct (v. 10), i.e. whose words fail to reflect and reshape their selves.

The irony latent in the request of v. 7a is heightened in the reproaches of vv. 8-9a—

8 *miqwēh yiśrā'ēl*
  môšî'ô bᵉ'ēt ṣārâ
  lāmmâ tihyeh kᵉgēr bā'āreṣ
  ûkᵉ'ōrēaḥ nāṭâ lālûn
9 *lāmmâ tihyeh kᵉ'îš nidhām*
  kᵉgibbôr lō'-yûkal lᵉhôšîaʿ

8 O thou hope of Israel,
    its savior in time of trouble,
  Why shouldst thou be like a stranger in the land,
    like a wayfarer who turns aside to tarry for a night?
9 Why shouldst thou be like a man confused,
    like a mighty man who cannot save? (RSV)

—which imply that there is a disparity between self and conduct on Yhwh's part, i.e. between God's self as revealed and actualized in the covenant and his present conduct of withholding help, his absence in the current 'time of trouble'. Such irony, however, is not a constitutive part of the request and reproaches *per se* but is rather a function of the particular people who lodge them. (And indeed it is realized only in the divine response of v. 10 which shows the disparity to be *theirs*, not his.) Hence, in its normative logic (as a standard element in the complaint *Gattung*) the reproach is less an unwitting self-indictment than a rhetorical means of acknowledging one's finitude, of confessing that one's distress has impaired the capacity to perceive God's hand

and understand his purpose. A reflection of faith's struggle with the hiddenness of God, the reproach is in fact a plea for clarity and presupposes that God *can* act decisively to save. Oddly enough, it is an expression of hope.

It is not incongruous, therefore, that the reproaches should address Yhwh as 'the hope of Israel' (*miqwēh yiśrā'ēl*, v. 8a). Suggestive once again of the covenant relationship, the epithet trades on the knowledge that God has saved Israel in the past, and it expresses the trust that he will keep covenant faith by doing so in the future. It thus characterizes Yhwh as trustworthy while it constitutes and defines the speakers, supposedly the covenant people, as hopeful. (The speakers become the covenant people and enact their identity as such by exercising hope, by praying to Yhwh precisely as 'the hope of Israel'.) Not incidentally, while the general concept 'hope' is hardly alien to the complaint psalms, the specific term *miqweh* appears to be the special province of Jeremiah.[74] Moreover, it occurs in the doxological invocation of 17.12-13, which functions in its present setting to introduce the individual complaint of 17.14-18, a complaint laden with overtones of reproach. Hence, when Jeremiah in ch. 17 complains as an individual, he too does so as one who hopes in the very God he reproaches. By employing the same term that appears in the communal complaint, which he prayed in the people's behalf, he now renders himself as one who is what the term implied the people to be, however ironic such implication may have been in their case. In effect, the self-constituting character of the epithet's use is made to apply paradigmatically to Jeremiah.

The confidence implicit in the divine epithet and reproaches fully emerges in the bold declarations of v. 9b:

wᵉ'attâ bᵉqirbēnû Yhwh
 wᵉšimᵉkā 'ālênû niqrā'
  'al-tanniḥēnû

Yet thou, O Lord, art in the midst of us,
 and we are called by thy name;
  leave us not. (RSV)

Correspondingly, these words go to the heart of the original covenant promise. Israel's only distinction is that by virtue of the covenant bond Yhwh is their God and they are his people (Gen 17.7-8; Exod 6.7; Jer 30.22; 31.1; etc.), and that as such God's presence goes with them (Exod 33.16). Both the Jerusalemite (P) and the deuteronomic

4. The Prophetic 'I' & its Ambiguities

tradition streams express the fact of God's in-dwelling in language similar to that of our first colon: e.g. Exod 29.45 and 1 Kgs 6.13 ($w^e\check{s}\bar{a}kant\hat{i}$ $b^et\hat{o}k$ $b^en\hat{e}$ $yi\acute{s}r\bar{a}'\bar{e}l$). Further, the Exodus and Kings passages are both accompanied by covenant formulas indigenous to their respective traditions. Thus, the hope of pardon and deliverance for the people who pray such a prayer as Jer 14.7-9 is fundamentally grounded in the fact of Yhwh's being in their midst as the God of the covenant. Once again, however, the affirmation of this fact contains a potential irony for petitioners who ignore their own covenant obligations, to wit, the irony 'that Yhwh's presence would mean judgment and not blessing'.[75]

The second colon (literally, 'thy name is proclaimed over us') is an extension of the first, thematically as well as syntactically. Rooted in legal custom pertaining to the acquisition of property, the formula declares the proprietorship of N, the name proclaimed, over X, the goods acquired.[76] Well-suited for appropriation into the legal-political imagery of Israel's covenantal thought, it comes to express 'the enduring election of Israel and her peculiar relationship to God'.[77] Thus, as can be seen in Deut 28.1-10, i.e. in the framework of covenant blessings and curses, the formula signifies Yhwh's lordship over and sovereign possession of his people, a fact which, like his in-dwelling with them, marks their distinctiveness among the nations and is at the core of their identity.[78] Needless to say, there is again the lurking irony that the expression's significance as blessing can be transformed into curse if the covenant stipulations are not heeded by those who employ it.

Even apart from its covenant setting, the formula's use presupposes that the proprietor can dispose of his property as he sees fit.[79] The negative implications of this situation, substantially heightened by the formula's covenant application, had already been laid out in Jeremiah's Temple Sermon of ch. 7. There the formula is used repeatedly in reference to Yhwh's 'house' (7.10, 11, 14, 30), which is earmarked for destruction by the proprietor because of the unremitting wickedness of the tenants. Significantly, the first prohibition against intercession occurs in this very context (7.16). Thus, while the normative force of the expression's use in prayer is positive (see 1 Kgs 8, especially vv. 35-36), it is rife with ominous reverberations in 14.9, however oblivious to this the petitioners may in fact be.

A final point to be observed regarding the formula is that in all the OT it is used only once of a specific individual, and this none other than Jeremiah. Moreover, Jeremiah applies it to himself (as the people had to themselves) in the individual complaint of 15.16, which as we have seen belongs to the companion piece of 14.2–15.4. Even more than with *miqwēh yiśrā'ēl*, which occurs both in the communal lament and in the individual complaint of ch. 17, the effect is to underscore the representative relation Jeremiah has to his people, to witness to the self-constituting quality of the language of the prayer in its normative use, and thus to make manifest the paradigmatic status which the text accords the prophetic persona.

To complete the discussion of vv. 7-9, let us now reconsider the remarks of Reventlow and Skinner quoted earlier. Though working with different aims and methods, both men concluded that the passage fails to reflect Jeremiah's own thought and feeling, Skinner on the premise that the passage 'contains nothing which rises above the popular religion of the time', Reventlow because of the passage's thoroughly traditional character (its cultically stamped language arranged according to a fixed liturgical schema—which reflects Jeremiah's purely representative role, in the 'sign'-sense, as official intercessor). However accurate their premises may be in themselves, the directness with which the conclusion is made to follow (and it by no means follows *necessarily* from the premises) might lead one to suspect both men of harboring a tacit prejudice against 'popular' or 'traditional' language *per se*, a prejudice which I think operates at a number of points throughout Reventlow's work in particular.

To be sure, Reventlow was arguing against the type of romantic interpretation that read v. 7 (as even Gunkel did and as Skinner often does with other such passages), as an instance of a 'heightened religious awareness', a spontaneous expression of spiritual genius attesting Jeremiah's own authorship.[80] Against this interpretation Reventlow's form-critical observations provide a necessary corrective. However, the danger inherent in both the romantic and form-critical perspectives (as evidenced by Gunkel, in whom the two perspectives are equally at home) is that spontaneity can be uncritically linked with authenticity, not just of authorship but emotion as well, while stereotypic language is tacitly associated with artificiality, as if the speaking of such language were just a perfunctory, rote activity performed in perfect self-detachment or, as it were, from behind a mask. Whether one attributes such a view to a certain form of Protestant anti-liturgical bias or to modernity's special regard for originality, or to a combination of the two, it is quite misleading and fails to do justice to the nature and purpose of liturgical prayer. A detached, mindless repetition of sounds, however common in practice, can only be regarded as an aberration, not the norm. Spontaneity and originality are irrelevant. Normatively, one must only mean what one says and the prayer becomes one's own in the praying of it. Submitting oneself to the prayer, the worshipper allows it to be his self-interpretation, and thereby allows it both to inform and reform who he is.

Now, precisely this difference between the aberrant and normative use of the prayer must be kept clearly in view for a proper appreciation of the divine word in v. 10:

> kōh-'āmar Yhwh lā'ām hazzeh
> kēn 'āhăbû lānûa'
>   raglêhem lō' ḥāśākû
> waYhwh lō' rāṣām
>   'attâ yizkōr 'awōnām
>   w^eyipqōd ḥaṭṭō'tām

Thus says Yhwh concerning this people:
Just so have they loved to wander,
   never checking their steps.
So Yhwh does not accept them,
  but now will remember their iniquity,
    and punish their sins.[81]

The irony that was latent in the prayer comes out here in full force. The expectations of what it would mean for Yhwh to act for his name's sake (v. 7), of the significance of his in-dwelling with the people, of his covenant lordship over them (v. 9)—all are suddenly and summarily overturned. Instead of 'iniquities' being forgotten and 'sins' forgiven (cf. Ps 79.8-9), they will be remembered and punished. The people's confidence of salvation is thwarted; wandering as they do, heedless of their steps, they are found quite unacceptable.

The invective's imagery (v. 10a) is of course reminiscent of many of the previous indictments against the nation, such as those that characterize the people as lightly gadding about changing their ways (2.36), as a 'restive young camel interlacing her tracks', unrestrained in lust (2.32-33), and as in constant need of admonishment for wavering (4.1 *nwd*; cf. *nw'* here). The themes of glibness, hypocrisy, complacency and false sense of security (4.30; 5.2, 12; 6.14; 7.4; 8-10; etc.) all resonate here. Certainly, the rather open-ended *kēn* ('just so', 'thus') in our verse has as its referent these earlier indictments and the form of life they cumulatively depict. At the same time *kēn* also points to the prayer just offered as itself an illustration of this glib and hypocritical form of life. Not that the fault is with the prayer *per se*, it is with the people who pray it, who pray it aberrantly, not meaning what they say. For the fact is that, as depicted in this book, they are *not* the obedient people of God, the keepers of covenant faith, that their words imply them to be. Their praying thus is no doubt to be seen in the light, and as proof, of what Jeremiah just two chapters earlier had accused them of being, people for whom God is 'near in their mouth and far from their heart' (12.2; cf. Deut 30.14); and the God 'who seest the heart and the mind' (20.12) sees through the prayer and recognizes them for what they are. Deviating from the covenant norm and subverting the normative logic of the prayer, the people put themselves in line for the covenant curses. Not surprisingly, the nature of the judgment, summarily formulated as punishment 'by sword, famine, and pestilence' in v. 12 (plus 'captivity' in 15.2), fits perfectly with that prescribed by Lev 26 and Deut 28, the listings of covenant blessings and curses.[82]

What should be said of Jeremiah's role in the prayer in light of the judgment oracle of v. 10? The third-person plural form of the oracle is not insignificant. Weiser had interpreted this as representing Yhwh's withdrawal and self-distancing from the community, and Reventlow appropriately criticized him for psychologizing the text.[83] Rather, the grammar reflects that stage of the intercessory process in which God announces his response to the prophet who had delivered the petition on the people's behalf. At the next stage the prophet would relay the response, presumably addressing the people as 'you' rather than 'they'. Thus, the effect of the present form of the text is to underscore Jeremiah's intercessory role. At the same time it is to make a distinction between the people's culpability, as those who do not mean what they say, and that of Jeremiah, who offers the prayer as their intercessor (and as such also personally participates in it).

To see this as implying a *positive* judgment on Jeremiah, as one who *does* mean what he says, would be to make an argument from silence, for the focus of God's attention is on the people, and Jeremiah's genuineness is not at this point an issue. However, when in ch. 15 the issue of his genuineness *does* come into play (note that Jeremiah addresses his complaint to Yhwh with the words 'thou knowest' in 15.15, i.e. God knows Jeremiah's heart and can therefore

4. The Prophetic 'I' & its Ambiguities

recognize the integrity and authenticity of his speech; cf. 2.3; 17.16; 20.12),[84] there the prophet receives only a conditional rebuke (in contrast to the people's in 14.10), a rebuke, moreover, which is only implicit in, and is overshadowed by, a promise of salvation.

Verses 11-12 make it clear beyond a doubt that the prayer of vv. 7-9 must be seen as the intercessory prayer of Jeremiah.

wayyō'mer Yhwh 'ēlāy 'al-titpallēl bᵉ'ad-hā'ām hazzeh lᵉṭôbâ (12) kî yāṣumû 'ēnennî šōmēa' 'el-rinnātām wᵉkî ya'ălû 'ōlâ ûminḥâ 'ēnennî rōṣām kî baḥereb ûbārā'āb ûbaddeber 'ānōkî mᵉkalleh 'ōtām

And the Lord said to me: 'Do not pray for the welfare of this people. (12) Though they fast I will not hear their cry, and though they offer burnt offering and cereal offering, I will not accept them; but I will consume them by the sword, by famine, and by pestilence.

The prophet himself later claims in 18.20 (cf. 15.11; 17.16) that in fact he *had* made intercession for the people, and perhaps the present arrangement of our materials intends 14.7-9 and 19-22 to be primary examples substantiating that claim. In any case he is here told, 'Do *not* pray for the welfare of this people', that they are beyond all hearing and are destined for destruction.

Though obviously related to the prayer's rejection in v. 10, the prohibition against intercession is not just 'one form among others which the denial of the intercession can assume', as Reventlow asserts.[85] Certainly, he is right that it does not reflect a prophetic polemic against the cult *per se* or that it is directed against intercession *qua* cultic activity. But in lumping it together with the denial, Reventlow fails to reckon with 7.16 and 11.14 where the intercession is forbidden *before the fact*. Far more emphatic and sweeping than a simple denial of a request, the prohibition constitutes a different *Gattung* altogether and represents something quite new in prophecy, reflecting the extraordinary quality of the time, a time so ripe with sin that judgment can no longer be deferred.[86] Accordingly, the prohibition represents a serious disruption of the standard expectations associated with the (Ephraimite) prophetic office and might be imagined to have compounded within the individual prophet the tension that was already inherent in his position.

Indeed, the acuteness of this tension immediately manifests itself in the prophet's response to Yhwh in v. 13:

wā'ōmar 'ăhāh 'ădōnāy Yhwh hinnēh hannᵉbi'îm 'ōmᵉrîm lāhem lō'-tir'û ḥereb wᵉrā'āb lō'-yihyeh lākem kî-šᵉlôm 'ĕmet 'ettēn lākem bammāqôm hazzeh

Then I said, 'Ah, Lord God, behold, the prophets say to them, "You shall not see the sword, nor shall you have famine, but I will give you assured peace in this place"'. (RSV)

Jeremiah's expression of perplexity has already been discussed in an earlier chapter. Suffice it to add that it vividly demonstrates the prophet's self-involvement in the general task of representing the people before God and in the intercessory prayer of vv. 7-9 in particular. For the (false) confidence which underlay the other prophets' message of *šālôm* to which Jeremiah here refers had as its basis essentially the same covenant promise as that which grounds the confidence motifs of vv. 7-9.[87] Jeremiah's perplexity, in other words, is at least in part a function of his participation in the confidence that belongs to the normative logic of the prayer.

wayyō'mer Yhwh 'ēlay šeqer hannᵉbi'îm nibbᵉ'îm bišmî lō' šᵉlaḥtîm wᵉlō' ṣiwwîtîm wᵉlō' dibbartî 'ălêhem ḥāzôn šeqer wᵉqesem wĕ'ᵉlîl wᵉtarmît libbām hēmmā mitnabbᵉ'îm lākem (15) lākēn kōh-'āmar Yhwh 'al-hannᵉbi'îm hannibbᵉ'îm bišmî wa'ănî lō'-šᵉlaḥtîm wᵉhēmmā 'ōmᵉrîm ḥereb wᵉrā'āb lō' yihyeh bā'āreṣ hazzō't baḥereb ûbārā'āb yittammû hannᵉbi'îm hāhēmmā (16) wᵉhā'ām 'ăšer-hēmmā nibbᵉ'îm lāhem yihyû mušlākîm bᵉḥuṣôt yerûšālaim mippᵉnê hārā'āb wᵉhaḥereb wᵉ'ên mᵉqabbēr lāhēmmā hēmmā nᵉšêhem ûbᵉnêhem ûbᵉnōtêhem wᵉšāpaktî 'ălêhem 'et-rā'ātām

And the Lord said to me: 'The prophets are prophesying lies in my name; I did not send them, nor did I command them or speak to them. They are prophesying to you a lying vision, worthless divination, and the deceit of their own minds. (15) Therefore thus says the Lord concerning the prophets who prophesy in my name although I did not send them, and who say, "Sword and famine shall not come on this land": By sword and famine those prophets shall be consumed. (16) And the people to whom they prophesy shall be cast out in the streets of Jerusalem, victims of famine and sword, with none to bury them—them, their wives, their sons, and their daughters. For I will pour out their wickedness upon them.' (RSV)

4. The Prophetic 'I' & its Ambiguities

The proof that their confidence that 'sword and famine shall not come on this land' was false, in fact 'the deceit of their own minds', is in their consignment to the very same judgment that awaits the people who listen to them.

Now, it is observed by many of the commentators that in the redactional unit vv. 11-16 the notion of the drought is replaced by the theme and imagery of war. The apparent shift leads some not only to reassert the composite character of the chapter (which is not unlikely) but to divide it into two parts that are taken as referring to separate historical moments. John Bright is a case in point:

> But the poetry itself does not all refer to the same date. In the bulk of it the situation is that of drought, without any hint of enemy invasion (cf. 14:2-6). In vss. 17-18, on the other hand, the situation (and it is not to be taken as predictive!) is precisely that of the ravages of war. The theme 'drought' in fact applies only to 14:2-9, 10, 19-22, while in the rest the theme is 'sword, famine, and disease' (14:12, 13, 15f., 18; 15:2.). The probability is that a piece originally composed in time of drought has here been expanded and adapted (and perhaps by Jeremiah himself) to a later situation.[88]

We have already noted that Reventlow relates the formula 'sword, famine, and pestilence' (plus 'captivity') to the covenant curses of Lev 26 and Deut 28. He is supported by Delbert Hillers who shows that the combination of drought and war imagery, plus that of many other phenomena, is common to these and other more ancient treaty-curse lists.[89] Reventlow is therefore well justified in arguing that the actual drought was seen as but the earnest for the curse of the 'sword' to follow; both belong to the unitary act of divine judgment.[90] Here, the form-critical perspective provides an invaluable corrective to a lock-step historically-referential reading and mentality. In Reventlow's words, 'The purely historical point of view proves misleading here. The basis [for the difference in theme] is rather a particular standardization of the distress in the traditional scheme of plagues which originated with the blessing-curse formulary.'[91]

While thoroughly damaging to Bright's position, Reventlow's argument was directed primarily against Weiser, who divided the chapter into the units, vv. 1-16 and 17ff.[92] Like Bright's, this division proves inappropriate in light of the covenant 'Plagenkette', which forms a thread that runs throughout the material and establishes a continuity of context across the supposed division.[93] Accordingly, we can see clear connections between the immediately preceding judgment oracle of Yhwh and vv. 17-18:

17 wᵉ'āmartā 'ălêhem 'et-haddābār hazzeh
   tēradnâ 'ênay dim'â
      laylâ wᵉyômām wᵉ'al-tidmênâ
   kî šeber gādôl nišbᵉrâ bᵉtûlat bat-'ammî
      makkâ nahlâ mᵉ'ōd
18 'im-yāṣā'tî haśśādeh
      wᵉhinnēh halᵉlê-hereb
   wᵉ'im bā'tî hā'îr
      wᵉhinnēh tahălû'ê rā'āb
   kî-gam-nābî' gam-kōhēn
      sāhărû 'el-'ereṣ
      wᵉlō' yādā'û

17 And you shall speak to them this word:
   'Let my eyes with tears overflow,
      by night and by day never ceasing;
   For a great breach has been broken in the virgin daughter of my people,
      a very grievous blow.
18 If I go out into the field,
      behold, those slain by the sword!
   And if I enter the city,
      behold, the diseases of famine!
   Indeed, both prophet and priest
      ply their trade through the land,
      but know nothing.'

The most obvious connection is the recurrence of the words 'sword' and 'famine' (*hereb* and *rā'āb*) which are here used in the dramatic visualization of the destruction promised in vv. 15-16. Further, vv. 17-18ab and 18c relate respectively to the dual focus of vv. 15-16 on 'people' and 'prophets'. Augmenting v. 15, 18c includes 'priest' with 'prophet' in the manner of a *Stichwort* based on such passages as 5.31, 6.13-14, and 8.10-11, which characterize both groups as 'false', the glib proclaimers of 'peace when there is no peace'. The final statement that prophet and priest 'know nothing' (cf. 2.8) summarizes their failings as Yhwh's intermediaries with the people, suggesting that the people's oft-cited lack of knowledge of Yhwh (4.22; 5.4; 8.7; 9.2, 5; etc.) is but a function of their own—a suggestion which informs the grouping of prophets with people in vv. 15-16 under the same judgment.[94]

While Reventlow's analysis of the *'Plagenkette'* makes it clear that a real relationship exists between vv. 17-18 and the preceding oracle, his assessment of the precise nature of that relationship seems badly amiss. As he sees it, vv. 17-18, while indeed a response to the divine word of 15-16, also mark the beginning of the 'liturgy's' second cycle. They are thus viewed in analogy to vv. 2-6, i.e. as the description of distress which is part and parcel of the standard complaint *Gattung*. This is to say that, just as 2-6 belong to 7-9, so 17-18 go uninterruptedly with 19-22 to form the complete lamentation pattern. The shift from first-person singular in 17-18 to plural in 19-22 poses no problem since it only reflects the intercessory character of the prayer, the prophet's 'I' being purely representative of, and therefore capable of moving smoothly into, the community's 'we'.[95]

With respect to the last point, we might digress for a moment to observe that Reventlow here addresses the question of whether v. 17 expresses 'a special tenderness of disposition, Jeremiah being so moved by the fate of his people that in a flood of emotion he cannot hold back his own tears'.[96] Characteristically, Reventlow answers in the negative on the basis of, again, the representative quality of the prophet's 'I' and the fact that the mention of tears is just a stereotypic motif common to ritual lamentation. Again, the argument has its point against a romantic, psychologically-referential reading, one that is motivated by an interest in the prophet's spirituality and so refers his words to his private experience and inherent temperament. But the case should not be so stated as to utterly depersonalize the language, for example, by dismissing the 'tears' motif as a *pro-forma* utterance. Once again, the expression's normative status must be respected, for the motif is common precisely because it is fitting to the occasion of crisis for which the liturgy would be employed. For the participant to use the motif seriously is to acknowledge its fittingness, to attest the congruence between the emotions it intends to express and the emotions one is in fact disposed to express (or feels are appropriate and *should* be expressed). Further, to use the motif seriously is to learn *how* to dispose oneself, to be *already* disposing oneself, to the occasion in the manner the motif indicates. It is a matter of allowing oneself to be conformed to the spirit of the prayer.

Now, to return to Reventlow's assessment, the question is whether vv. 17-18 *are* in fact a prayer and so are to be seen as part of the intercessory complaint vv. 19-22. In fact, they seem even *less* a prayer-like description of distress than do vv. 2-6, which were actually found to be a prophetic attestation of judgment. Not only does 18c have the distinctive ring of an invective, but 17 ('And you shall say to them this word') explicitly casts what follows as a word of Yhwh. However, just as Reventlow struck v. 1 as redactional in order to read vv. 2-6 as part of the people's lament, so also he strikes 17a, treating it as a 'gloss... which has *misunderstood* its *Vorlage*'.[97] Convinced that the text must be read according to his hypothetically reconstructed model of the 'complaint liturgy', Reventlow prejudicially denigrates the redactional process and violates the text in its present shape. He thus puts himself out of position for assessing the *effect* of this shaping process.

As indicated above, the effect of 17a is to preclude reading 17-18 as part of the communal lament. We should note in particular that the introductory *wāw* connects this verse with the final statement of the judgment oracle in v. 16:

> w^ešāpaktî 'ălêhem w^e'āmartā 'ălêhem
> 'et-rā'ātām 'et-haddābār hazzeh
>
> And I will pour out upon them their evil,
> and you shall speak to them this word.

A statement of what Yhwh will do is thus coupled with a statement of what Jeremiah is to do. The clear impression is that 'this word' which Jeremiah is commanded to speak is to be in some way explanatory or interpretive of Yhwh's act of judgment; it is meant to fill out the judgment's reason (v. 18c) and entailments (vv. 17a-18b). The first of these entailments is emotional: the tears motif represents grief. Although its context is not that of a prayer, much of what was said above concerning this motif should still be borne in mind. It is not to be dismissed as *just* a rhetorical device for the purpose of heightening the effect of the announcement by, for example, emphasizing the judgment's inevitability. Rather, as the content of the interpretive word which Yhwh commands Jeremiah to speak, the motif serves to illuminate the quality of the divine action with reference to the actor. Itself a part of the message, the grief is shown to be part of Yhwh's own pathos and purpose.

It is relevant at this point to remark on the ambiguity of the first-person singular usage in 17-18. Yhwh has commanded Jeremiah to deliver a word which is spoken by an 'I'. Is this 'I' Yhwh's or Jeremiah's? The overall redactional shaping of the book makes it difficult to answer the question by correlating the terms of vv. 17-18 with other passages, since what clear distinctions may have originally existed between the words of Yhwh and those of Jeremiah have been largely blurred. For instance, the tears motif and the term *bat-'ammî* also occur in context together in 8.18-23, but this passage presents the very same ambiguity that ours does.[98] In the absence of definitive evidence to the contrary, and in keeping with our general thesis of how such ambiguity works, we answer that the 'I' belongs to *both* Yhwh and Jeremiah, or more precisely, to Jeremiah as Yhwh's representative.

To summarize the argument, vv. 17-18 function as a word of Yhwh entrusted to the prophet, to be delivered to the people, for the purpose of explicating the previous oracle of vv. 15-16. The prophet is therefore *not* being depicted by the text as one who responds to a scene of suffering simply on the basis of an innately sympathetic temperament unconditioned by a socio-religious role. Here Reventlow is right. Rather, and the rest Reventlow misses, by virtue of the fact that his words are directed by Yhwh, Jeremiah stands over against the people, speaking not for them but *to* them, and from Yhwh's side as Yhwh's agent. Thus, the sympathy that his words express, being part of the word which Yhwh commands him to perform, is a function not of innate temperament but of his representative role *qua* prophet. But this is not to say that his words are impersonal, that his 'I' and his grief are not actually *his*. He himself (and this means '*qua* prophet') has been placed in the position of owning his words, entertaining the vision of destruction, and expressing the grief over it—all in behalf of Yhwh and in the service of confirming and explicating the preceding judgment oracle. In essence, the prophet's self has become a part of his message, which is to say, a part of the divine message. Person and office have fully merged. Jeremiah constitutes himself, becomes who he truly is, precisely as he performs the office, however unbearable the tension.

Given that vv. 17-18 are a prophetic word of Yhwh and not part of the people's lament, the transition from the first-person singular to the plural of vv. 19-22 is somewhat more problematic than Reventlow thought. Not that it presents any longer a problem of interpretation, rather it is a matter of the tension mentioned above, the tension that resides within the prophet and comes to clearest expression in the individual confessions. For now the prophet must, as it were, switch sides and pray again as the people's representative.

19 hămā'ōs mā'astā 'et-yᵉhûdâ
   'im-bᵉṣiyôn gā'ālâ napšekā
   maddû'a hikkîtānû
   wᵉ'ên lānû marpē'
   gawwēh lᵉšālôm wᵉ'ên ṭôb
   ûlᵉ'ēt marpē'
   wᵉhinnēh bᵉ'ātâ
20 yāda'nû Yhwh riš'ēnû
   'ăwōn 'ăbôtênû
   kî ḥātā'nû lāk
21 'al-tin'aṣ lᵉma'an šimᵉkā
   'al-tᵉnabbēl kissē' kᵉbôdekā
   zᵉkōr 'al-tāpēr bᵉrîtᵉkā 'ittānô
22 hăyēš bᵉhablê haggôyim magšimîm
   wᵉ'im-haššāmayim yittᵉnû rᵉbibîm
   hălō' 'attâ-hû' Yhwh
   'elōhênû ûnᵉqawweh-llāk
   kî-'attâ 'āśîtā 'et-kol-'ēlleh

19 Hast thou utterly rejected Judah?
   Does thy soul loathe Zion?
   Why hast thou smitten us
      so that there is no healing for us?
   We looked for peace, but no good came;
      for a time of healing, but behold, terror.
20 We acknowledge our wickedness, O Lord,
      and the iniquity of our fathers,
      for we have sinned against thee.
21 Do not spurn us, for thy name's sake;
      do not dishonor thy glorious throne;
      remember and do not break thy covenant with us.
22 Are there any among the false gods of the nations that can bring rain?
   Or can the heavens give showers?
   Art thou not he, Yhwh our God?
   We set our hope on thee,
      for thou doest all these things. (RSV)

Similar in logic and structure to vv. 7-9, the prayer is basically a variation on the themes of the first lament. As in the first, the reproaches (v. 19) are put in question form, although their rapid, staccato-like succession, plus their expansion by the declarative 'We looked for peace...' (cf. 8.15), effects an intensification of the complaint. The confession (v. 20) employs a triad of terms for sin, as in v. 7, and culminates in the same phrase, though chiastically arranged and prefaced by a *kî* (perhaps for emphasis, 'surely' or 'how against thee we have sinned!'). The petition (v. 21) involves an appeal to Yhwh's name (cf. v. 7a), to his in-dwelling with them ('throne'; cf. v. 9b), and to the 'covenant' (only implicit in 7-9). Once again, however, there seems to be a heightening effect here through the use of four verbs in the imperative as opposed to two in 7-9, and by virtue of the explicit mention of covenant. Moreover, the verbs used in petition in 7-9 (*'ăśēh*, v. 7a; *tanniḥēnû*, v. 9b) are pale in comparison with the more urgent, almost presumptuous, *tin'aṣ*, *t^{e}nabbēl*, and *tāpēr* here.

As might be expected, the intensification in tone of the second complaint results in a deepening of the potential irony resident within it. The more severe the reproaches, the more urgent and condemnatory toward Yhwh the requests—the greater and more threatening is the gulf between an aberrant, self-justifying praying and the normative use of the prayer; in other words, the more likely is the prayer to operate as a self-indictment. In this regard, the prayer's explicit mention of covenant merits attention, since, as we have seen, the covenant provides the basis for the very possibility of such an ironic self-indictment, there being built into it curses which automatically come into effect as a consequence of the people's deviation from the norm. Thus, the more direct the appeal to covenant, the more clearly its negative implications come into view.

Accordingly, it is significant how closely the language of our passage conforms to that of the covenant sanctions in Lev 26. Specifically, the parallel verbs *m's* ('reject', 'spurn') and *g'l* ('loathe', 'abhor') in v. 19 and *prr* ('break', 'violate') in v. 21 are grouped together in both Lev 26.15 and 26.44. In the former they are used of the people: 'if you spurn my statutes, and if your soul abhors my ordinances, so that you break my covenant, (v. 16) I will do this to you . . . ' In the latter their subject is God: 'I will not spurn them, neither will I abhor them so as to destroy them utterly and break my covenant with them . . . ' It is to the point of the irony that when the people use these terms in their prayer, they do so with Yhwh as the subject, i.e. in the manner of Lev 26.44. To the extent that their confession of sin in v. 20 is only perfunctory and fails to reckon honestly with their *own* spurning, loathing, and violating covenant, then their appeal to the promise of forgiveness articulated in Lev 26.40 reflects a false confidence and their rejection by Yhwh becomes a foregone conclusion.

As with vv. 7-9, there is evidence of Jeremiah's self-involvement in this second intercessory prayer, evidence which indicates both his identification *with* the people and his differentiation *from* them. For example, the term 'glorious throne' (*kissē' kābôd*, v. 21) occurs later in the preface to the prophet's individual lamentation in ch. 17, which, as we have seen, also expresses 'hope', just as in 14.8 and here in 14.22 ('we set our hope on thee'). Similarly, the imperative to 'remember' ($z^e kor$) in the same verse anticipates 15.15 and 18.20 where the prophet calls on Yhwh to keep his part of the special relationship between them just as Jeremiah has kept his. But we should note the contrast between Jeremiah and his people at this point, since the people's calling on Yhwh to 'remember' covenant has behind it an unbroken history of their own forgetting (2.32; etc.). Further, Jeremiah, like his people, suffered perplexity at the failure of *šālôm* to materialize (4.10; 14.13), although, being privy to God's counsel, he could not avoid the truth of the explanation for this failure (as apparently they could). Finally, he shared the people's 'wound' (8.21), and in his own laments he both prayed for 'healing' (17.14) and complained of the lack of any (15.18). However, he also knew his wound to be a matter of obeying Yhwh and that, because he *was* obedient, he suffered it at the hands of a people who were *not*.

Again, the point of these linguistic and thematic parallels between the present passage and Jeremiah's own speech is to evince his own participation in the intercessory prayer. There is nothing here that he cannot say, indeed does not say, of himself. Still, while his words reflect his solidarity with his people, the way they connect with his life is different from the way they connect, or fail to connect (as they normatively should), with the people's. Prophet and people can thus be differentiated according to the different stances they adopt toward the subject matter of their prayer—just as we saw with regard to vv. 7-9.

Accordingly, just as vv. 10-12 hint at this differentiation, by focusing judgment upon the people on the basis of their 'wandering' (their glibness and hypocrisy), so too hints the oracular response of 15.1, though in a different manner:

> Then the Lord said to me, 'Though Moses and Samuel stood before me, yet my heart would not turn toward this people. Send them out of my sight, and let them go!' (RSV)

The rejection of the petition and the prohibition against intercession are conflated, which completes the heightening effect in this second round of complaint and answer. More importantly, the statement that not even the archetypal prophetic intercessors, Moses and Samuel, could dissuade Yhwh from judgment implies *via negativa* not only that Jeremiah's own self *is* fully engaged in his praying but that normatively the quality of the person who intercedes does in fact count in the way the prayer is received. That it does *not* count in the present situation is an index, again, of the extraordinary character of the circumstances, namely the people's proven incorrigibility. To the extent that intercession had come to be construed as a guaranteed system of propitiation that can tolerate every form of hypocrisy, it had to be forbidden. The identification between prophet and people cannot be absolute. God can in fact distinguish between them, must do so for his name's sake, and so now announces that he will.

Thus, Yhwh prohibits the prophet from interceding (cf. 15.19c), and without the prophet to turn to, the people are left to the curses they have brought upon themselves:

15.2 And when they ask you, 'Where shall we go?' you shall say to them,
    'Thus says the Lord:
  Those who are for pestilence, to pestilence,
    and those who are for the sword, to the sword;
  those who are for famine, to famine,
    and those who are for captivity, to captivity'. (RSV)

The oracle remains focused entirely on the people through v. 4, only continuing in order to elaborate the horror of the coming judgment and to relate it to the people's true representative in sin, Manasseh.

Where does this oracle then leave Jeremiah? In banning intercession and thus preventing the prophet from performing an activity felt to be constitutive of his identity, Yhwh has changed the rules of the prophetic game midstream and subverted Jeremiah's very self-understanding. Jeremiah's differentiation from the people seems therefore to work only negatively, i.e. only to permit the confirmation of the judgment which the people richly deserve but which they thought conveniently to avoid through the mechanism of intercession. Jeremiah appears to be left alone, no doubt confused and clearly unvindicated.

Of course, this is to ignore what Gerstenberger has already shown, namely that the passage ends not in 15.4 but 15.21 and that in the second act of the drama Jeremiah's differentiation from the people works positively, resulting not in the unconditional rejection which the people receive but in a promise of salvation. And the promise proves that Jeremiah's representative status does not terminate with his intercession. Rather, he remains *Yhwh's* representative such that all that we said of him in relation to 14.17-18 continues to apply. As in his grieving *with* Yhwh and at Yhwh's command *for* his people, Jeremiah's life illustrates the divine pathos and interprets the divine word/action. The prophetic life becomes a medium for the message.

But even with regard to the people, Jeremiah's representative status does not come to an end. Rather, it shifts in character, in fact gets expanded. To be sure, he can no longer represent the people as their intercessor, i.e. with just words, even words he truly means. Now he represents them, again, with his life—both in what he suffers and in what he is promised. For just as his identification with the people is not total, neither is his differentiation from them total. Being mortal, having to confess sins, he remains subject to judgment, is in fact rebuked, and must suffer with the people in the hard realities of the national disaster. However, the fact is that he also has reconfirmed to him the original promise of God's presence and deliverance (cf. ch. 1). This same promise is in turn extended to the exiles in Babylon (24.4-7), to the disciple Baruch (ch. 45), and ultimately to the people as a whole (chs. 30-33). Gerstenberger was right: Jeremiah's life becomes a paradigm in the divine economy of judgment and salvation. The medium *is* the message.

Jer 14-15 makes a climactic statement on the prophetic persona's theological significance, and with our references to 15.10-21 we would appear to have crossed the threshold into Jeremiah's individual confessions, which will be the subject of the next chapter. Yet it is not an entirely superfluous regression if we turn back to an earlier passage, 8.4–9.25, to continue our analysis of the role of first-person speech in the delineation of the relationship between people, prophet, and God. That passage will reinforce the conclusions achieved so far, but in a differently nuanced and novel way that will reward our consideration. At the same time its complexities are such that we can best discern its direction and import only on the basis of what has already become clear in Sections I and II.

III. *Jeremiah 8.4–9.25 (9.26 English versions)*

We begin by addressing the scope of the passage. Even here the decision as to where the unit begins and ends has been informed by

4. *The Prophetic 'I' & its Ambiguities* 103

the results of the previous investigation, to be exact, by the picture of the prophet-as-paradigm drawn in chs. 14-15. Without that picture and the light it throws upon the material that precedes it in the book, the inclination might be to mark the beginning of the unit at 8.14, with its first-person plural speech,[99] and the conclusion at 9.21, in the process dismissing 9.22f. as 'miscellaneous sayings' and giving short shrift to crucial wisdom motifs that run throughout the material.[100] However, in the light of that picture these boundaries prove too restrictive, and the neglect of the wisdom motifs results in a serious interpretive loss. For when viewed from the vantage point of chs. 14-15, the passage can be seen as an adumbration of Jeremiah's paradigmatic status, the principal vehicle for which is precisely the idea of wisdom, which arises not only well within the midst of the unit, in 9.11 especially, but in the disputed periphery as well, namely in 8.4-13 and 9.22-23.

At the outset it might be well to specify the wisdom motifs present here in order both to lay the groundwork for our analysis of this adumbration of the prophet's status and, more proximately, to demonstrate the connection of 8.4-13 and 9.22f. with the rest of the passage. Hence, we note first the use of the root *ḥkm* in 8.8, 9; 9.11, and 22. In 9.11 'wise' is accompanied by another basic wisdom term, *byn*, 'to understand' (cf. *śkl* in 9.22-23). In light of this pairing, perhaps we may be permitted to hear a resonance of wisdom in 9.16: 'Consider (*hitbôneṇû*) . . . and send for the skillful women (*haḥăkāmôt*) to come'.[101] Similarly, perhaps we can catch a wisdom flavor in the 'instruction' of 9.19: 'let your ear receive the word of his mouth and teach your daughters a lament' (cf. Prov 1.8; 4.1, 10, 20; 5.1, 7, etc.). Further, the idea of knowing Yhwh, of the knowledge of God (*yd'*, *da'at*), paramount in both prophecy and wisdom (e.g. Prov 1.7; 2.5; 30.3), occurs in 8.7; 9.2, 5; and, again, in 9.23, here in the same context as 'wise' and 'understand' (*śkl*). Finally, and most significantly, all of these motifs revolve around the central theme in the passage, the contrast between right, fitting, and proper speech and speech that is deceitful, slanderous, and treacherous (e.g. 8.6, 8, 11; 9.2-6, 8). This same theme is at the heart of wisdom thought (e.g. Prov 4.24; 8.7-8; 10.31-32; 17.7; 24.26, 28; 25.11; 31.26).

It makes sense that the concern with the quality of speech should be developed with the frequent use of quotations. This accounts in part for the prevalence of first-person language in the passage. Within 8.4-13 in particular the people's words are cited twice as positive evidence of the failures for which they merit judgment. And once there is a (negative) citation of words they should have said but did not. To wit, after a wisdom-styled opening (v. 4) cast in the form of rhetorical questions that appeal to the world of experience (in which people are normally observed to get up after they fall, to return [i.e. repent] after they turn away [from sin, cf. 4.1]), the indictment is laid against Yhwh's people that they have been singularly unnatural in 'holding fast to deceit' and 'refusing to repent' (v. 5). Although Yhwh has strained to hear a fitting word of remorse, 'they have not spoken aright' (in the RSV's felicitous translation), with no one taking sufficient stock of his condition to ask 'What have I done?' (v. 6).

The negative citation is followed by another wisdom-type appeal, this time to the animal realm where even mute creatures can be seen to observe the ordinance of seasonal migration that God has prescribed for them—whereas, by contrast, 'my people know not the ordinance of Yhwh' (8.7). The first positive citation occurs at this point, in a context charged with irony. The people are quoted as attributing to themselves a wisdom which they presume to have by virtue of possessing the *Tôrâ* of Yhwh: 'How can you say, "We are wise, and the law of the Lord is with us"?' (v. 8).

This citation marks the center of the subsection, vv. 4-13, the remainder of which is devoted to its refutation. The second citation, the words 'Peace, peace' of the prophets and priests (v. 11), is but an illustration of the falseness of this claim to wisdom, the prophets and priests being false dealers, superficial healers, there being in fact no peace at all. The falseness of the self-attribution of wisdom, the text indicates, is evidenced by falseness in other forms of speech. Falseness is of course disobedience which, though in speech being quintessentially 'expressive', can be enacted in all other modes of human behavior as well. Thus, greed for unjust gain (v. 10) and the shameless commitment of abomination (v. 12), like 'apostasy' and 'wickedness' in general (vv. 5, 8), are also cited in the refutation of the claim.

The crux of the matter is that wisdom is conceived as obedience to Yhwh. It is in light of this conception that the sense of the harvest imagery of v. 13 becomes clear. By professing wisdom on the grounds of having God's law, the people mean to lay claim to Yhwh's approval, to commend themselves as a crop fit for an appreciative ingathering. But in the eyes of the harvester, who sees the law given the lie by disobedience (v. 8b) and the word rejected that was intended as nourishment (v. 9b), the professed wisdom evaporates ('What wisdom is in them?', v. 9b), leaving behind nothing to gather but 'withered leaves'.[102] Both Yhwh and the people had desired (the latter presumptuously) a rewarding and positive harvest. That hope being frustrated, we have the sense that dire consequences will follow. This sense is confirmed by the use made of the root *'sp* ('gather') in 8.13-14.

13 *'āsōp 'ăsîpēm n*^{e}*'um-Yhwh*
   'ên 'ănābîm baggepen
   w^e*'ên t*^{e}*'ēnîm bat'ēnâ*
   w^e*he'āleh nābēl*
   wā'ettēn lāhem ya'abrûm
14 *'al-mâ 'ănaḥnû yōš*^{e}*bîm*
   hē'ās^e*pû w*^{e}*nābô' 'el-'ārê hammibṣār*
   w^e*nidd*^{e}*mâ-ššām*
   kî Yhwh 'ĕlōhênû hădimmānû
   wayyašqēnû mê-rō'š
   kî ḥāṭā'nû laYhwh

13 When I would gather them, says the Lord,
       there are no grapes on the vine,
     nor figs on the fig tree;
       even the leaves are withered,
       and what I gave them has passed away from them.
14 Why do we sit still?
       Gather together that we may enter the fortified cities, and perish there.
     For the Lord our God has doomed us to perish,
       and has given us poisoned water to drink,
       because we have sinned against the Lord.

The root *'sp* serves to connect the two verses, and thereby the material that precedes and follows them. Disputing such a connection, Holladay argues that the repetition of *'sp* in vv. 13 and 14 is only 'a verbal link with the next cycle [his 'Supplementary Foe Cycle'], for 8.14 replicates diction from 4.5, and we are off into something new'— as if the 'verbal link' is something mere and naked, having no semantic significance. Holladay is of course right about 8.14 replicating diction from 4.5; both verses have 'Gather together (*hē'ās*^{e}*pû*) that we may enter the fortified cities'. And he is right about their difference: In 8.14 the walled cities are no longer the refuge they were in 4.5 but rather 'traps for the victims within'. Further, whereas 4.5 has God telling the people what to say, 8.14 has the people actually saying it, adding sarcastically, 'and perish there' (literally, 'that we may be silenced there', *wᵉniddᵉmâ-ššām*), such that 8.14 'is a kind of response to God's command in 4.5'.¹⁰³ Now, it is clear that in both cases *hē'āsᵉpû* occurs in the context of judgment. What Holladay ignores is that this same context also holds for *'sp* in 8.13.

It is not only that v. 13 follows immediately upon an announcement of judgment in v. 12 ('Therefore they shall fall among the fallen; when I punish them, they shall be overthrown, says the Lord'). It is also that the negative overtones we sense in the people's failure to measure up as a crop suitable to Yhwh are dramatically intensified by an ominous pun on *'sp* in the first colon. The present form of the text has *'āsōp 'āsîpēm*, i.e. the infinitive absolute of *'sp* plus the hiphil first-singular imperfect of, apparently, *swp*, 'to cut off'. While most commentators seek to circumvent the grammatical oddity by emendation, it seems best to let the text stand as is and see here a poetic assonance designed to associate the harvest imagery precisely with the theme of judgment.¹⁰⁴ We might then read paraphrastically, 'When I would gather (I must cut them off), there are no grapes on the vine . . . '

Accordingly, if, as Holladay suggests, 8.14 represents a sarcastic play on 4.5, the people realizing that gathering to flee will result not in safety but destruction, it only does so in the vein already established by the pun of 8.13: their gathering means their end. Further, in view of this connection the literal sense of the people's sarcastic *wᵉniddᵉmâ-ššām* takes on unexpected significance. It is as people who have not *spoken aright*, who have spoken boastfully of a wisdom that they continually betray, and who have proclaimed 'peace' and expected well-being when in fact they deserve 'terror' (v. 15) that they are to be cut off. False speakers, they are gathered 'so that we may be silenced'. It turns out that the 'verbal link' provided by *'sp* really belongs to the larger wisdom/speech matrix and that, as such, it *does* serve to establish continuity of context between 8.4-13 and 8.14f.

With 8.14 there begins the kind of first-person speech and interchange of voices that is our special concern. For much of this material the formulas and narrative elements that typically serve to identify speakers are lacking (e.g. *kōh 'āmar Yhwh*, *nᵉ'um Yhwh*, *lē'mōr*, or 'Then I said', 'How can you say', etc.). The issue of where different voices are blended and where they are distinct will again have to be addressed, and, as in Sections I and II, there are no general rules that definitively resolve the matter for every case. Each case

4. The Prophetic 'I' & its Ambiguities

will have to be evaluated in terms of the logic of its given context. In this regard the one rule we shall follow (in contrast to the majority of commentators) is to grant the ambiguities that the text presents sufficient room in which to work and not to obscure their effect by precipitously seeking to eliminate them. We shall observe in this material that ambiguities are effected by the overlapping, blurring, and foreshortening of perspectives.

Recalling the first-person material in ch. 14, we might ask at the outset to what extent Jeremiah's own voice can be heard in the people's speech in 8.14-15. We have already seen that by one (quite legitimate) reading of $w^e nidd^e mâ$ the people's persona is characterized by sarcasm. On the other hand, the passage is unique in this depiction. While perfect consistency in characterization cannot be expected from a work of this sort (it is not after all a novel), nowhere else do the people evince the sort of realization presupposed here of the end that awaits them. On the contrary, they are elsewhere oblivious to its approach and heedless of, or hypocritical in their response to, its warnings. In this sarcasm, it may be suggested, an authorial voice is making its presence felt, that of the *writing* prophet putting words, *his* words, into the mouth of his personae.[105] For it is really the prophet's awareness and knowledge that the people articulate. His perspective has crept into their speech or been overlaid upon it.

But it is not *just* as an authorial voice that Jeremiah can be heard in vv. 14-15. As the sarcasm gives way to confession ('for the Lord our God has silenced us and has given us poisoned water to drink, because we have sinned against the Lord'), the sense of Jeremiah standing behind the text as its author diminishes and that of his presence *in* the text, as a persona participating in the confession, begins to grow. For it cannot be the case that the perspective from which these words are spoken is suddenly all the people's own, as if they were any more capable of a remorseful acknowledgement of their situation than a sarcastic one. Rather, as in 4.19-21, 10.19b-21, and the confessions of ch. 14, they can make confession only as the prophetic intercessor makes it for them. By way of confirmation, it needs only be recalled that v. 15—

$qaww\bar{e}h\ l^e š\bar{a}l\hat{o}m\ w^e \hat{e}n\ \underline{t}\hat{o}b$
$l^{e'}\bar{e}t\ marp\bar{e}h\ w^e hinn\bar{e}h\ b^{e'}\bar{a}t\hat{a}$

We looked for peace, but no good came,
    for a time of healing, but behold, terror. (RSV)

—recurs verbatim in the intercessory lament of 14.19 and that in 4.10 and 14.13 the failure of the expectation of peace was a source of dismay to the prophet himself.[106]

Most of the commentators group v. 16 with vv. 14-15 as part of the people's speech.[107] The third-person singular pronominal suffixes (e.g. *sûsāyw*, 'his horses', presumably Yhwh's) correspond to the third-person references to Yhwh in v. 14, and the grammatically ambiguous *nišmaʿ* can easily be taken as the qal imperfect 'we hear', thus as a continuation of the preceding first-person plural verbs. Holladay assigns the verse to Yhwh, believing there to be a rhetorical parallelism between vv. 14-15 and 16-17 (*yšb* and *ʿîr/ʿārê* appearing in 14 and 16, *ʾên* in 15 and 17) that reflects a dialogical structure.[108] This reading would necessarily take *nišmaʿ* as the niphal perfect 'is heard'. It does not, however, reckon with the third-singular suffixes. In my opinion, a definitive identification of the speaker is not called for. Thematically and stylistically, the verse is reminiscent of the battle scenes, the so-called 'Scythian songs', that punctuate the book and, like objective data open to public scrutiny, are announced, perceived, and responded to from a variety of angles (see especially 4.13-17; 6.22-27; 10.22).[109] Verse 16 can therefore be heard as either the people's *or* Yhwh's voice, or either in concert with Jeremiah's. No single perspective dominates. In any case, it has very little the quality of self-characterizing speech.

There are no significant ambiguities in v. 17. Marked by a divine-word formula, Yhwh's announcement of judgment is the stark reality to which the preceding and following first-person utterances are ordered.

Similarly, though without explicit markers, the identity of the speaker in vv. 18-19a and 21 cannot be mistaken. As in 4.19 and 23.9, Jeremiah articulates the personally shattering impact of the reality of judgment through the metaphor of the heart:

> *mablîgîtî ʿălê yāgôn*
> *ʿālay libbî dawwāy*
>
> Beyond all healing for me is the grief,
>   within me my heart is sick.[110] (v. 18)

(Such words—a grief-speaking—are once again constitutive of a self, and if fitly spoken, we shall return to ask, do they not also constitute the self as wise?) Jeremiah grieves, however, not just for himself or from a self-contained perspective as just one victim among many. As

4. The Prophetic 'I' & its Ambiguities

in 4.19-21 and 10.19b-20, he speaks as the prophet whose ear is tuned to 'the cry of the daughter of my people', and who makes himself recognizable in suffering not just with but *for* and *over* his people:

'*al šeber bat-'ammî hošbārtî*
qādartî šammâ heḥĕziqātᵉnî

For the wound of the daughter of my people I am wounded;
I mourn, dismay has seized me. (v. 21)

That it is as a *prophet* that he suffers so is to say that his perspective, like his identity, is a compound one. Something of Yhwh's point of view is at work here, informing Jeremiah's speech.

It is to the point of this compound perspective that the speech in 8.18f. begins as Jeremiah's but ends as Yhwh's (note the divine-word formula for 9.2, 5, and 6-8) and that we cannot tell exactly where the transition takes place. Already in the dialogical exchange of v. 19bc the first-person singular response, while presumably Yhwh's, is formally undistinguished from the first-singular voice of 19a. The exchange is patterned with three rhetorical questions introduced by *ha-*, *'im-*, and *maddûaʿ* respectively.[111] The speaker of the first two questions is identified by the prophet's 'Behold, the sound of the cry of the daughter of my people from the furthest reaches of the land'. The content of the people's cry follows immediately:

haYhwh 'ên bĕṣiyôn
'im-malkāh 'ên bāh

Is Yhwh not in Zion?
Is her King not in her?

As in 14.19 ('Hast thou utterly rejected Judah? Does thy soul loathe Zion?'), the questions reflect the people's consternation at Yhwh's apparent enmity, which, given the presumed fact of his indwelling with them (also presumed to guarantee his aid and protection), they find quite unintelligible. Here formulated negatively, the questions presuppose a *positive* answer (e.g. '*Of course* Yhwh is in Zion') and serve as a reproach designed to hasten the expected salvation. But instead of a positive answer affirming God's presence and intention to save, there follows the third question—

maddûaʿ hikʿîsûnî bipsilêhem
bᵉhablê nēkār

Why have they provoked my anger with their graven images,
with their foreign idols?

—which is in effect a *negative* response, Yhwh implying that indeed he is *not* in Zion, or at least not there to save but to condemn, having been provoked to anger by their idolatry. At the same time the third question implies that the first two are viewed as inappropriate and hypocritical. We might paraphrase, 'Why do they suddenly invoke *my* name when heretofore they've been content with idols? Don't they know such behavior can only be provocative?'

The significance in the lack of an explicit differentiation between Jeremiah's voice and Yhwh's here can be seen in a comparison with the use of the *ha/'im/maddûa'* triple-question pattern in other passages (cf. 2.14, 31; 8.4-5, 22; 14.19; 22.28; and 49.1). With the exception of 14.19, where it is part of the people's complaint, and 8.22 which will be discussed below, all occurrences belong to a context of judgment, usually on Israel (Moab in 49.1, Coniah in 22.28). The three instances preceding our verse, most notably 8.4-5 which begins our unit, establish the pattern as a characteristic means by which Yhwh himself interrogates his people. In these instances, as typically, the first two questions work as a foil for the third, hinting at some peculiarity or disorder in the persons being interrogated. The third question then reformulates the first two to make the implied disorder explicit and to give the indictment a severe pointedness. Thus, all *three* questions originate out of the same point of view and work to the same purpose, that of accusing the miscreant. It is ultimately the same with our verse. The people's words provide the first two questions but have only been cited to set up the clinching line. In effect, they are but the data or evidence for, thus a constitutive part of, the indictment; and the perspective of the one who cites them, i.e. Jeremiah, is precisely that of the final accuser, Yhwh.[112]

In light of the above analysis it is evident that Jeremiah's suffering for and over his people, poignantly articulated in 8.18, 21, and 23, represents not just a sympathetic identification with them but, by virtue of his enlistment in Yhwh's case *against* them, a suffering that entails anger as well, an anger that has them as its object. This corresponds with our conclusions regarding 4.19f. (and with Gerstenberger's on 15.10.).[113]

The compound perspective with its complex emotional structure continues into v. 22, but now Jeremiah's anger seems directed against Yhwh (which in light of the Confessions is by no means an impossibility):

4. The Prophetic 'I' & its Ambiguities

haṣorî 'ên bᵉgil'ād
'im-rōpē' 'ên šām
kî maddûa' lō' 'alᵉtâ 'ărukat bat-'ammî

Is there no balm in Gilead?
Is there no physician there?
Why then fails the healing of the daughter of my people?

Again we have the triple-question pattern, this time all of which is spoken by Jeremiah, though again there are no formulas to indicate so, only the epithet *bat-'ammî* favored by the prophet. Even here, however, the fact that *Yhwh* uses the term in 8.11 (cf. 6.14) and 9.6 makes this an ambiguous instrument for distinguishing Jeremiah's voice from God's.

In any case, the *ha/'im/maddûa'* pattern operates here just as it does elsewhere, the third question proceeding upon the obvious answer to the first two. Just as surely as there is balsam in Gilead, Yhwh is Israel's healer (cf. 3.22 and 17.14); but if so, where is he? Why hasn't he done his job? Hence, now it is Jeremiah interrogating Yhwh, and with an unmistakable tone of reproach.

However, the close proximity of this verse to the questions of v. 19 adds another dimension to the prophet's words. There just as here the issue was Yhwh's absence and enmity, but the force of the third question was to turn the people's reproach back upon themselves. In effect, that question provides the answer to the third question here as well. The reason why the people's wound remains unsalved lies within themselves, not in some failure of Yhwh. However much the prophet's third question in 8.22 remains an open one, burdening him with grief and dismay (v. 23 is the evidence that it does), it has simultaneously a rhetorical quality. The answer has already been given, and the prophet better than anyone knows it. To the extent that the question has this rhetorical quality, the prophet's words are informed by the divine perspective, and his anger is in part a sharing of Yhwh's own.

The first-singular speech continues uninterruptedly, and without identification of the speaker, through 8.23 and 9.1 (MT):

8.23 *mî-yittēn rō'šî mayim*
  wᵉ'ênî mᵉqôr dim'â
  wᵉ'ebkeh yômām wālaylâ
   'ēt ḥalᵉlê bat-'ammî
9.1 *mî-yittᵉnēnî bammidbar mᵉlôn 'ōrᵉḥîm*

w^e'e'$ez^eb\hat{a}$ 'et-'$amm\hat{i}$ w^e'$\bar{e}l^ek\hat{a}$ $m\bar{e}$'$itt\bar{a}m$
$k\hat{i}$ $kull\bar{a}m$ m^ena'$\bar{a}p\hat{i}m$ '$\bar{a}ṣeret$ $b\bar{o}g^ed\hat{i}m$

8.23 Oh that my head were waters
and my eye a fountain of tears
that I might bewail day and night
the slain of the daughter of my people!
9.1 Oh that I had in the wilderness a wayfarers' lodgings
that I might leave my people, get away from them,
for all of them are adulterers, a company of crooks!

Whether one associates 9.1 with Elijah's flight in 1 Kgs 19 (in which case the speaker becomes a type of Elijah) or with the psalmist of Ps 55.7ff., a human figure who desires to flee in the face of betrayal by a companion, the conclusion seems unavoidable that Jeremiah is speaking here.[114] If so, then it is as one who is capable of moving instantaneously from the profoundest grief (v. 23 being another illustration, perhaps the most powerful one, of prophetic sympathy) to bitter accusation, while directing both the grief and the bitterness toward the same object.

It is precisely this sudden shift in mood (along with the parallel structure effected by $m\hat{i}$-$yitt\bar{e}n$/$yitt^en\bar{e}n\hat{i}$) that impels Holladay to go against virtually all other commentators by assigning 9.1, with the following verses, to Yhwh. He believes that this proposal will 'open up the possibility of a far more acute understanding of Jeremiah's perception of the tension between himself and Yahweh in their respective attitudes toward the people'.[115] But as we have already seen both in the preceding verses and in other passages, Jeremiah's attitude is itself composite, containing both the sympathetic grief and the bitter anger. He is quite capable of such a shift in mood precisely because it is Yhwh's perspective and attitude(s) that he shares. The 'tension' between Jeremiah and God is rooted not in their *attitudes* toward the people, which are identical, but in how Yhwh chooses to *enact* those attitudes (and in how he chooses to act toward the prophet—see the Confessions).

Obviously, this is not to say that 9.1 should *not* be heard as Yhwh's voice but rather, and once again as suggested by the text's refusal to attach an identifying formula, as not *exclusively* Yhwh's voice. The hinted Elijah typology and the analogy to Ps 55 (enforced by the close linguistic correspondence between the latter and 9.1) continue to push Jeremiah's persona to the forefront here. On the other hand, neither is the voice in 8.23 to be heard as exclusively Jeremiah's, for if he has a share in Yhwh's anger, so Yhwh has a share in his grief. Specifically, we need to recall the ambiguity related to the 'tears' motif in 14.17, how in that passage Jeremiah's 'I' was representative of Yhwh's, his tears an expression of God's emotion. The same motif is present in 13.17, a passage which, like the present one, begins as Jeremiah's speech but at some point (v. 18? 20? 24?) turns into Yhwh's. Most relevant, however, is the fact that in 9.9 the destructiveness of his judgment prompts Yhwh himself to 'take up weeping' ($b^e k\hat{\imath}$).

Now, the ambiguity attending the identity of the first-singular speaker from 8.18–9.1 is admittedly subtle and not especially problematic. Although the voices of the people and God break through that of the dominant persona at certain points, overtly manifesting the presence of other perspectives that are covertly present throughout, the fact that Jeremiah is the dominant persona seems obvious. However, when 9.2 ends with 'and they do not know *me*' and the 'I' we have become accustomed to hearing as Jeremiah's explicitly and suddenly becomes Yhwh's, the ambiguity becomes deep and systematic. Just how much so is evidenced by the number of commentators who emend $w^e\,'\bar{o}t\hat{\imath}$ to $w^e\,'\bar{e}t\ Yhwh$ and delete $n^e\,'um\text{-}Yhwh$ so as to read the verse as a continuation of Jeremiah's speech.[116] Others try to resolve the ambiguity by positing the final bi-cola as a citation by Jeremiah of a word he had previously received from Yhwh.[117]

Neither move has objective criteria to support it. Even from the diachronic perspective that seeks to establish the 'original' text, the emendations are only partially justified.[118] As for the citation hypothesis, the question is how one justifies restricting the quoted material to just the final bi-cola. For it is not the case, at least in the final form of the text, that the formula $n^e\,'um\text{-}Yhwh$ is used *only* for citations, brief or otherwise, within larger units of the prophet's speech or that it applies *only* to an immediately preceding statement. Its recurrent use in ch. 2, an extended speech of Yhwh, as well as in 3.1, 12; and 4.1 (where the material that it governs preceding it is of exactly the same order [e.g. first-singular] as that which comes after it), offers evidence to the contrary. Finally, it is interesting that in his study on the prophetic use of citations H.W. Wolff effectively acknowledges the systematic ambiguity of the relation between the word of Yhwh and that of the prophet and so reserves the designation 'citation' for words the prophets quote from parties other than God.[119]

Thematically, 9.2 develops the implications of the last word of 9.1, *bōgᵉdîm* (literally, 'treacherous men'), and begins an extensive metaphorical elaboration of the people's disobedience in terms of the 'false speech' theme (cf. 8.6, 8, 11, etc.). The verse thus effects a continuity between the voice that was heard predominantly as Jeremiah's in 8.18–9.1 and the one which is here marked as Yhwh's.

Beyond what has already been discussed, vv. 2-4 present no urgent problems. It is, however, worth observing the relentlessness with which they pursue the theme:

2 *wayyadrᵉkû 'et-lᵉšônām*
    qaštām šeqer
        wᵉlō' le'ĕmûnâ gābᵉrû bā'āreṣ
  kî mērā'â 'el-rā'â yaṣā'û
    wᵉ'ōtî lō'-yādā'û nᵉ'um-Yhwh
3 *'îš mērē'ēhû hiššāmērû*
    wᵉ'al-kol-'āḥ 'al-tibṭāḥû
  kî kol-'āḥ 'āqôb ya'qōb
    wᵉkol-rēa' rākîl yahălōk
4 *wᵉ'îš bᵉrē'ēhû yᵉhātēllû*
    we'ĕmet lō' yᵉdabbērû
  limmᵉdû lᵉšônām dabber-šeqer
    ha'ăwēh nil'û

2 They have bent their tongue,
    their bow is a lie,
        and not for truth have they become strong in the land;
  for from evil to evil they proceed,
    and me they do not know, says the Lord.
3 Each ought beware his neighbor,
    nor any brother trust;
  for every brother is a cheating Jacob,
    and every neighbor peddles slander.
4 Each the other deceives,
    and truth they will not speak,
  having taught their tongue to speak deceit,
    straining to act perversely.[120]

The speech reaches a penultimate climax in v. 5, and here there *are* problems:

  šibtᵉkā bᵉtôk mirmâ
  bᵉmirmâ mē'ănû da'at-'ôtî nᵉ'um-Yhwh

> Your dwelling is in the midst of treachery;
> in treachery they have refused to know me, says the Lord.[121]

The same commentators who in v. 2 emend the first-singular objective pronoun and delete the divine-word formula do so again, and again without full justification. The sudden incursion of the second-person address (šibt^{e}kā) leads some, the RSV included, to follow the Greek by redividing the consonants, assigning šb to the end of v. 4 and reading v. 5 as tōk b^{e}tôk mirmâ b^{e}mirmâ ... ('Wrong on wrong, deceit on deceit').[122] Berridge maintains the vocalization of the MT but relocates the entire fifth verse after v. 6 and sees it as part of the judgment oracle (vv. 6-8) that is introduced by the messenger formula and by which Yhwh confirms Jeremiah's analysis of the people's abhorrent conduct.[123]

As before, we shall let the present form *and* sequence of the text stand and accept its resultant ambiguities. The ambiguities permit two optional readings (I and II), each of which contains two internal options (A and B). If only the second colon is read as Yhwh's word (I), then the first would appear to have Jeremiah addressing either Yhwh, 'your dwelling' referring to God's earthly temple-abode which is surrounded by human fraud (A), or the people, the 'dwelling' then not being in any way something standing over against the fraud but a part of it (B). The B reading would be reinforced by another parallel with Ps 55. Verses 7-9 of the psalm were the words of a human figure seeking escape from a treacherous companion: the correspondence with 9.1 suggests Jeremiah as the speaker there. Then, with five different references vv. 10b-12 of the psalm locate the corruption (cf. 'fraud'), of which the friend's betrayal is but a specific instance, within and throughout the city (cf. 'your dwelling'): 'For I see violence and contention in the city. Day and night they go around it on its walls; and mischief and trouble are in its midst. Ruin is in its midst, and from its market place there does not depart either oppression or treachery.'[124] The parallel thus suggests that it is a ubiquitous malaise in Jer 9.5a, one constitutive of the city in general. The idea of God's dwelling does not enter the picture.

If on the other hand, and by analogy with 9.2 (cf. 3.1; etc.), *both* cola are read as the n^e'um-Yhwh (II), then 5a would be heard as God addressing either Jeremiah (as Berridge recommends) (A), or again the people (B)—which is more likely given the present sequence of the text. Indeed, the continuity of tone in 9.2-5 plus the repetition of the divine-word formula, which tends to attract into its orbit all the intervening material, gives this reading a saliency equal to that provided its rival by the parallel with Ps 55.

An objection to both IB and IIB (the same that prompted the RSV's emendations) would be that whereas the people are referred to in the third-plural in all the surrounding context, v. 5a employs a second-singular address. Hence, the addressee must be Jeremiah or God, not the people. However, equally abrupt shifts occur in 2.14-16 and 2.26-28, both of which are spoken to or about the people by Yhwh (note 'they have forgotten *me*' in 2.13 and 'they have turned their back on *me*' in 2.27). Even if these shifts are only the product of a secondary juxtaposition of originally separate units, the very fact of the juxtaposition indicates that the 'you' and the 'they' were heard as having the same referent, i.e. the people.

In sum, at 9.5 the text attains a radical open-endedness, there being no definitive means of excluding any of the four readings adduced. While IB (Jeremiah addressing the people in 5a, Yhwh responding in 5b) and IIB (Yhwh speaking in both cola, addressing the people in the first) prove more likely than their counterparts, the ambiguities reduce no further. Each of the preferred readings has its own compelling logic and justification. The important point, however, is that the double-reading we are left with reflects the simultaneity or conflation of perspectives we have been observing all along. Specifically, from 9.2 through v. 5 Jeremiah's perspective on the people is indistinguishable from Yhwh's.

Verses 6-8 are introduced by the messenger formula, and from this point on the chapter is dominated by the voice of Yhwh. Verse 7 is a clear reprise of the 'false speech' theme from vv. 2-4:

ḥēṣ šwḥṭ lᵉšônām mirmâ dibbēr
   bāpîw šālôm 'et-rēʿēhû yᵉdabbēr
      ûbᵉqirbô yāśîm 'ārbô

A deadly arrow is their tongue which speaks deceit;
   with his mouth each says 'Peace' to his neighbor,
      but within his heart he plans an ambush.

Given the conflation of perspectives in vv. 2-4 (and 5), v. 7 is hardly Yhwh's 'answer to Jeremiah's lamentation', as Berridge maintains, but is rather a summary statement that authorizes the preceding verses as deriving ultimately and unambiguously from Yhwh's word.[125] In the same vein v. 6, which speaks of Yhwh's intention to refine and test the people, is not quite a matter of God's taking over the task that Jeremiah was commissioned to do in 5.1 and 6.27, as if the prophet had somehow failed. As 8.6 would suggest, in which Yhwh states that he has 'given heed and listened', i.e. to test the people's faith, Jeremiah's assaying was Yhwh's work all along. But by 9.6 that previous investigation into the moral life of the people is completed, and the refining and testing are now a matter of punishment: 'For what else can I do because of my people? ... Shall I not punish them for these things? says the Lord; and shall I not avenge myself on a nation such as this?' (vv. 6b, 8).

The note of reluctance in these questions is significant for what follows. It hints that Yhwh's anger, like Jeremiah's, is colored by sadness. In 9.9 the hint becomes fact in a statement of exquisite pathos:

> 'al-hehārîm 'eśśā' b^ekî wānehî
> w^e'al-n^e'ôt midbar qînâ
> kî niṣṣ^{e}tû mibb^{e}lî-'îš 'ōbēr
> w^elō' šām^e'û qôl miqneh
> mē'ôp haššāmayim w^e'ad-b^ehēmâ
> nād^{e}dû hālākû

> For the mountains I shall take up weeping and wailing,
>   and for the pastures of the wilderness a lamentation;
> because they are laid waste so that no one passes through,
>   and the lowing of cattle cannot be heard,
> both the birds of the air and the beasts
>   having fled; they are gone.[126]

That Yhwh himself should so anthropomorphically weep and lament may be startling, but to try to avoid the offense by emending the text (to the Greek) is to rob the MT of one of its more profound expressions of the Creator's involvement with his Creation (cf. 14.17). It is further to obscure the text's unique depictive force of having its personae enact their identity of interrelatedness through self-constituting language. That is to say, Yhwh's 'weeping' identifies him with the prophet who would 'weep' for his people in 8.23; his 'wailing' identifies him with the people he instructs to 'wail' in 9.17.

Of course, if it were *Jeremiah* speaking here, as Bright maintains, the force of these observations, and the offense as well, would be considerably diminished.[127] However, the persona whose 'I' announces judgment in the next verse—'I will make Jerusalem a heap of ruins, a lair of jackals; and I will make the cities of Judah a desolation, without inhabitant'—and whom everyone recognizes as Yhwh, is no more explicitly identified as such than the persona whose 'I' weeps in 9.9. There are no speaker-formulas in either verse. It seems to be the text's intent to let the prominence and obviousness of Yhwh's 'I' in the surrounding verses govern our reading of the 'I' in 9.9. There is, however, one grammatical point that can provide objective corroboration: v. 10 begins with a *wāw*-consecutive, $w^e n\bar{a}tat\hat{i}$; thus, 'I will take up... (v. 9) *and* I will make...' (v. 10). Verses 9-10 are therefore one sentence. The speaker is Yhwh.

The scene of devastation, perhaps with the spectacle of a grieving God, induces the series of questions that follow in v. 11:

> Who is the man so wise that he can understand this? To whom has the mouth of the Lord spoken, that he may declare it? Why is the land ruined and laid waste like a wilderness, so that no one passes through?

This may easily be heard as the blended voices of Jeremiah, the people, and, similarly to the 'authorial voice' in 8.14, the tradition that composed the book.[128] It is noteworthy that only the last question receives an answer, which is supplied by Yhwh in vv. 12-13. The first two remain open, at least for the time being. The fact that the 'wisdom' and 'speech' themes are so directly coordinated is, of course, a matter of no slight consequence. There is a strong sense that the questions are driving toward a point that will eventually have to be made clear. They will in fact be answered.

Following a judgment oracle in vv. 14-15 comes a summons to lamentation directed toward the women of Judah. Verses 16-18 and 19-20 are roughly parallel in structure, a series of imperatives followed by a *kî* clause in each case. There is nothing to contradict the impression created by this structure that all five verses should be heard as the same voice.

16 *kōh 'āmar Yhwh ṣ^ebā'ôt*
    hitbôn^enû w^eqir^e'û lamqôn^enôt ûtĕbô'ênâ
        w^e'et-haḥăkāmôt šil^eḥû w^etābô'nâ
17 *ût^emahērnâ w^etiśśenâ 'ālênû nehî*
    w^etēradnâ 'ênênû dim'āh
        w^e'ap'appênû yizz^elû-mayim
18 *kî qôl n^ehî nišma' miṣṣîyôn*
    'ēk šuddādnû bōšnû m^e'ōd
    kî-'āzabnû 'āreṣ
        kî hišlîkû misk^enôtênû

19 kî-šᵉma'nâ nāšîm dᵉbar-Yhwh
    wᵉtiqqaḥ 'oznᵉkem dᵉbar-pîw
    wᵉlammēdnâ bᵉnôtêkem nehî
    wᵉ'iššâ rᵉ'ûtāh qînâ
20 kî-'ālâ māwet bᵉḥallônênû
    bā' bᵉ'armᵉnôtênû
    lᵉhakrît 'ôlāl miḥûṣ
    baḥûrîm mērḥōbôt

16 Thus says the Lord of hosts:
    Consider, and call for the mourning women that they may come.
    Send for the wise women that they may come.
17 Let them make haste and raise a wailing over us
    that our eyes may run down with tears
    and our eyelids gush with water.
18 For a sound of wailing we hear/is heard from Zion:
    'How we are ruined! We are utterly ashamed,
    because we have left the land,
    because they have cast down our dwellings.'
19 Hear well, O women, the word of the Lord,
    and let your ear receive the word of his mouth,
    and teach your daughters a wailing,
    and each her neighbor a dirge.
20 For death has come up into our windows,
    it has entered our palaces,
    to cut off the children from the streets
    and the young men from the squares.

Among the points to be emphasized, the voice that issues the imperatives (v. 16) refers to itself in the first-person plural (vv. 17 and 20).[129] Further, v. 17 employs *nehî* 'wailing' from 9.9, which was Yhwh's own lamentation, and the 'tears' motif from 8.23, which was heard primarily in Jeremiah's first-singular voice. Again, note the plural here: 'that *our* eyes may run down with tears and *our* eyelids gush with water'.

None of this would be peculiar for a speech by the prophet, and the passage might well have been originally composed as an intercessory communal lament. But in the present form of the text it has been prefaced by the messenger formula so as to be heard as God speaking.[130] This raises the scandal of v. 9 to an altogether higher level. Not only will Yhwh weep *over* his creation, he will weep *with* it, as if a fellow victim. It is now not just Jeremiah, but Yhwh himself, the divine judge, who is ranged alongside those who must suffer the divine judgment, who in fact ranges *himself* alongside them through his speech. It is hardly an exaggeration to say that here the nature of the divine-human relationship takes on a mysterious, if not paradoxical, quality. At the same time, by providing this glimpse of God as a co-sufferer, the text hints again at the deep significance of the prophet's suffering. The dual character of Jeremiah's grief, a grieving with the people by virtue of his humanity and a grieving over them by virtue of his sharing *qua* prophet in the divine pathos, serves to mirror the dual suffering of the transcendent and immanent God. Once again, Jeremiah's life is metaphoric of God's, and interpretive of the divine action.

In the succeeding verses the mystery is first exacerbated and then 'explained'. It is exacerbated in v. 21 when the co-suffering God immediately reasserts the cold fact of imminent judgment:

dabbēr kōh n^e'um-Yhwh
w^{e}nāp^{e}lâ niblat hā'ādām
    k^{e}dōmen 'al-p^{e}nê haśśādeh
ûk^e'āmîr mē'aḥărê haqqōṣēr
    w^e'ên m^e'assēp

Speak, Thus is the word of Yhwh:
And the carcasses of men shall fall
    like dung upon the open field,
and like sheaves after the harvester,
    which no one gathers.

It is 'explained' in vv. 22-23:

kōh 'āmar Yhwh
'al-yithallēl ḥākām b^{e}ḥokmātô
    w^e'al-yithallēl haggibbôr bigbûrātô
        'al-yithallēl 'āšîr b^e'ošrô
kî 'im-b^{e}zō't yithallēl hammithallēl
    haśkēl w^{e}yādōa' 'ōtî
kî 'ănî Yhwh 'ōśeh ḥesed mišpāṭ ûṣ^{e}dāqâ bā'āreṣ
kî-b^e'ēlleh ḥāpaṣtî n^e'um-Yhwh

Thus says the Lord:
Let not the wise man glory in his wisdom,
    neither let the mighty man glory in his might,
        nor the rich man glory in his riches.
But let him who glories glory in this,
    that he understands and knows me.

4. *The Prophetic 'I' & its Ambiguities* 121

For I am Yhwh, working steadfast love, justice, and righteousness in the earth;
for in these I delight—the word of Yhwh.

The burden of the explanation rests on the penultimate *kî* clause, specifically, the formula of self-disclosure (*Selbstvorstellung*), *'ănî Yhwh*, which is closely associated with the giving of covenant and grounding of the Law (see especially Exod 20.2, 5; Lev 18-26; Pss 50.8 and 81.11) and in which virtually all the important content of revelation is implicit (to know the divine name being in some measure to understand the divine nature, will, and action).[131] The formula's use here has an illuminating analogy in ch. 32. God's command that Jeremiah buy the field in Anathoth is followed by the prophet's prayer in which he first confesses in (deuteronomic) credo-style his understanding of the national disaster as a divine judgment but then professes perplexity at the command, since the city has already been 'given into the hands of the Chaldeans' (v. 25). In the confession he twice refers to the divine name; the first reference seems especially to anticipate the self-disclosure formula in Yhwh's response. Jeremiah prays, 'Nothing is too hard for thee, who showest steadfast love (*'ōśeh ḥesed*) to thousands but dost requite the guilt of fathers to their sons after them, O great and mighty God whose name is *Yhwh ṣᵉbā'ôt* ...' (vv. 17-18). Yhwh's first words are then 'Behold, *'ănî Yhwh*, the God of all flesh; is anything too hard for me?' (v. 27). The point is that the salvation symbolized by the command to buy the enemy-occupied field and then explicitly promised in vv. 36-41 is no less ingredient to the covenant God's nature than is the judgment.

Relevant in the analogy is that the formula in 9.23 is expanded by the phrase *'ōśeh ḥesed mišpāṭ ûṣᵉdāqâ bā'āreṣ*, which is uniquely expressive of the covenant relationship and was seen in shortened form in 32.18 (*'ōśeh ḥesed*). Thus, just as the formula explains the enigmatic command in ch. 32 as part of an action the very possibility of which is given in the divine name and which expresses God's fidelity to the covenant, it similarly explains the incongruity of God's determination to destroy being coupled with his suffering under the destruction. Both the determination and the co-suffering are a function of the integrity of the divine nature; it is a matter of God's being true to the divine name by maintaining the covenant relationship, which is to say, by exercising love, justice, and righteousness toward the creation. As the final *kî* clause indicates, such action is the direct expression of the divine will: 'for in these things I delight, says the Lord'.

To what extent do vv. 22-23 have a bearing upon the persona of Jeremiah? As we answer this question, we begin the elucidation promised at the outset of the way the passage adumbrates the portrait of the prophet-as-paradigm. It was stated that this adumbration is achieved in terms of the wisdom/false-speech theme. It is therefore noteworthy that v. 21, part of the incongruity that vv. 22-23 explain, employs the harvest imagery from 8.13-14 (note the root *'sp*), which functioned in the refutation of the people's claim to be wise, and that v. 22 echoes that claim and its refutation by stating as the first of its three negative imperatives the injunction against boasting of one's own wisdom: 'Let not the wise man glory [= boast] in his wisdom'. Such boasting would be an instance of the false speech for which the people have been roundly condemned already, and the human wisdom so gloried in would be of no account whatsoever. If one must boast, v. 23 contends, it should be in the fact that one 'knows and understands' Yhwh. The implication is that true wisdom, like true 'might' and 'riches', resides in this knowing and understanding. To answer our question, it needs to be shown how the text makes Jeremiah the subject of these qualities.

As it happens, the self-disclosure formula is relevant in this connection as well. Among its other functions it expresses Yhwh's self-glorification over against any who would seek to usurp his glory, especially rival gods. This is particularly evident in Deutero-Isaiah (e.g. 42.8; 43.11; 45.5),[132] and in that same prophet the formula has close thematic and grammatical affinities with the self-asseveration form *'ănî/'ānōkî hû'* (43.10, 13; 48.12; and note the addition of the participle in 51.12). Given the immediately following oracle in Jer 9.24-25, an oracle directed against both the nations and Israel, it seems likely that the formula in v. 23 is also pointing toward 10.1-16, the case against 'the way of the nations', which has as its theme idolatry and false-glorying in one's own products, and in vv. 10, 12 of which we see a third-person refraction of the self-asseveration form:

10a *waYhwh 'ĕlōhîm 'emet*
    hû'-'ĕlōhîm ḥayyîm ûmelek 'ôlām
12a *'ōśēh 'ereṣ bekōḥô*
    mēkîn tēbēl beḥokmātô
    ûbitbûnātô nāṭâ šāmāyim

4. The Prophetic 'I' & its Ambiguities 123

10a But *Yhwh* is the true God;
　　he is the living God and the everlasting King...
12a *It is he who* made the earth by his power,
　　who established the world by his wisdom,
　　and by his understanding stretched out the heavens.

By means of the introductory summons to hear in 10.1 and the messenger formula in 10.2, this speech is cast as a divine oracle, the bearer of which is the prophet. Jeremiah, then, is here performing what Yhwh prescribes in 9.23. His participation in Yhwh's glorification involves precisely the sort of knowledge and understanding that Yhwh requires and that manifests genuine wisdom, which is ultimately the acknowledgment of *Yhwh's* wisdom (10.12). Recalling the concluding remarks in Section I, we might add that Jeremiah's participation is reinforced by the confessional prayer he offers in 10.23-25, the prayer in which he directly submits himself to the wisdom of Yhwh and thereby constitutes himself 'as the wise, obedient, and humble servant of both his God and people'. Significantly, he begins his confession with the verb *yāda'tî*, 'I know [= acknowledge] that the way of man is not in himself'.

The prophet's self-submission to Yhwh's wisdom is amply attested at other points within our passage. Accordingly, we have here to take up the question posed earlier as to whether Jeremiah's expression of grief in 8.18 serves to characterize him as wise. Again, this verse has to be seen in context with the refutation of the people's claim to wisdom, a refutation that was based on their disobedience, which in turn expressed itself most vividly in their false and inappropriate speech. The fittingness of the prophet's grief, as a response to both the announcement of Yhwh's judgment in 8.17 and the ill-suited 'cry' of the people (their questions in v. 19 being self-serving), places him in stark contrast to them. By virtue of the contrast, he enacts the wisdom that they only pretend to have.

It bears emphasis that the grief represents wisdom in so far as it reflects a knowing and understanding of Yhwh, and that analytic in this concept of knowledge is the concept 'obedience'. Part of what it means to know Yhwh is thus to discern his activity in history, to perceive in some measure his plan, and to order oneself appropriately to it. It is evident that both Jeremiah's grief in 8.18 and his glorification of Yhwh as prescribed in 9.23 fit this description. At this point the connection we saw between the latter verse and ch. 32 becomes relevant again. Relating Yhwh's name to his sovereignty in

32.17-18, Jeremiah knows even amidst his perplexity that the enigmatic command, as also his obedient performance of it, must have its point, since 'nothing is too hard for thee'. Further, the prayer in that chapter is the text's fullest and most explicit statement of the prophetic persona's discernment of the divine plan. Chapter 32 thus helps confirm and fill out our passage's depiction of Jeremiah as a model of wisdom. (It thereby helps illustrate the fundamental continuity of the book's identity description of the prophet across its various strata and despite the differences in style and orientation that exist between those strata.[133])

But that is not the only point at which later portions of the book connect with and illuminate our passage. Accordingly, we may recall the earlier comment that the two unanswered questions in 9.11 'are driving toward a point that will eventually have to be made clear'. Combining wisdom and prophetic motifs, the questions ask for the sage who can understand the ruination of the land, for someone who has been made privy to Yhwh's counsel (and 'council') so as to be able to declare the fact and meaning of the divine judgment.

Now, in 23.9f. there is an extended polemic against the false prophets. Incorporating a series of prophetic oracles, the argument has two basic points: 1. The prophets are false because disobedient, their own ungodliness promoting disobedience among the people as a whole (vv. 10-17). 2. They are false (and disobedient) because they speak without having 'stood in the council of the Lord to perceive and to hear his word' (v. 18; see also 21-22). Condemning the false prophets, the passage clearly wants to legitimate Jeremiah, who is not merely the bearer of the oracles but in v. 9 a first-person witness to their divine origin and veracity. By clear implication and as attested throughout the book, Jeremiah is the true prophet standing in Yhwh's council, receiving the word of his mouth, then declaring it, all in obedience.

Given 23.9f. and the centrality of the book's claim for Jeremiah as the true prophet, it seems unavoidable to read the first two interrogatives of 9.11 as leading questions which have 'Jeremiah' as their answer. Surely, this conclusion is consistent with the movement of 8.4–9.25, indeed 8.4–10.25, as a whole. Jeremiah, the true prophet, is everywhere recommended, either implicitly or explicitly, as a paradigm of wisdom by virtue of his obedient knowing and understanding of Yhwh.

Summary

The three sections of this chapter have attempted an analysis responsive to the specific literary configurations of the selected texts and to the self-constituting quality of the first-person language. Our close readings have shown that neither the theory of the blending of voices, which everywhere sees Jeremiah's 'I' as a direct reflection of the community's 'we', nor the theory which at every point seeks a clean separation of voices, is adequate. We have seen that at one moment Jeremiah may speak in a voice that is purely his own (10.19b), while at the next speak as or with the voice of the people (10.20, 23-25; 14.7-9, 19-22; 8.14-15), and in the next speak in a voice indistinguishable from Yhwh's (14.17-18; 9.1-5). We have also maintained that, whenever he speaks, he speaks *qua* prophet. It is therefore inappropriate to refer his speech to his 'private' experience, or to explain it in terms of innate temperament or spiritual genius. Jeremiah's personal and prophetic identity are one.

Further, we have argued that when he speaks as an intercessor and employs the stereotypic terminology of the cult, his language is no less self-constituting than when he speaks in other capacities. The normative logic of the concept 'intercession' and of prayer itself entails his self-involvement. This self-involvement is then substantiated by specific statements such as 14.13 and 15.1 and by passages in the Confessions which employ the same terms and motifs as in the communal laments.

Finally, our results are consistent with those of the previous chapter concerning Jer 4 and the depiction of the prophetic persona: Through his first-person speech Jeremiah enacts a prophetic identity of identification with both God and people. We found, however, that the identification cannot be total on either side, and with this point we began to see more nuanced lines in the characterization. Representing each party to the other, Jeremiah is subject to an extraordinary tension. He not only entertains the grief and anger proper to each toward the other but comes personally to embody the divine-human event such that his life becomes a vehicle for the event's interpretation. Jeremiah's life becomes his message. Thus, we observed that the text assigns the figure a paradigmatic status. The facts that all three of our passages meet in this depiction (8.4f. and 10.17ff. literally so) and that other portions of the book could directly illuminate the way our passages execute this depiction (chs. 23 and

32) attest something of its scope and import in the total scheme of the book. The Confessions will be seen to provide further evidence along these lines.

Chapter 5

THE CONFESSIONS:
THE PROPHET AS EXEMPLAR AND METAPHOR

The Confessions of Jeremiah stand out from the other first-person speeches in the book by their length, their sustained emotional intensity, and their quality as direct address to God.[1] For these and related reasons they have long been the object of intense scholarly interest. In the present century they have been a primary point at which on-going biographical interests in the historical figures of the Old Testament converged with the form-critical method. Hence, in Baumgartner's seminal monograph the Confessions were identified as belonging to the individual lament *Gattung* so numerous in the Psalms, yet as having been adapted by the prophet to reflect his unique experience, his innermost person, indeed his private, non-professional self.[2]

Baumgartner, however, did not adequately address the theological relevance of this data, e.g. how the Confessions fit into the book as a whole. Von Rad therefore, while agreeing both that the Confessions are adaptations of the individual lament and that they relate to the actual experience of the historical Jeremiah, sought to break down the professional-private distinction by showing that the material presents Jeremiah's person entirely within the context of his prophetic vocation. Thus, as a witness to the way the whole life of a prophet could be taken up into the service of God's word, the Confessions for von Rad function theologically as part of the prophet's proclamation.[3]

Already, and especially in von Rad, one can see that our effort to demonstrate Jeremiah's paradigmatic status in the other first-person materials has been foreshadowed by the scholarship on the Confessions. At the same time it is clear that such work was largely motivated by the belief that the Confessions offer direct insights into the historical Jeremiah, whence they derive much of their value. In this respect

Gerstenberger's study of Jer 15.10-21 marked a significant turning point.[4]

As we have seen, Gerstenberger not only crystallized for us the notion of 'paradigm'; he also recognized at least implicitly the distinction between the 'Jeremiah of history' and the textual 'persona'. That is, Gerstenberger understood the first-person speaker as a literary-theological construct and hence identified the meaning of the text elsewhere than in any supposed reference to the experiences of the historical figure. Nevertheless, his orientation remained diachronic in that he was still mainly concerned with reconstructing the process of composition and as a consequence tended to identify the text's meaningfulness with the original occasion and purpose of the redaction.

In each of these respects more recent scholarship has followed Gerstenberger's lead.[5] Building on Baumgartner's observations of the close parallels between the Confessions and the complaint psalms, A.H.J. Gunneweg (1970) and Peter Welten (1977) have proposed that the Confessions represent a deliberate redactional effort to render Jeremiah in terms of the exemplary 'I' of the individual lament *Gattung*, the purpose being to console and encourage members of the exilic communities who had heeded, supported, and were now invited to identify with the prophet from Anathoth.[6] The following precis of Gunneweg's position applies equally well to Welten's:

> A.H.J. Gunneweg has more recently developed a rather similar thesis [to Gerstenberger's] that all the 'confessions', far from offering any biographical information about Jeremiah or insight into the prophet's psychology, are interpretations of Jeremiah's preaching and person. They portray Jeremiah as the righteous sufferer who is an exemplar for the community of the period in which they were incorporated into the Jeremiah material. They do not seriously distort our picture of the historical Jeremiah, who is represented broadly as such a figure in the authentic Jeremiah traditions, but their occasion is to be sought outside the life and ministry of Jeremiah himself.[7]

There is much to commend in Gunneweg's and Welten's theses. The notion of Jeremiah as the exemplary 'I', the righteous sufferer of the psalms, is immediately applicable to the interpretive model 'prophet-as-paradigm' which we have explored in other materials. The connections which they identified between the Confessions and their literary contexts belong to an important area of investigation

5. *The Confessions*

still largely unexplored even after Gerstenberger's study. Gunneweg and Welten have thereby taken us an important step toward a holistic reading and an appreciation of the synchronic dimensions of the text. However, their analysis was quite general, and it remains for a close reading to substantiate the thesis in detail and explore its fuller implications.

Several qualifications are first in order. Clearly, Gunneweg was opposed to psychologizing interpretations that either seek to gain access to the text through the psyche of the prophet or, conversely, seek to gain access to the prophet's psyche through the text.[8] We share this opposition. However, for Gunneweg the issue ultimately comes down to an opposition between 'piety' (ostensibly, the main concern of psychologizing interpretation) and 'kerygma'. He writes, 'The prophecy as well as its subsequent interpretation contains less piety to be explicated psychologically but for that all the more kerygma to be explicated theologically'.[9] Here we register our first qualification. For analytic in the concept 'exemplar', one would think, is the concept 'imitation', and it is precisely the prophetic persona's piety, i.e. his obediential faith, that configuration of beliefs, trust, praise, and anguish expressed in the Confessions, which is to be imitated by the reader—and explicated by the exegete. In other words, since Jeremiah's person is inextricably bound up with his proclamation, the piety is really part of the kerygma, not something extrinsic to it.

Consequently, a psychological interpretation *is* still appropriate. However, it must be of an entirely different sort from the kind Gunneweg rejects. Its concern cannot be with reconstructing the Jeremiah of history in order to identify there a watershed in the history of human consciousness and religious spirituality.[10] Rather, it is to limn the features of the persona rendered by the text as a model of obediential suffering. This in our opinion is the locus of the theological value and interest of the text, when understood as scripture. From this perspective the 'psychological' dilemma reflected in the Confessions, most acutely in 20.7-18, poses serious problems of theological interpretation and will have to be addressed.

A second qualification has to do with the continuing diachronic orientation (and prejudices) of Gunneweg's and Welten's theses. It is not the purpose here to take sides in the debate over the occasion of the Confessions; whether they are the work of redactors or the prophet himself remains an issue highly intractable to literary analysis. Rather, and as indicated earlier, the point is to question the relevance of the debate itself. However the text achieved its present shape, it is that shape that confronts the reader and is the primary determinant of meaning (as well as the primary witness to what the writers may have intended). More specifically, I would object to the assumption that in giving the text its final shaping the redactors were addressing only an immediate religio-political situation. Relatedly, I object to the somewhat tendentious limitation of the Confessions' theological significance that results from evaluating their meaning primarily in terms of their occasion.

The problem is particularly acute with Welten. He wants to identify as precisely as possible the way suffering is treated in each stratum of the book, which of course is a fully legitimate enterprise. Within the prose speeches (Source C), for example, ch. 16 is described as showing how Yhwh imposes upon the prophet restrictions that isolate him from the community, the point being to symbolize in Jeremiah the suffering that the coming judgment will bring upon the nation as a whole. However, this material says nothing of Jeremiah's oppression by the authorities; that is the subject of the biographical (B) narratives. The Confessions take a still different tack. They register 'Jeremiah's' personal response to his plight and render him as the innocent sufferer at the hands of enemies, i.e. the authorities who are reported to oppress him in the B material.[11]

While Welten acknowledges a certain continuity in the development of the theme, it is the discontinuities that receive the greater emphasis. These are exaggerated, I believe, and here is where the difficulty begins. The motif of the prophet's isolation, for instance, is not unique to the C material as Welten claims, but can already be detected in the 'authentic' words, as observed in the previous chapter with respect to 9.1.[12] Neither is the element of innocence absent from the picture of suffering in the B narratives, only to be later introduced by the Confessions.[13] In 37.18 Jeremiah begins his plea to Zedekiah by asking, 'What wrong have I done to you or your servants or this people that you have put me in prison?' (See also 26.15-19 and 38.9, 15.)

The difficulty turns into a muddle when Welten shifts back and forth from speaking of the different strata's application of 'additions' and 'further aspects' to the situation of suffering, to saying that the strata actually offer distinct 'theologies' of suffering.[14] The implied equivalence (between 'additions' and 'theologies') is misleading because the two ways of speaking are of quite different logical orders. Moreover, the latter term is singularly unsuitable.[15] For it is only after the 'further aspects' are reified, etiologically linked with specific (but hypothetical) historical occasions, and speculatively blown up into programmatic statements which the various tradents are conjectured to be addressing to their particular audiences, that they can be mistaken for 'theologies'. In actual fact, the substantive differences between the book's several witnesses to Jeremiah's suffering are considerably less than the differences within Welten's own terminology. And finally, although Welten makes an effort to picture how the strata function in the book as a whole, the picture cannot help but be distorted by his attempt to retain intact the several separate suffering theologies and keep them bound to the purposes for which they were constructed.

Qualifications made, let us turn now to a close reading of the text. Limitations of space require that the analysis be confined to but two of the Confessions, and in unequal measure. Jer 17.(12-13)14-18 will be the primary focus. More frequently passed over than the other Confessions, yet set into a unique context (e.g. the wisdom fragments of vv. 5-11), this was also the passage least adequately explicated by Gunneweg and Welten. The procedure here will be to attend first to the passage itself, observing its typicality as a psalm-like individual lament as well as the particularity it has by virtue of its adaptation to the book of Jeremiah and application to the prophetic persona. Then we shall explore the effects of the Confession's incorporation into its literary context. The same procedure will be followed for the second passage, Jer 20.7-18, though in briefer compass. An object of perennial critical interest, this Confession more than any other taxes our interpretive model. At the same time it promises much in the way of rewards, particularly in terms of the connections it suggests with the book's biographical narratives. As always, with both passages our purpose is to give due consideration to the synchronic dimension of the text as we chart the status and function of its first-person speaker.

I. *Jeremiah 17.(12-13)14-18*

In both vocabulary and structure the Confession bears the unmistakable stamp of the lamentation of the individual. Formally, only the vow and thanksgiving are lacking; otherwise it can be neatly analyzed into a request for alleviation from an affliction (v. 14), the lament proper with a citation of the words of the godless (v. 15), an affirmation of innocence (v. 16), renewed request and an expression of confidence (v. 17), and again requests, now combined with a curse against the godless (v. 18).[16] Broadly outlined so, this prayer is a type abundantly attested in the Psalms. Its speaker, too, is a type, one whose 'I' is interchangeable with that of any faithful Israelite who finds himself the innocent victim of violence and suffering and in trust implores Yhwh to right the wrong by restoring the oppressed and vanquishing the oppressor. As this typical prayer is taken up in the book of Jeremiah, it gains a particular context and the prophet becomes an instantiation of the general type.

More difficult to fit into the standard pattern of the individual lament are the opening two verses, 12-13:

12-13 *kissē' kābôd mārôm mēri'śôn*
m^eqôm miqdāšēnû miqwēh yiśrā'ēl Yhwh
kol-'ōz^ebêkā yēbōšû
y^esûray bā'āreṣ yikkātēbû
kî 'āz^ebû m^eqôr mayim-ḥayyîm 'et-Yhwh

12-13 O glorious throne, primordial height!
Place of our sanctuary, O Yhwh, thou hope of Israel!
All who forsake you shall be put to shame!
Those who turn away from me shall be written in the earth!
Truly, they have forsaken Yhwh, fountain of living water!

To take vv. 12-13a as a series of vocatives is already to treat them as an invocation, thus as an integral part of the prayer, as Baumgartner and Berridge have done.[17] Otherwise they remain only a 'separate fragment' of unspecified function.[18] Acknowledging the rarity of such a hymnic introduction among the complaint psalms, Baumgartner nevertheless finds parallels in Ps 80.2-3, several late narrative texts (e.g. Neh 1.5ff.; 9.6ff.; and Dan 9.4f.), and numerous Babylonian-Assyrian lamentations.[19]

However, the parallels are not exact. The narrative texts, for example, all employ portions of the formula for the revelation of the divine name found in Exod 34.6ff. While perhaps originally used in covenant-renewal ceremony, the formula lends itself particularly well to the penitential function these texts perform.[20] The Jeremiah passage is not penitential. As for Ps 80, a communal lament, the hymnic elements of vv. 2-3 are already a part of the request: 'O shepherd of Israel, give ear! O thou who leadest Israel like a flock, who sittest above the cherubim, shine forth...! Stir up thy might

5. The Confessions

and come to save us!' Admittedly, the distinction fades if *yēbōšû* in 13b of our passage is taken as a jussive and the statement is translated '*Let* all who forsake you be put to shame!'

A closer analogy might be Ps 48.2-3: 'Great (is) Yahweh and greatly praised in the city of our God, his holy mountain, beautiful in elevation, joy of all the earth, Mount Zion in the far north, city of the Great King!' The string of epithets and adjectives plus the fact that Yhwh and his city are extolled indistinguishably offer a striking similarity with our text. However, such features are especially suited to the genre of Ps 48, a Zion psalm, which may explain why Baumgartner did not cite it.

All things considered, the inclusion of vv. 12-13a might be taken as evidence of the freedom with which the individual lament *Gattung* has been adapted to the prophetic text and setting. In any case, we regard them as part of the Confession, specifically as a hymnic invocation that serves to particularize both the prayer and its speaker with respect to the standard form of the lament and its purely anonymous 'I'. The terms 'glorious throne' and 'hope of Israel' are found in the prophet's intercessory prayers (14.8, 21) and help to identify the voice here as Jeremiah's.[21] With the first-person plural 'our sanctuary' Jeremiah renders praise to God while affirming his identification with his people, which is as much a matter of his prophetic vocation as it is of his citizenship. One should not think, however, that by praising Yhwh under the image of the divine throne and mountain sanctuary Jeremiah necessarily contradicts his own condemnation of the inflated temple-ideology of his compatriots (ch. 7).[22] The normative logic of the epithets here is to ground the ensuing requests in praise to the God who has established relationship with his covenant-people, which at the same time means to acknowledge the sovereignty of God's will over one's own and his authority to dispose of one's requests according to his good pleasure and purpose. In no way need the words suggest an idolatrous faith in the cult and temple *per se* at the expense of either God's transcendence or his radical demand for obedience. To construe them so would be an exercise in the hermeneutics of suspicion. More reasonably, the praise ought to be seen as an expression of trust in God himself, a point not incidental to our later remarks on the Confession's context, 17.7 in particular.

While hardly incompatible with the hymnic quality of the opening epithets, v. 13b can also be construed as an expression of confidence characteristic of individual laments.[23] Interestingly, the verb *bwš* is equally frequent in the Psalms (thirty-three times, mostly in laments) and Jeremiah (thirty-five times). A close analogy to its use here in the indicative is Ps 6.11: 'All my enemies shall be ashamed (*yēbōšû*) and sorely troubled; they shall turn back and be put to shame (*yēbōšû*) in a moment'. The major difference is that in this lament the enemies are primarily the psalmist's and Yhwh's only by implication, whereas in the Jeremiah passage it is just the reverse.[24] This difference is reflected in the use of *'zb* elsewhere in the two books. Of twenty-two instances in the Psalms only three times is Yhwh (more exactly, Yhwh's law) the object of the verb (Pss 89.31; 119.53, 87); otherwise the psalmist-complainant is the object. But in Jeremiah (twenty-five instances) Yhwh is almost always the object, as here. That Yhwh's enemies, those who forsake him, are indeed *also* Jeremiah's is confirmed by v. 18 of the Confession where the prophet asks that *his* persecutors (*rōd^{e}pay*) be put to shame (*yēbōšû*); that is to say, Yhwh's forsakers and Jeremiah's persecutors are the same.

In v. 13c the enemies who were referred to in the previous colon with the second-person suffix (*'ōz^{e}bêkā*, 'those who forsake *you*') are now spoken of with the first-person suffix (*y^{e}sûray*, 'those who turn from *me*'). Suddenly, it is Yhwh speaking, pronouncing a threat. As he does, the difference between the Confession and its psalmic analogue becomes accentuated, the verse now assuming the character of distinctly prophetic proclamation. Not coincidentally, the last colon grounds the threat in the identical words of Jer 2.13 (except that now Yhwh is referred to in the third-person rather than the first).

The resulting shape of vv. 12-13 is striking. As an invocation coupled with a threat and reason, the passage is a blend of psalmic and prophetic, indeed Jeremianic, elements. The role of the speaker is equally striking. The one who praises Yhwh in the language of the people and as one of the people, and in praising manifests the trust and confidence normative for the people's praying, is also the particular individual chosen to convey to the people Yhwh's word of judgment against them at a specific moment in their history. From the outset, typicality and particularity are ingredient in the Confession and characterize its speaker.

The request of v. 14 is no exception.

r^{e}pā'ēnî Yhwh w^e'ērāpē'
hôšî'ēnî w^e'iwwāšē'â
kî t^{e}hillātî 'āttâ

5. *The Confessions* 135

> Heal me, O Yhwh, and I shall be healed;
> save me, and I shall be saved;
> for thou art my praise!

As Baumgartner has shown, the verbs *rp'*, 'heal', and *yšc*, 'save', are frequent in the individual laments of the psalter, especially the latter.[25] Along with their nominal forms they are also significant terms in Jeremiah where again they function to connect the prophet with his people. 'Healing' (*marpē'*) is requested for the people in 8.15 and 14.19, both of which are probably to be seen as intercessory prayers offered by Jeremiah, the latter definitely so.[26] In 15.18 Jeremiah complains of his own need for healing, and the lack of any, a situation that pertains to the people as well (8.22; cf. 30.13).[27] Similarly, *yšc* is a staple element in the people's requests (2.27; cf. 11.12) and complaints (8.20; 14.8-9), and occurs in an admonishment directed to them by the prophet (4.14). Moreover, Yhwh's promise of 'salvation' is granted both to the prophet personally in 15.20 and to the people in 23.6 (= 33.16); 30.7, 10-11; 31.7; 42.11; and 46.27. The upshot is that, in Berridge's words, 'verse 14 might then be said to have had a paradigmatic significance for the people to whom this word was spoken, indicating the words which every member of Yahweh's people should be speaking...'[28]

In other words, while manifesting the clear parallels with the individual laments of the Psalms, our verse bears the particularity of the Jeremianic context. It also reflects a distinctively Jeremianic style. Again, Berridge:

> Especially noteworthy is Ps. 6, a lamentation of the individual, with its *rᵉpā'ēnî* (v. 3) and *hôšî'ēnî* (v. 5). But already the formulation of Jer. 17:14 discloses an individual application of this terminology. We have here two examples of a stylistic device employed by Jeremiah on numerous occasions, namely, two conjugations by the same verb used together. By this means, Jeremiah is not only able to lay stress upon the fact that healing and salvation come from Yahweh alone, but he may also voice his assurance that when Yahweh acts, he will be healed and saved.[29]

Mentioned here are two important thematic elements in the request, the prophet's dependence upon God and his assurance of God's ability to heal and save. These are implicitly conjoined and summarily emphasized in the concluding colon of the verse: 'for/surely thou art my praise'. Of the twenty-nine occurrences of *tᵉhillâ* in the psalter, slightly more than one-third are in individual laments or the lamentation portions of mixed types. Most often the term occurs in the psalmist's vow or other directly motivational statements: e.g. 'Be gracious to me... that I may recount all thy praises' (Ps 9.15; cf. Pss 35.28; 51.17; 71.8, 14). Closer to its use in our passage, however, are the verbless constructions of Pss 22.26 and 71.6: 'From thee (is) my praise in the great congregation' and 'My praise (is) always in thee', respectively.

There may well be more significance to such assertions than meets the eye. Certainly, the form-critical rubric 'motivation' is hardly adequate for describing their logic, since more is at work here than a calculated effort to win God's approval, assuming of course that the sensibility of the individual who prays can match the potential depth and maturity of the prayer itself.[30] To be specific, these statements entail emotion, gratitude in particular, and not simply by way of anticipation of God's favorable response but as a present and enduring disposition toward the God who has called one into relationship with himself.[31] To claim that God *is* one's praise, and mean it, is to have God always in view as both creator and redeemer, the giver and restorer of life, and thus to view life itself as a gift, even in the context of suffering. Obviously more than a neutral statement of fact, the claim has the performative quality of *ascribing* praise *to* God, and to ascribe praise *is* to praise.

In its present position in the Confession, this performative utterance has a two-fold effect. On the one hand, while augmenting the confidence registered by the indicatives of 14a and b, it explicitly grounds the imperative requests, i.e. roots them in the grateful acknowledgment of Yhwh as the source of life and healing. Thereby it qualifies the requests as a form of praise as well. And this is to say that 14c mirrors the function of the hymnic elements of vv. 12-13a, which ground the entire prayer in praise, but now with respect to a specific moment within the prayer. The result is to enhance the prayer's formal and thematic coherence.

On the other hand, in that many performative utterances are a self-involving, self-constituting form of behavior, and given the use of the word *t^ehillâ* elsewhere in the book, the ascription of praise in 14c qualifies its speaker in a special way. In this regard Berridge's observation that v. 14 has a paradigmatic significance for the people must also extend to the prophet. As one whose praise is Yhwh and who in affirming so actually renders praise to Yhwh, Jeremiah becomes in part what Israel as a whole was intended but failed to become: In Jer 13.11 Yhwh says, 'I made the whole house of Israel and the whole house of Judah cling to me so that they might be for me a people, a name, a praise (*t^ehillâ*), and a glory, but they would not listen'. As a paradigm who stands over against and in contrast to the people, Jeremiah also foreshadows, paradigmatically, the fulfilment of the divine purpose for the nation, a fulfilment promised in Jer 33.9: 'And this city shall be to me a name of joy, a praise (*t^ehillâ*), and a glory before all the nations'.[32]

Thus, in *t^ehillâ* we see once again the interplay between the typical and the particular, an interplay ingredient in the very concept 'paradigm'. The prophet and his prayer gain typicality by means of a common feature in the Psalms. At the same time the significance of the term is here conditioned by its specific uses within the book of Jeremiah. Hence, the ascription of praise in the Confession gains its particularity through its prophetic, Jeremianic context.

The reason for the request for healing and salvation would seem to be specified in the complaint of v. 15. This verse and the following 'affirmation of innocence' have been the focus of considerable debate.

15 *hinnēh-hēmmâ 'ōm^erîm 'ēlāy*
    'ayyēh d^ebar-Yhwh yābô' nā'
16 *wa'ănî lō'-'aṣtî mērō'eh 'aḥārêkā*
    w^eyôm 'ānûš lō' hit'awwêtî
    'attâ yāda'tā môṣā' s^epātay
    nōkaḥ pānêkā hāyâ

15 Behold, they say to me,
    'Where is the word of Yhwh? Let it come!'
16 But as for me, I have not shirked being a shepherd after thee;
    neither have I desired the day from which there is no recovery.[33]
    Thou knowest, the issue of my lips
    was manifest before thee.

From Baumgartner into the past decade the issue has been whether there are here uniquely prophetic features, elements without analogy in the complaint psalms, the foremost candidate being the reference to the 'word of Yhwh'. For Baumgartner, this 'word' is unambiguously and singularly prophetic.[34] In the Gunneweg–Welten thesis, however, whereby Jeremianic redactors have adapted a psalmic *Vorlage* and inserted it into the present text, the *d^ebar Yhwh* originally referred not to a prophetic judgment oracle but to a priestly assurance of salvation which, having been earlier granted to the psalmist, nevertheless failed to materialize and so exposed him to mockery. Welten points out that Ps 107.17-22, though late, refers to the 'word of Yhwh' in connection with healing (v. 20) and may reflect an ancient thanksgiving ceremony which could have been the *Sitz-im-Leben* for our passage in its original form. Numerous other psalms also speak of God's word, though perhaps only Ps 130.5 is a very apt parallel. Neither Gunneweg nor Welten, however, can cite close psalmic parallels for v. 16a or actually bother reconstructing the supposed *Vorlage* of non-prophetic content.[35]

Regardless of the material's origin, the point of interest is the extent to which it prompts and sustains analogies between the persona of the Confession and the righteous sufferer of the complaint psalms. From this synchronic perspective, one can argue in favor of Gunneweg and Welten's position that the analogy which they perceive does not in fact depend upon their redactional hypothesis. For the hypothesis does not generate the analogy; rather, it is the analogy (resident in the ambiguous status of the 'word') that generates the hypothesis. For them the notion of the psalmic *Vorlage* only serves to confirm the analogy prompted by the text itself. Thus viewed, their position is generally compatible with that of Baumgartner who, while indeed overlooking the ambiguity in the d^ebar-$Yhwh$, still sees in the prophet's situation vis-à-vis his enemies a clear parallel with the 'I' in the cultic laments. Now, a completely different view of the matter is held by Berridge. He presents a thorough and often compelling analysis that requires detailed consideration.

His argument turns on the nature of the charge and the status of the enemies in v. 15. Baumgartner had argued that the citation 'Where is the word of Yhwh? Let it come!' represents a personal attack upon Jeremiah with the insinuation that he actually desired the doom he predicts:

> As if he himself should take satisfaction in the word's fulfilment! They have no idea how deeply such prophecies of judgment afflict him. That the word will come to pass, of that he has no doubt. Thus he does not shrink at that reproach. What pains him is the complete misunderstanding of his nature. How can they slander him as the evil foe of Israel—him, the people's best friend, their tireless intercessor![36]

Thus, for Baumgartner the Confession as a whole revolves around a personal conflict between Jeremiah and his enemies and focuses attention on the distress their attack brings upon him, just as in many of the complaint psalms.

5. The Confessions 139

Berridge agrees that the $d^e bar$-$Yhwh$ refers to Jeremiah's earlier proclamation of judgment and not to an outstanding salvation oracle. For substantiation he directs attention to the use of the verb bw' ($yābô' nā'$, 'Let it come'), which occurs three more times in the OT in conjunction with the prophetic 'word of Yhwh': Ezek 33.31-33, the programmatic statement of Deut 18.22, and the latter's companion piece, Jer 28.9.[37] However, the fact that all three of these texts, the latter two especially, pertain to the issue of true and false prophecy indicates that the charge lodged by the enemies in our passage bears much less on Jeremiah's personal motivations than on the larger question of his legitimacy as a prophet: 'If Jeremiah is a true prophet, then the word which he has been proclaiming must materialize'.[38] But even more, it is Yhwh himself who is called into question. And to Berridge's point, we might note the similarity in tone and content to the people's words quoted elsewhere in Jeremiah: e.g. 'They have spoken falsely of Yhwh and have said, "He will do nothing; no evil will come upon us, nor shall we see sword or famine. The prophets will become wind; the word is not in them"' (5.12-13); and 'Men have said, "He will not see our latter end"' (12.4).

Therefore, the enemies' words in v. 15 represent an arrogant challenge both to Yhwh's power and authority and to Jeremiah's legitimacy. They thus reflect 'the critically skeptical attitude which had been adopted by the people as a result of Jeremiah's repeated and unfulfilled predictions of catastrophe'.[39] As for the enemies themselves, they should not be identified with a restricted circle of the speaker's personal opponents (as would be the case in the individual lament psalms), but rather 'are to be recognized as the people of Judah *in toto*'. Hence, instead of the Confession's centering on a personal conflict between prophet and enemies, and on Jeremiah's sense of injury, its true subject is 'Judah's attitude concerning the non-actualization of Yahweh's earlier word of judgment' and, in light of that attitude, the necessity for the judgment's fulfilment to vindicate both Yhwh and his prophet.[41]

It is evident that for Berridge the purpose (and effect) of the Confession is not to depict Jeremiah in analogy with the righteous sufferer of the complaint psalms but to advance his proclamation of Judah's guilt and inevitable punishment. The obvious question is whether these purposes and effects are really mutually exclusive.

Certainly, Berridge's thesis gains credibility from his analysis of the terms $yôm$ '$ānûš$ (v. 16) and $yôm$ $rā'â$ (vv. 17-18). He recognizes that this or similar terminology (*yôm ṣārâ/ṣār, yôm 'ēd, 'ēt ṣārâ, 'ēt rā'â*) is frequent in the complaint psalms where indeed it always refers to a situation of personal and individual distress in the life of the psalmist.[42] In Jeremiah, however, as in the prophetic literature generally, such terminology corresponds to the eschatological concept of the 'Day of Yhwh' and refers to the time of God's final judgment upon Judah/Israel.[43] So it is in the Confession: Like the *d^ebar-Yhwh* of v. 15, *yôm 'ānûš* and *yôm rā'â* speak of the imminent national catastrophe.[44] Still, it remains my inclination to think that the very prevalence of such language in the complaint psalms gives Jeremiah a certain typicality, while the semantic shift effected by the language's use in the prophetic context marks the prophet's particularity.

In any case the detailed strokes of Berridge's interpretation follow cogently from his linguistic analysis. Verses 15-16 do not represent so much a personal accusation and defense as simply a *contrast* between a cynical Judah and the faithful prophet. The quality of contrast is rhetorically enhanced by the pronouns which introduce each verse (*hinnēh-hēmmâ, wa'ānî*). Following the MT for 16aα, Berridge then suggests that Jeremiah's radical application of the word 'shepherd' to himself is designed to emphasize his faithfulness to his divine commission over against the failure of Judah's official leadership to be the shepherds (*'aḥărêkā*, 'after you', i.e. in the manner of Yhwh) that they were appointed to be.[45]

Two alternative readings are then proposed for 16aβ. By the first, Jeremiah contends that he has demonstrated his faithfulness by proclaiming Yhwh's judgment, i.e. the *yôm 'ānûš*, even though he himself has not desired it (*hit'awwêtî*). By the second, Jeremiah is seen as playing on Amos 5.18 ('Woe to those who desire [*hammit'awwîm*]) the day of Yhwh'—to indicate that he does not share the distorted view of Yhwh's 'day' (as one of 'light' for Israel rather than 'darkness') that was held by Amos's audience,[46] as also by his own to the extent that they refused to believe that Yhwh could or would wage holy war *against* them.

Once again, Berridge's point with vv. 15-16 is the contrast between the prophet and his compatriots. Obediently proclaiming God's word, Jeremiah knows and accepts what it means; they do not. I want to acknowledge the viability of Berridge's suggestions for 16aα and point out that, whichever reading one prefers for 16aβ, *via* the contrast Jeremiah is again being rendered as a paradigm of obediential faith.

5. The Confessions 141

Appeals to God's knowledge such as we have in v. 16b are frequent in the Confessions (12.3; 15.15; 18.23) as well as in the Psalms, but they function variously in both places. Here, Berridge proposes, *'attâ yādā'tā* refers to God's knowledge not of the speaker's inner thoughts and motives (as in 12.3 and Ps. 139.1-6), but of his open and public behavior (as in 15.15 and Ps 40.10), namely, his public proclamation (*môṣā' sᵉpātay*) of divine judgment. While *môṣā' sᵉpātay* is hardly a distinctively prophetic formula, given the context it is clear to Berridge that it refers to the prophetic word.[47] This is a sound conclusion. It should be asked, however, whether this analysis necessarily precludes an expanded interpretation that admits Jeremiah's inwardness into the picture.

For the present we may note that if v. 16 *were* an expression of injured innocence (*contra* Berridge), the tone of urgent need and anger in vv. 17-18 would be well motivated:[48]

17 *'al-tihyēh-lî limḥittâ*
   maḥăsî-'attâ bᵉyôm rā'â
18 *yēbōšû rōdᵉpay wᵉ'al-'ēbōšâ 'ānî*
   yēḥattû hēmmâ wᵉ'al-'ēḥattâ 'ānî
   hābî' 'ălêhem yôm rā'â
   ûmišneh šibbārôn šābrēm

17 Be not a terror to me;
   thou art my refuge in the day of evil.
18 Let my persecutors be put to shame, but let not me be put to shame;
   let them be dismayed, but let not me be dismayed.
   Bring upon them the day of evil,
   and with double destruction destroy them!

To interpret accordingly, v. 17 recapitulates the basic movement of v. 14 from request to ascription, but here the speaker assumes a more defensive posture. The negative imperative, 'Be not a terror', suggests a mild reproach: since it was God who commissioned the prophet to speak the word for which he is now scorned, it is almost as if God himself were assaulting him (cf. 15.15, 18; 20.7-8). Yet in faith he knows that God must be his refuge, and that only God can be a refuge, in this situation of distress. So in v. 18 he vents his spleen on the true enemies and does at last what he has just protested he has not done, namely, wish upon them the full fury of divine judgment. As Baumgartner observes, the same paradoxical shift is found in the Psalms: 'First the psalmist swears to have done only good to the enemies (35.12-14; 109.5): then he deluges them with the most gruesome curses (35.22-26; 109.6-20).'⁴⁹

Again, for Berridge the traditional analysis is mistaken since in his opinion, as we have seen, vv. 15-16 do not represent a conflict over the prophet's motivations nor does *yôm rā'â* refer to Jeremiah's present, personal distress. While the terms 'refuge' (*maḥseh*), 'shame' (*bwš*), and 'dismay' (*ḥtt*) do figure in the complaint psalms, Berridge points out that the parallel use of the latter two and the employment of all three in relation to Yhwh's *yôm rā'â* mark a clear break from the psalmic analogy. Accordingly, vv. 17-18 are for him less an expression of the prophet's desire for vengeance upon personal enemies than a reflection of the need for vindication through the fulfilment of Yhwh's word. At the same time the passage reflects Jeremiah's own fear of the impending general doom because he knows that this doom must fall upon himself as well as his people. Even so, having been faithful, he hopes that he would 'at least not receive the same full measure of punishment as those who have been fully apostate'. Hence the petition for the 'double destruction'.⁵⁰ But is the tone of v. 18 really as modest as this description would suggest? Does it not in fact reflect a situation of bitter conflict?

Berridge's interpretation begins to unravel here, and with it his attempt to diminish the analogy with the complaint psalms. For simply on the face of it the tone of v. 18 is nothing short of vitriolic. More importantly (and less subjectively), the mention of 'my persecutors' in the context of a curse implies conflict by definition. It is, moreover, hard not to see some significance in the fact that 18a so closely mirrors 1.17b—'Do not be dismayed (*ḥtt*) by them lest before them I dismay you'—which of course belongs to the commissioning sequence in which Yhwh warns the prophet of conflict to come. In light of this resemblance it seems more than likely that the prophet's requests in vv. 17-18 have in view the promises God made to him at the outset, namely, to fortify and be with him in the face of opposition, to deliver him when 'they' fight against him (1.8, 17-19; cf. 15.20-21). In short, the Confession depicts not just a *contrast* between a faithful Jeremiah and an apostate Judah but a genuine *conflict* in which the prophet sees himself as suffering persecution.

If this is so, can it be the case, as Berridge proposes, that the 'day of distress' of which Jeremiah speaks always refers to the final judgment alone and never to the present, personal distress which he experiences at the hands of the foes who persecute him? It would seem that in

v. 17 in particular the prophetic and the psalm-like applications of the *yôm rāʿâ* have flowed together, the latter perhaps even being the dominant current. That is, God is Jeremiah's refuge, not just at the time of the word's fulfilment, but now in the moment of his current affliction, the affliction that prompts his request for healing in the first place (v. 14). Note, however, that for Berridge even that initial request has only the final judgment as its objective. But as he admits, such a view of v. 14 'must remain a conjecture'.[51] So then must the view that the *yôm rāʿâ* refers only to the final judgment.

In my opinion the fluidity of the 'day of distress' in v. 17 is a significant feature in the text's depiction of the prophetic persona. What Jeremiah suffers now, his present time of trouble, is directly related to what the nation will suffer under Yhwh's judgment. In causing his *yôm rāʿâ*, his compatriots assure their own. Rejecting him, they reject Yhwh. Jeremiah's suffering is therefore doubly metaphoric. It represents both the rejection Yhwh suffers at the hands of the people and that which they shall suffer, and in the person of their prophetic representative already do, at the hand of Yhwh. We can see that in the metaphoric operation of the *yôm rāʿâ*, typicality and particularity blend together once again to render the prophet as a paradigm of suffering, though at this point an inimitable one. (That is to say, imitation of the prophet's piety is not a likely factor in the dynamic at work here.)

To summarize the interpretation vis-à-vis Berridge: 1. Jeremiah does in fact take the enemies' charge in v. 15 'personally'. 2. The situation is therefore one of conflict and not just contrast. 3. Accordingly, Jeremiah's requests are oriented not simply to the speedy fulfilment of his judgment oracles but also to an intermediate healing in order that he might continue to carry out his commission. 4. The Confession renders Jeremiah as a particular, prophetic instantiation of the righteous sufferer, the unfairly persecuted, exemplary 'I' of the complaint psalms. It should be noted in due respect to Berridge, that for all this the Confession is no less proclamation than prayer. With regard to Gunneweg, however, it must be emphasized that because it is proclamation *through* prayer, the 'kerygma' proclaimed contains a notable measure of 'piety'. The appropriateness of the emphasis is fully confirmed by an analysis of the Confession's immediate context, to which we now turn.

The opening material, 17.1-11, bears more directly on the Confession than does the Sabbath sermon that concludes the chapter (vv. 19-27).[52]

The following remarks are therefore restricted to the opening eleven verses. At the outset there are several features that interconnect the two sections of the context, the prophetic judgment oracle of vv. 1-4 and the wisdom poem of vv. 5-11, both with the Confession and with each other. In v. 1 the sin of Judah is 'written' ($k^e t \hat{u} b \hat{a}$) with a pen of iron; in v. 13 the sinners themselves will be 'written' ($yikk\bar{a}t\bar{e}b\hat{u}$) in the earth. Read synchronically, the *Stichwort* connection helps to identify the enemies of the Confession as the apostate Judah condemned in the opening judgment oracle (thus confirming Berridge's diachronic conclusion about the enemies' identity[53]).

A similar situation obtains between vv. 5 and 13. The use of the root *swr*, in both places with Yhwh as the object, suggests an equivalence between the enemies and a general type, that of the 'cursed man'. Note also the use of the term 'heart' ($l\bar{e}b$) in vv. 1, 5, 9-10. Specifically, the motif of the 'deceitful' and 'desperately corrupt' heart which is to be read, as it were, by Yhwh (vv. 9-10) is anticipated by v. 1 in the notion that Judah's sin is engraved on, and thus can be read off, its heart. Judah's sin-engraved heart in v. 1, in other words, should be identified with the apostate and desperately corrupt heart of vv. 5 and 9.

Finally, the image in v. 3 of Judah's sudden loss of wealth in payment for its sin is mirrored in v. 11 in the picture of the evaporation of the rich man's unjust gain 'in the midst of his days'. It may even be that through the root '*zb* this connection is meant to extend into v. 13: As the man's unjust gain 'abandons him' ($ya\,'azbenn\hat{u}$) and he proves at the last a fool, so those who 'abandon' Yhwh ('$\bar{o}z^e b\hat{e}k\bar{a}$, '$\bar{a}z^e b\hat{u}$) are appointed to folly's ultimate shame, abandonment by Yhwh.

Just this much shows that there are definite analogies between the personae of the context and those of the Confession. Indeed, the context provides a framework by which the personae of the Confession are to be understood. Correspondingly, it is quite striking how the particularity and typicality ingredient in the Confession are emphasized by each portion of the context respectively. As we observed above, the prose portion vv. 1-4 identifies the enemies particularistically as Judah, the 7th-6th century audience of the prophet Jeremiah, while the poetic verses 5-11 cast them in terms that are essentially universal in scope.

This latter operation is largely a function of the material's genre. For it is the style and categories of wisdom (rather than the

5. *The Confessions*

individual lament psalm) that stamp the poetry and are there applied to the enemies. The style is immediately evident in the antithetical parallelism of vv. 5-8. The contrast between the cursed and blessed man displays wisdom's propensity to perceive the world in terms of antithetical types (e.g. the wise/foolish, righteous/wicked, poor/rich contrasts in Proverbs and the wisdom psalms).[54] The style is also evident in the nature analogy of v. 11 and in the didactic tone throughout. 'Trust' (vv. 5, 7) is of course a fundamental category in wisdom's thought world,[55] and wisdom's lexical stock is well represented by such terms as *mibṭaḥ*, *geber*, *ḥqr*, *bḥn*, and *'ōšer*. Finally, the near replication of Ps 1.3, a classic wisdom psalm, by v. 8 is a striking generic signal.

Now, if the enemies in the Confession are to be viewed through the lens of wisdom (vv. 5-11) as having universal typicality, what of Jeremiah? Clearly, he would be the enemies' counterpart in the antithetical sayings of vv. 5-8. That is, the wisdom poem would have us read the exemplary 'I' and righteous sufferer of the lamentation-styled Confession in terms of an even broader type, the blessed man who trusts in Yhwh. Let us inspect this operation more closely.

5 *kōh 'āmar Yhwh*
  'ārûr haggeber 'ăšer yibṭaḥ bā'ādām
    wᵉśām bāśār zᵉrō'ô
    ûmin-Yhwh yāsûr libbô
6 *wᵉhāyâ kᵉ'ar'ār bā'ărābâ*
    wᵉlō' yir'eh kî-yābô' ṭôb
    wᵉšākan ḥărērîm bammidbār
    'ereṣ mᵉlēḥâ wᵉlō' tēšēb
7 *bārûk haggeber 'ăšer yibṭaḥ baYhwh*
    wᵉhāyâ Yhwh mibṭaḥô
8 *wᵉhāyâ kᵉ'ēṣ šātûl 'al-mayim*
    wᵉ'al-yûbal yᵉšallaḥ šārāšāyw
    wᵉlō yir'e kî yābō' ḥōm
    wᵉhāyâ 'ālēhû ra'ănān
    ûbišnat baṣṣōret lō' yid'āg
    wᵉlō' yāmîš mē'ăśôt perî

5 Thus says Yhwh:
  Cursed is the man who trusts in man,
    and makes flesh his arm,
      whose heart turns from Yhwh.

> 6 For he is like a shrub in the desert
>   and cannot see when good comes.
>   And he will dwell in the parched places of the wilderness
>   in a land of salt, uninhabited.
> 7 Blessed is the man who trusts in Yhwh,
>   whose confidence is Yhwh.
> 8 For he is like a tree planted by the waters,
>   stretching out its roots by a stream.
>   He will not fear when the heat comes,
>   but his leaves will remain green;
>   nor in the year of drought will he be anxious,
>   or cease to bear fruit.

The poetic form of wisdom is manifest in the antithetical construction of vv. 5-8—and not just the form but the mode and substance of its thought as well. Distilling from experience fundamental truths of life, wisdom propounds a doctrine of man. Here an anthropocentric anthropology is spurned and a theocentric one endorsed, since the one leads to curse while the other to blessing. This corresponds with similarly formulated sage-like statements in the Psalms: e.g. 'Happy the man who takes refuge in Yhwh' (Ps 34.9), and 'Happy the man who puts his trust in Yhwh' (Ps 40.5). And underlying such statements is the basic wisdom principle, 'The steps of a man are from Yhwh' (Ps 37.23), i.e. 'A man's mind plans his way, but Yhwh directs his steps' (Prov 16.9). Now, as we saw in an earlier chapter, Jeremiah affirmed the very same principle when he confessed 'that the way of man is not in himself, that it is not in man who walks to direct his steps' (10.23), and we noted then that this affirmation contributed to the depiction of the prophet in chs. 8-10 as a paradigm of wisdom.[56]

A similar depiction is underway here. Indeed, it is a perfect expression of the wisdom maxim in 10.23 when in the Confession of ch. 17 Jeremiah claims Yhwh as his hope (v. 13), his praise (v. 14), and his refuge (v. 17)—in short, as his trust and confidence. From the vantage point of the wisdom poem, in other words, Jeremiah's Confession articulates the trust in Yhwh that characterizes one as 'blessed' and, by implication, as wise.[57]

Now, as much as vv. 5-8 fit a wisdom pattern, there are some peculiarities. To be sure, we have already cited two psalms that display the formula used in vv. 5 and 7: namely, adjective + *haggeber* + finite verb + object. To these may be added Pss 94.12, 127.5, and numerous others which show only slight variations of the formula.[58]

5. The Confessions

However, while many of these include a negative contrast, never does the contrast use the word 'cursed' (*'ārûr*). Moreover, in all cases the positive term is *'ašrê*, 'happy', not *bārûk*, 'blessed'. As it turns out, the *'ārûr/bārûk* antithesis is primarily found not in the wisdom literature but in the covenant sanctions of Deut 27-28. Significantly, Jer 11.3 employs *'ārûr* with *bĕrît*, 'covenant', in the formulaic pattern of 17.5:

> *kōh 'āmar Yhwh 'ĕlōhê yiśrā'ēl*
> *'ārûr hā'îš 'ăšer lō' yišma' 'et-dibrê habbᵉrît hazzō't*
> Thus says Yhwh, God of Israel:
> Cursed is the man who heeds not the words of this covenant.

Further, like 11.3, 17.5-8 begins with the messenger formula.

The point is that wisdom and covenantal/prophetic speech forms have intersected in our passage. The universal scope of the one has been qualified (but by no means negated) by the historical particularity of the other. A subtle but significant semantic shift is thereby effected. What at first glance would seem to be the empirical observations of wisdom are in fact a divine pronouncement by which a covenant norm is invoked and its curse and blessing are activated. Thus, the antithesis of trust-in-man vs. trust-in-Yhwh, while always implicitly an ethical opposition, becomes explicitly one of disobedience vs. obedience, the consequences of which do not follow simply by 'natural law' or merely as a matter of course, but as a judgment that has Yhwh as its agent. Verses 5-8, therefore, are very much performative statements: in 5-6 Yhwh threatens, in 7-8 he promises.

The performative quality gives the description of consequences in vv. 6 and 8 a special pathos, particularly the *r'h/yr'* word-play. Whether one follows the *kᵉtîb* in v. 8 and reads 'will not fear' or the *qᵉrê*, 'will not see', the point is the contrast with v. 6. As in 4.18 and 5.25, at stake is the self as a function of faculties and capacities by which one reads and responds to the world. The judgment upon the disobedient, i.e. the self-centered person, is ironically the diminution of the self, even to the point of an incapacity to recognize the good when it comes. Conversely, it is God's promise to the obedient, God-trusting person that he will not be incapacitated by fear when he is under heat; rather, he will flourish, bear his fruit, even in a time of drought.

The implications for Jeremiah's Confession are profound. The prophet's conflict with the enemies is set in the (covenantal-wisdom) context of the conflict between obedience and disobedience. Identified as those who make flesh their arm, the enemies prove their disobedience by spurning the word of Yhwh and its bearer. Jeremiah demonstrates obedience to God through trust. In effect, then, vv. 5-8 answer the lament in advance, God condemning the enemy to self-dissolution while promising courage and vitality to the prophet in the face of 'heat' from the adversary.

Verses 9-10 work similarly. They too interpret the Confession by anticipation:

9 *'āqōb hallēb mikkōl*
    wᵉ'ānuš hû' mî yēdā'ennû
10 *'ănî Yhwh ḥōqēr lēb*
    bōḥēn kᵉlāyôt
    wᵉlātēt lᵉ'îš kidrākāw
    kiprî ma'ălālāyw

9 The heart is deceitful above all things
    and desperately corrupt. Who can understand it?
10 I, Yhwh, search the mind
    and try the heart,
  to give to each according to his ways,
    according to the fruit of his doings. (RSV)

Recall that at v. 16b of the Confession we questioned Berridge's decision that Jeremiah's inwardness is not at issue in his appeal to Yhwh (*'attâ yādā'tā*).[59] Now, in view of vv. 9-10 (and note the root *ydʿ*), we can see that it *is* an issue. The human heart—i.e. the intricate relationship between one's outward behavior and inner motivation, between deed, word, and thought—is notoriously difficult to read and fathom; yet it is only if the heart is read that it can be known whether one trusts man or God, is obedient or disobedient. This is the problem posed by v. 9—*mî yēdā'ennû*, 'who can know it?'. The answer is provided by v. 10. Yhwh knows. Employing the self-disclosure formula which elsewhere attests his covenant fidelity, justice, and righteousness, Yhwh here presents himself as the one true interpreter of the human heart and the ultimate arbiter of human affairs.[60] The juxtaposition of the wisdom poem with the Confession makes it reasonable, therefore, to read Jeremiah's appeal in v. 16 ('thou knowest') as grounded upon this pointed self-asseveration by Yhwh. Thus, in the face of persecution Jeremiah appeals to Yhwh's knowledge of his public behavior, of course, but also of the heart out of which the behavior springs, for Yhwh searches the heart and tries the kidneys, i.e. knows the behavior inside-out.

5. The Confessions 149

There may be another dimension to the relation between vv. 9-10 and 16. In 11.20 Jeremiah uses the same terminology employed in 17.10, i.e. *bōḥēn kᵉlāyôt wālēb*, and shortly thereafter in 12.3 this language is combined with the opening phrase of 17.16b, to wit:

*wᵉ'attâ Yhwh yᵉda'tānî tir'ēnî
ûbāḥantî libbî 'ittāk*

But thou, O Yhwh, knowest me, thou seest me
and triest my heart toward thee.

God's knowing, seeing, and trying the heart are intimately related. Given Yhwh's statement in 17.10 and the way the appeal works in 12.3, it seems likely that in appealing to God's knowing in 17.16, Jeremiah either presupposes or invites testing by God.

Now, 'testing' (*bḥn*) and 'searching' (*ḥqr*) can indicate not only God's ability to see into the heart, but even more the *process* of the seeing, or the situation through which one's heart is revealed to God.[61] That is, they can refer to events and experiences that 'test' one's metal, indeed perhaps even forge it, to situations in other words where the strength or weakness of one's commitment cannot fail to be exposed. It seems likely that the Confessions in general reflect such an ordeal of testing and searching. The divine responses in 12.5-6 and 15.19-20 would tend to confirm this. The same seems to be the case in ch. 17.

Thus, vv. 9-10 of the wisdom poem serve two purposes. First, as an affirmation of God's ability to understand the heart and to discriminate between obedience and disobedience, they anticipate and ground Jeremiah's appeal in 16b. Thereby they also prepare us to read it specifically as an appeal for vindication of the integrity of Jeremiah's heart, his behavior in its internal as well as external dimensions. Second, vv. 9-10 suggest that the Confession be seen in the context of an ordeal in which the prophet's obedience is being tried, and his self is being formed.

In this regard it may seem curious how the wisdom poem ends.

*qōrē' dāgar wᵉlō' yālād
'ōśeh 'ōšer wᵉlō' bᵉmišpāṭ
baḥăṣî yāmāw ya'azbennû
ûbᵉ'aḥărîtô yihyeh nābāl*

Like the partridge that gathers a brood which she did not hatch,
  so is he who gets riches but not by right;
in the midst of his days they will leave him,
  and at his end he will be a fool.

Verse 11 appears to fill out the thought of v. 10b ('to give to each according to his ways and the fruit of his doings'), but only with respect to the cursed, disobedient man. A balancing statement on the fate of the blessed man would be in order. However, none appears. Instead there follow Jeremiah's own words, the Confession with its doxological invocation. In effect, prophetic complaint and curse, being grounded in and issuing out of praise and trust, are the counterbalance to v. 11's reflection on the way of the wicked—and complete the symmetry of curse and blessing.[62] Jeremiah, then, praying his way through the conflict-laden situation in which Yhwh tests him, instantiates the way of the righteous who suffer innocently yet bear the blessing granted to those who trust in Yhwh and make him their confidence.

To summarize, verses 1-11 have a decided influence on the way the Confession is to be read. They first of all enhance, not annul, the Confession's proclamatory quality. When read in light of the initial judgment oracle (vv. 1-4) and the wisdom poem-turned-divine word (5-11), the Confession becomes all the more a witness to Judah's rejection of Yhwh. Forsaking Yhwh, turning their heart from him (v. 13), scorning his word and persecuting his prophet (v. 15), Judah manifests its sin-engraved heart and pursues the way of the cursed (vv. 1, 15). Appropriately, the Confession also witnesses to the judgment (v. 18) that will come upon Judah 'according to its ways and the fruit of its doings' (v. 10).

At the same time the context amplifies the 'personal' component of the Confession. It sees the conflict between prophet and persecutors as a test of hearts, and it describes that conflict in terms of qualities of the heart such as trust and folly (vv. 5, 7, 11). Ultimately, the issue is obedience. Corollary to this is an emphasis on Jeremiah's exemplary significance. As the context heightens the personal, it broadens the type, yet without diminishing the particular. Even as he becomes an exemplar of trust, a wisdom-styled model of obedience in suffering, Jeremiah remains the prophetic figure of a definite time, place, and mission.

It is obvious by now that particularity and typicality are by no means mutually exclusive categories, even less 'kerygma' and 'piety'. On the other hand, neither are the four qualities everywhere present in the same proportion, functioning in the same way and to the same effect. Their interrelationships and functions are exceedingly fluid and complex. For example, while Jeremiah may nearly always typify

5. *The Confessions*

something, it is not always in his piety that he does so, and certainly there are aspects of his persona that go beyond imitability. This was observed in v. 17 where the circumstances and sheer fact of his suffering (which had elements of both typicality and particularity) were more the focus of interest than was the manner in which he bore it, and consequently the imitative aspect of his paradigmatic status receded for the moment behind the metaphoric or symbolic aspect. In that instance the kerygma, what was being proclaimed in and through the persona, was the pathos and judgment of God. In the instances where the imitative aspect is more prominent (e.g. 'Heal me . . . for thou art my praise'), the kerygma is directed more to the possibility and grammar of relationship with God, and more to the divine promise and consolation.

Finally, there is a special problem that concerns the concept 'imitation' and the prophet's typicality. It arises with the curse of v. 18 and has been formulated by Baumgartner so: 'The curse may not be ethically irreproachable, but psychologically it is perfectly understandable'.[63] That is, the curse represents a typical human response to adversity. But how can it be commended as an act of obediential faith? Is the modelling function operative even here?

The text seems not to recognize any difficulty here, and perhaps there is no reason that it should. As the psalmic parallels attest, a curse on one's enemies, who are understood as God's enemies, was hardly an aberrant feature of ancient Israelite piety and could even be taken as an expression of one's commitment to Yhwh's cause. The problem would seem to be a modern one, therefore, and a hermeneutical (rather than an exegetical) issue. But we should note, the concept 'imitation', which is clearly relevant to exegeting the text's depiction of its main persona, invites the problem by its very nature, for it is inherently a highly existential, reader-involving concept. Having unleashed such a concept, or image, the intentionality of the text cannot be restricted to that of its authors and to one historical moment and milieu. The problem is therefore not really extrinsic to the text and the text's exegesis, though it permits no once-and-for-all solution. It is part of its burden that the text simply indicates that the persona *is* to be imitated, primarily in his trust, but without indicating in every respect how. It is left to the reader of every age to assess, in light of the fullest witness available, to what extent and in what manner vengeful anger toward the oppressor is congruent with trust in Yhwh.

Clearly, the notion of imitation demands much in the way of reader discernment and ethical-theological sophistication. Of course, there is also a kind of discernment required when it is granted that part of what Jeremiah does in v. 18 is the particularly prophetic, and hence inimitable, action of proclaiming the divine word that has been entrusted uniquely to him. This is only to say that in certain respects Jeremiah's typicality, and imitability, is limited by his particularity, and that the lines of analogy between persona and reader are, once again, fluid and quite complex.

With these considerations we have begun to enter the territory of our last chapter. However, the problems involved in 17.18 recur in even more pressing form in Jeremiah's final Confession. Consequently, before addressing the hermeneutics of the prophet-as-paradigm, we turn to Jer 20.7-18.

II. *Jeremiah 20.7-18*

Chapter 20 can be treated more summarily than ch. 17, with the focus on salient points of contact and development between the two. The task is made easier by the recent work of D.J.A. Clines and D.M. Gunn. While contesting the redactional theories of Gerstenberger and Gunneweg by locating the occasion of vv. 7-18 in the ministry of the historical Jeremiah, Clines and Gunn offer a very careful analysis of the original form and function of the text. They then go on to evaluate the shift in meaning effected by its incorporation into the present context.[64] In my opinion the analysis and results at both stages of the inquiry are highly illuminating and, with a few notable exceptions to be addressed in excursuses, help to advance the present thesis and provide a valuable springboard for further reflection.

Form critically, 20.7-18 appears to be a composite structure. Verses 7-13 fit the pattern of the individual complaint psalm while vv. 14-18 are a self-curse which is basically extrinsic to the lament *Gattung*. Accordingly, the first seven verses resemble the Confession of ch. 17 with an invocation or address (v. 7a), the lament proper, again including a citation of the words of the enemy (7-10), a succession of expressions of trust, certainty of hearing, and petition (11-12), and finally praise (13).[65]

Against those who would dispute the unity of vv. 7-9 and 10-13 on the basis of the prophetic cast of the former, Clines and Gunn point out features in 7-9 that are fully characteristic of the individual

5. The Confessions

lament psalm. Like the psalmist, the prophet is beset by enemies. The language describing both is typical: The enemy is stronger (*ḥzq*) than and threatens to prevail (*ykl*) over the complainant (Pss 35.10; 13.4-5). The complainant is a laughingstock (*śḥq*: Pss 37.13; 59.9), the object of mockery (*l'g*: Pss 22.8; 35.16; 59.9), reproach (*ḥrp*: Pss 22.7; 31.12; 39.9; 42.11), and derision (*qls*: Pss 44.14; 79.4).[66] The prophetic, and Jeremianic, particularities such as the word-pair *ḥāmās wāšōd* ('violence and destruction'), the motif of speaking in God's name, and the closely related notion of prophetic compulsion all serve as in ch. 17 to establish an identification between the righteously suffering, exemplary 'I' of the complaint psalms and the prophet Jeremiah.

Excursus A

For *ḥāmās wāšōd* see Isa 59.6-7, 60.18, Ezek 45.9, Amos 3.10, Hab 1.3, 2.17, and not least Jer 6.7. Clines and Gunn have addressed the interpretation of *ḥāmās wāšōd* in a more recent article, '"You Tried to Persuade Me" and "Violence! Outrage!" in Jeremiah 20:7-8', *VT* 28 (1978), pp. 20-27. They identified four basic alternative interpretations that are or have been variously represented in the discipline. Their choice, reflected in the earlier article, is that *ḥāmās wāšōd* does not refer to the content of Jeremiah's proclamation but is rather the prophet's cry of distress to Yhwh, indeed a protest against him 'who has behaved towards Jeremiah in the manner of the enemies'.[67]

The primary support for this position is that *z'q*, 'cry out', in v. 8 is 'not an appropriate term for introducing a judgment or an oracle of doom; rather, it is virtually a technical term for a cry of appeal made by an innocent sufferer against unjust oppressors'.[68] However, *z'q* is not the only verb in the statement's predicate. Note the bi-cola's structure:

kî-middê 'ădabbēr 'ez'āq
ḥāmās wāšōd 'eqrā'

For whenever I speak, I cry out,
'Violence and destruction!' I cry.

I agree that *'ădabbēr* refers to the divine word that the prophet speaks.[69] As for *z'q*, one could argue either that *'ez'āq* in 8aα has *no* object (and should be punctuated with a semi-colon), or that it *shares* its object (*ḥāmās wāšōd*) with *'eqrā'* in 8aβ, *qr'* being able to designate a prophetic word as well as a general utterance (e.g. Isa 40.6).

Not incidental to this is the fact that when the word-pair occurs earlier in Jer 6.7 it refers to the activity of those who stand under judgment; i.e. it is a prophetic characterization of Judah/Jerusalem's moral life. It works similarly in the other prophetic passages listed above, even with Hab 1.3, for the *ḥāmās wāšōd* which Habakkuk surveys, while indeed the effect of oppression by the enemy, are also *attributes* of the enemy qualifying *him* for judgment (Hab 2.17).

The complexity of the situation in Habakkuk is really quite significant. In Hab 1.3 what is felt as oppression was itself Yhwh's act of judgment upon Judah, which, as 2.17 indicates, will be repaid in kind, *qua* divine judgment, to the human instruments of that judgment for their *own ḥāmās wāšōd*. A basic trait of prophetic reason-and-judgment speech is at work here: the punishment ironically mirrors the crime. A people's *ḥāmās wāšōd* reaps the divine *ḥāmās wāšōd* in retribution. (See Amos 3.11; also the general statement of the principle in Isa 59.18, 'According to their deeds, so will he repay'; cf. Jer 17.10.)

In light of the evidence I think it likely that there is a complex, poetic ambiguity at work in Jer 20.8. The prophet has already characterized Judah's life as filled with *ḥāmās wāšōd*. The divine word which he delivers has been that Judah would be repaid in kind, and indeed *that* word too could be easily characterized as one of 'violence and destruction'. In Jer 28.27 the prophet identifies his message with that of his precursors, describing it as the prophecy of 'war, famine, and pestilence'. That same formulaic characterization of his word occurs in 14.11-16; 15.2; 18.21; etc. In the language of the commissioning sequence and related passages, the message is one of plucking up and breaking down, destroying and overthrowing (1.10; cf. 45.4; etc.). The imagery of judgment in the book seems abundant and diverse, but actually it is all quite similar in basic thrust (cf. also *šeber*, *makkâ*, *šᵉmāmâ*, *rā'â*, etc.). *Ḥāmās wāšōd* fits in easily (and I see no form-critical reason for denying that it could be used to characterize Jeremiah's message). At the same time it is because Jeremiah has been compelled to speak that word repeatedly that he himself suffers persecution, is himself threatened with a violence and destruction the ultimate source of which he sees as Yhwh.

It might be added that the very diversity in opinion over the interpretation of this phrase is itself indicative of the text's ambiguity. It is a functional ambiguity, which if allowed to stand (which is only to grant that poetic meaning is not always univocal) further attests the paradigmatic status of the prophetic persona. Once again, the conflict between God and people in its manifold aspects is focused, crystallized, and held up to view in the life and person of the prophet.

Alongside the form-critical connections, Clines and Gunn can demonstrate a strong thematic coherence between vv. 7-9 and 10-13. Whereas Baumgartner regarded the repetition of *ykl* (vv. 7 and 9, 10

5. The Confessions

and 11) and *pth* (vv. 7, 10) as an artificial *Stichwort*-method of linking originally disparate units, Clines and Gunn regard it as having 'deliberate structural significance'.[70] Their explication is brilliant:

> *Ykl*, in fact, is a key term in v. 7-13, for the notion of 'prevailing' or 'having power' lies at the heart of the poem. It epitomises the prophet's complaint: Yahweh who has prevailed over him (*ykl*, v. 7) has compelling power, the prophet has not (*lō' 'ûkāl*, v. 9); on the other hand, this very 'enemy'-like quality of Yahweh becomes in turn the source of the prophet's confidence: while his enemies imagine that *they* will prevail over him (*ykl*, v. 10), Jeremiah knows that with Yahweh on his side they cannot succeed (*lō' yukālû*, v. 11).
>
> It is precisely because in the prophet's own experience Yahweh is an oppressive and irresistible God, who is stronger than his victim, prevails over him and commits violence and outrage against him (v. 7f.), that he may be called on in turn to become the irresistible divine oppressor of the prophet's human oppressors (v. 11). The irony is strikingly captured in the phrase, 'But Yahweh is with me *as a dread warrior* (*gibbôr 'ārîṣ*)': he is both 'mightily heroic' (*gibbôr*, a term of approbation, found often in Ps, but rarely in a psalm of lament) and 'terribly ruthless' (*'arîṣ*, normally applied to the wicked 'enemies' or 'men of violence'; all occurrences in Ps are in individual laments; cf. 37.35; 54.5; 86.14).
>
> The repetition of *pth*, moreover, underlines this fundamental parallelism between Yahweh and the persecutors: in v. 7 the prophet cries that he has been 'persuaded' (*pth*) and that *Yahweh* has overcome him (*ykl*); in v. 10 the enemies hope that Jeremiah will be 'persuaded' (*pth*) and that *they* will overcome him (*ykl*).[71]

It is evident that the undercurrent of reproach in the prophet's request 'Be not a terror to me' in 17.17 has in ch. 20 been considerably amplified.[72] Yhwh is here directly accused; the prophet's 'refuge' (17.17) *is* a terror to him. At the same time, God can be appealed to in order to 'shame', or terrorize, the prophet's persecutors (20.11). Two issues may be noted here to be developed later. The first is that this description, like the second paragraph in Clines and Gunn's quotation above, is in part a psychological interpretation; i.e. it makes it intelligible how the persona can simultaneously regard God with anger, dread, and trust. Apparently, for Clines and Gunn the conventionality of the language and generic pattern does not obviate the need for showing how one would use and *mean* the prayer, nor does it preclude the possibility that the language expresses emotion on the part of the person who prays it. The second issue is the same that was raised in relation to 17.18. The severity of the prophet's reproach of God might seem to place into question his role as a model for imitation.

However, it is the expression of trust and other positive emotions that is the remarkable thing about this poem, in light of the acridness of the reproach and complaint. And it is in this latter section (vv. 11-13) that the point of the petitionary lament is to be found.[73] Clines and Gunn identify v. 12a as 'the center of gravity of the poem, not the outrageously unconventional, and therefore attractively "modern", protest against Yahweh of v. 7a'.[74] Employing the motif of Yhwh's knowing from 11.20, 15.15, and 17.10a, 16b (which we discussed at length), v. 12 gives the prophet's obedience a crucial status in the poem. And if v. 12 is the poem's center of gravity, v. 13 is its climax.[75] The trust expressed in the previous two verses is here raised into outright praise of the God who 'has delivered the life of the needy from the hand of evildoers'. The effect is the same as in 17.12, 14c: Jeremiah's praise testifies 'before a doubtless sceptical audience the authority and authenticity of the oracles which Jeremiah delivers as Yahweh's prophet'.[76] The praise is therefore part of the proclamation of the divine word. No less importantly, the praise characterizes the persona who offers it and constitutes his personhood, mobilizing capacities that give the self definition and, given the circumstances, no small degree of complexity.

Like the Confession in ch. 17, we can see that 20.7-13 contains elements of psalmic typicality and prophetic particularity and, moreover, that its proclamatory function does not preclude its 'personal' dimension, or in the words of Clines and Gunn, 'does not remove the element of "spiritual struggle" from the poem'.[77] Further, and also as with ch. 17, the effect of the lamentation's juxtaposition with the preceding material, 20.1-6, is to heighten the personal dimension dramatically. The major difference with the situation in ch. 17 is that here the context gives the poem greater historical specificity but very little universality, if any (cf. 17.5-11).

The juxtaposition of the two passages completes a parallel rhetorical pattern between ch. 18 and chs. 19-20, the pattern consisting of 1. a symbolic act and speech, 2. scenic comment, 3. persecution of the prophet, and 4. lament. Clines and Gunn comment:

5. *The Confessions*

From three different sources ('I'-narrative; 'He'-narrative; laments) the Deuteronomistic editor has shaped a narrative of a single situation to depict a stylized scene in the preaching of Jeremiah, representing his typical preaching and the typical reaction of his audience. The lament may then have been deliberately inserted at this point to fill out a pattern which the editor was creating in order to offer a stereoscopic picture of Jeremiah.[78]

Specifically, by virtue of the juxtaposition the reader recognizes the repetition of 'terror on every side' (*māgôr missābîb*) in vv. 3 and 10 and associates Pashhur, so nicknamed in v. 3, with the impinging danger so described in v. 10. Similarly, the phrase 'all your friends' (literally, 'loved ones', *kol-'ōhăbêkā*) in vv. 4 and 6 resonates in 'all my familiar friends' (*kōl 'enôš šᵉlômî*) of v. 10. Consequently, Pashhur and cohorts are identified with the friends-turned-'persecutors' (v. 11) and 'evildoers' (v. 13) in the lament. Moreover, the rift between Pashhur and his friends suggested in v. 4 of the prophet's doom oracle comes to be seen as the just deserts for the betrayal Jeremiah complains of in the lament. Finally, the cry 'Violence and destruction!' (*ḥāmās wāšōd*) in the lament can be heard as a characterization of the oracle(s) in vv. 3-6 and/or as a reference to the persecution suffered at the hands of Pashhur and, because suffered in Yhwh's service, at the hands of Yhwh himself.

In sum, the narrative context leads one to identify the situation of vv. 7-13 with the Pashhur incident.[79] We might question, however, whether this identification should be taken as an exhaustive one, as Clines and Gunn seem to take it.[80] That is to say, does the redactional shaping intend for us to read the lament as referring *only* to the Pashhur incident and as having no surplus significance such that when read with the other Confessions in mind (and indeed with other first-person utterances of the prophet) it could be seen as characterizing a *pattern* in the prophet's experience? I am inclined to think that the poem does *not* yield all its allusiveness to the narrative context of 20.1-6, and that while the Pashhur incident does indeed give the poem greater historical specificity and concreteness, it does so as a particularly salient illustration of the *kind* of crisis the poem reflects.

A still more basic point merits emphasis: The redactors apparently saw no obstacle in taking the rather generally formulated conventions of persecution and mockery in the lamentation *Gattung* as an expression of the personal experience of their prophetic persona. It will be useful to keep this in mind for the discussion of vv. 14-18.

What effect does the lament have on the narrative? According to Clines and Gunn, the psalm adds emotion and human interest to the narrative's relatively flat account.[81] This is true enough, but there is more to be said. In my opinion the poetic lament gives the prose story an emblematic quality. As with the adaptation and application of psalm-like material to the book of Jeremiah as a whole, the poem gives this particular story typicality. Jeremiah's suffering at the hands of Pashhur and his announcement of his doom typify the suffering of the righteous in general and God's promise for their vindication.

Now, how do vv. 14-18 fit into the picture? To say the least, the contrast in mood between the self-curse and the lament (7-13) is severe. It raises the question of whether there is any fit at all. Is it possible to read the two units together and construe them as spoken by the same person into the same situation? One (form-critical) answer might be that the contrast is a false one, that in fact the mood of vv. 14-18 is not personal and does not express the persona's actual emotion the way vv. 7-13 do. This answer stands on three legs: 1. The words *'āmāl* ('toil'), *yāgôn* ('sorrow'), and *bōšet* ('shame') in v. 18 are more objective than subjective in orientation; i.e. they describe not the prophet's private anguish but the objective situation of the people.[82] 2. As evidenced by the parallel passage of Job 3.2-10, the curse in Jer 20.14-17 has a formulaic, stereotypic quality which makes it 'naive to read the passage as a direct transcript of the prophet's feelings'.[83] 3. Relatedly, the self-curse is like 'the conventional description of dismay at the hearing of bad news', which functions in the prophetic literature to emphasize the distressing *content* of a proclamation, not the speaker's personal reaction to it.[84]

Excursus B

Clines and Gunn take the above position respecting the unit's original function. It is impressive that they then carry their exegesis a step further to observe how this function is transformed (suppressed) when the material is placed in its present setting in the book (*Sitz-im-Buch*). Nevertheless, the argument may be flawed even with regard to the original *Sitz-im-Leben*. To take each leg in order:

1. The clear sense of the question in v. 18 ('Why did I come forth from the womb to see toil and sorrow and spend my days in shame?') is that what the speaker has seen has not been to his liking. However objective the terms 'toil', 'sorrow', and 'shame' may be, the people's distress has obviously become a source of distress to the prophet.

5. *The Confessions* 159

2. To be sure, formulaic and conventional speech forms must be interpreted very cautiously, but do they, as Clines and Gunn say, quoting D.H. Hillers, 'prevent us from drawing *any* conclusions as to [the poet's] individual psychology'?[85] Actually, Hillers' exact words are 'psychological *reaction*', and he goes on to add, 'We can only say that he was concerned to describe himself as reacting in a *typical, normal* way'.[86] Hence, our caution should not be of drawing *any* conclusions, only those that try to establish the *uniqueness* of the speaker's psyche on the basis of his conventional utterances, as if he were the only one in the culture that could express emotion so. What needs to be affirmed is that anyone in the culture who employs the convention appropriately probably does so to express the relevant emotion.

3. To illustrate their point about the self-curse, Clines and Gunn cite Hillers' remark, 'Recast in unemotional terms, [the prophet's] words mean: "Yahweh's word is very bad news indeed"'.[87] But is it legitimate to recast the expression in unemotional terms and still claim to convey its meaning? Now, to observe that the self-curse can and does have an objective quality, that it says something about the content of the proclamation, is quite appropriate. Emotion statements (such as 'Cursed be the day on which I was born!', v. 14) have both an expressive and a descriptive (fact-asserting) force. That is, as they express the emotion (e.g. despair), they also imply beliefs (e.g. that the situation is desperate, that a general destruction is inevitable, that Yhwh's word is bad news). However, it must be recognized that normally the descriptive component is an entailment, an implication, of the expressive part. Again, the speaker *implies* that the situation is bad by showing how he feels. The listener *infers* the beliefs (the description) from the emotion. But in the form-critical position of Hillers, Clines, and Gunn, this logic is reversed. How is this reversal justified? In my opinion extraordinary evidence would have to be furnished as to why the normal situation does not obtain. The kind of evidence that would support nullifying or discounting the emotive quality of the statement (such as direct verbal denials of the emotion by the speaker, or physical gestures and subsequent behavior to the same point) is simply not available. In sum, it must be assumed that the self-curse asserted the direness of the situation that prompted it *as* and *while* it expressed the emotion of dire dismay.

It is not just for the reasons given in the excursus that the contrast in mood between vv. 7-13 and 14-18 cannot be dismissed. The immediate juxtaposition of the two units of first-person speech, without any hint of lapse in time or altered situation, impels that they be read as the words of a single persona torn by radically conflicting emotions. This is also to say that like vv. 7-13, and in sequence with them, vv. 14-18 are to be read in the context of the Pashhur incident of 20.1-6. If in that incident the prophet can move from protest to praise of the God who will ultimately vindicate him, he can also return to bitterly decry the fact that the toil, sorrow, and shame which he now knows at the hands of his enemy (his people) he will see again as it overtakes his people (his enemy).[88] In this case the persona is rendered in terms of the peculiarly prophetic blend of sympathy and antipathy, hence again as a metaphor of the divine-human relationship.

As for how the prophet could be a model for imitation, the passage's total thrust is ambiguous and all the options seem dark at best. The prophet who in the midst of persecution exemplifies righteousness by praising God is at the same time the suffering sage (cf. Job 3.2-10) whose testing carries him to the brink of despair. Obviously, there is no simplistic piety being commended here. Is it the element of sympathetic identification with the plight of the enemy/people that the persona here embodies and the text commends? Is a model of obediential faith to be seen in the struggle itself, in the very tension between praise and anguish? Is it in the fact that the prophet simply persists in his task?

Though the text's intention remains hazy, it may be significant that the book does not end with 20.18. If unlike in the first three Confessions there is no accompanying divine word to address the self-curse,[89] there is at least the reportage in ch. 21 of Jeremiah's continuing prophetic activity—and confrontation with the authorities.[90] Moreover, that chapter *does* contain a divine word, part of which (vv. 8-9) turns out to be pregnant with implications for Jeremiah's destiny. Perhaps for this reason ch. 21, especially vv. 1-10 which are in the form of a prose speech (C material), was developed by the biographical narratives (B) which depict the interrelated fate of the prophetic word and person.[91]

Specifically, in 21.8, in words recalling Deut 30.15, Jeremiah is told to set before the people the two ways, life and death. Verse 9 gives the details: 'He who stays in this city shall die by the sword, by famine, and by pestilence; but he who goes out and surrenders to the Chaldeans who are besieging you shall live and shall have his life as a prize of war'. The biographical development of the material is complex, indeed, baroque. In 37.11-15 Jeremiah is captured and accused of defecting to the Chaldeans, as if having heeded his own oracle, although it appears that he was only going to take possession of the plot he had purchased in Anathoth (Benjamin) at Yhwh's command (ch. 32), ironically, an action that symbolized the divine promise of redemption. One might speculate that in fact the action

5. The Confessions

did entail a defection (and hence that the promises of 21.9b and ch. 32 amounted to the same thing), but Jeremiah denies any treasonous intent in 37.14. In any case, if anyone sought to seize and silence the prophet—and chs. 20.1-6, 26-29, and 36 indicate that there were those who did, from Jehoiakim's reign right through Zedekiah's— here was the pretext. Jeremiah was imprisoned. The incident thus seems a further illustration of 20.10 where the prophet complains that his familiar friends (*'enôš š^{e}lômî*) seek to denounce him, watch for his fall, and hope that he will be 'persuaded' (*pth*, by Yhwh) so that they might 'prevail' (*ykl*) over him.

Then the oracle of 21.9 is recapitulated in 38.2, now for the sake of reporting its repercussions. The king's counsellors demand the death penalty, and with Zedekiah's permission they cast him into a cistern, leaving him to die (38.6). At this point the narrative presents two contrasting patterns of response to the prophet and his message.

First, Ebed-melek intercedes for Jeremiah and draws him out of the pit, saving his life (38.7-13).[92] Interestingly, his action is interpreted in 39.18 as manifesting 'trust in Yhwh', which as we have seen is a primary quality of Jeremiah's Confessions, i.e. a quality of which the prophet is a model. Further, the oracle that attributes this trust to Ebed-melek is again a version of the one announced in 21.8-10 and recapitulated in 38.2-3. In particular, it employs the same key phrase, 'you shall have your life as a prize of war' (*hāy^{e}tâ l^{e}kā napš^{e}kā l^{e}šālāl*). There is only one other place where this formula occurs, namely, in 45.5, in the oracle to the prophet's faithful secretary, Baruch. Again, one might find a suggestion of the imitation of the prophet in that oracle's quotation of Baruch's brief lament (v. 3) and in its repetition of the vocabulary of Jeremiah's commission (v. 4: *bnh, hrs, nt', ntš*; cf. 1.10). And it might be asked to what extent the question posed by Yhwh in v. 5 ('And do you seek great things for yourself?') answers Jeremiah's final complaint as well as Baruch's. At any rate, a promise (form-critically different from, but) in substance the same as that granted to the prophet himself in 1.8, 18-19, and 15.20-21 is declared to two figures who have aligned themselves with Yhwh's prophet and hence with Yhwh himself. Imitators of Jeremiah through their obedience in the face of personal danger, Ebed-melek and Baruch share in his promise.[93]

The second pattern of response is represented by Zedekiah. After Ebed-melek retrieves Jeremiah from the cistern (again, with the king's permission), Zedekiah summons the prophet who repeats essentially the same conditional word he had delivered in ch. 21: If the king obeys Yhwh and surrenders to the Chaldeans, he is told, 'your life shall be spared' (38.17, 20; cf. 21.9b). If he refuses, judgment will follow (38.18, 23; cf. 21.7, 10). Of primary interest is the vision depicting this judgment. Women being led out of the palace to their captors are heard singing a dirge for the king:

> *hissîtukā wᵉyākᵉlû lᵉkā*
> *'anšê šᵉlōmekā*
> *hoṭbᵉ'û babbōṣ raglekā*
> *nāsōgû 'āḥôr*

They have incited you and prevailed over you,
    your familiar friends!
Now that your feet are sunk in the mire,
    they have turned away from you!

The first bi-colon clearly replicates the thought and language of Jeremiah's last Confession,[94] while the second one recalls 38.6, Jeremiah's sinking (*ṭb'*) into the mud at the bottom of the cistern. Jeremiah's own experience, in other words, now provides the terms for describing the fate of the weak-willed and ultimately disobedient king. The prophet's own suffering has become metaphoric of Zedekiah's, and the nation's, judgment. There is also implied a causal relation: the judgment on the king results from his response to Jeremiah and the prophetic word.

In sum, while Jeremiah's self-curse in 20.14-18 appears to go unanswered, we have seen that the immediately following C material in ch. 21 opens out into the biographical narratives which offer further reflection on the significance of the prophet's suffering. Jeremiah's question of meaning ('Why did I come forth from the womb...?') receives its answer in the nation's story and in the divine purpose and action. His life interprets the nation's life with God. In particular, he provides the pattern for understanding the judgment on Zedekiah and the promises to Ebed-melek and Baruch. Finally, in that judgment and those promises, as in the ultimate victory of the divine word, God vindicates the prophet and refuses to let self-curse be the final word on his fate.

Chapter 6

SUMMARY AND CONCLUDING
HERMENEUTICAL REFLECTIONS

It is evident from the previous chapter that Jeremiah's Confessions manifest the same qualities and bear upon the same range of topics that have occupied our attention throughout this study. Poetic form, metaphor, the language of the heart, self-constituting behavior, the representation of a paradigm—all are closely interwoven there, just as in the other first-person speeches of the prophet. The following remarks, focusing mainly on the Confessions, will attempt to summarize our procedures and findings in these matters and to adduce several implications for scripture's mode of meaning-making and the religious reading of the text.

Poetry and Metaphor

Like our other passages, the Confessions are patently poetic. The parallelism is as regular as one has any right to expect, and rhetorical devices abound. Specific instances receiving attention included the parallel repetition of the roots *rp'* and *yš'* in 17.14, the contrasting pronouns introducing 17.15 and 16, and the structurally crucial *ykl* and *pth* in 20.7-13, to name but a few. Likewise, metaphors, the heart of poetry, proliferated. Yhwh is addressed as 'glorious throne', 'hope of Israel', 'fountain of living waters', 'praise', and 'refuge', in 17.12-13, while in 20.11 he is described as a 'dread warrior'. God's enemies, it is said, will be 'written in the earth' (17.13) and Jeremiah's will 'stumble' (20.17). God's word has become for Jeremiah a 'reproach and derision' (20.8), and within his 'heart' is 'a burning fire shut up in my bones' (20.9). He wishes his mother had been his 'grave' (20.17).

It is not a trivial matter to make these observations. Poetry's careful patterning of sound and thought, its clothing of thought with feeling, its proclivity for connotation, for assertion by indirection, for the abrupt juxtaposition, in all, for the forms of reality which are better implied and evoked than explicitly defined—all this only heightens features that are already found in ordinary language and, indeed, that are fundamental to the language process itself. In particular, the general linguistic requirement for understanding-in-context, for always seeing the part in relation to the whole, is the *sina qua non* for poetry, and is well illustrated, say, by the way praise qualifies reproach in chs 17 and 20.

The force of context, the effect of juxtaposition and sequence, is felt even more vividly when the opening oracle, the wisdom poem, and the Confession of ch. 17 (or in ch. 20 the Pashhur narrative, the lamentation, and the self-curse) are read sequentially and permitted to interact. It was our position, which our synchronic approach was designed to accommodate, that the juxtapositions of form-critically diverse materials are not necessarily random and arbitrary. Rather, they often combine to forge larger units which structure the communication event and generate meaning. Again, it is the material's poetic quality that invites the exploration of these juxtapositions and rewards the effort with the perception of unifying patterns and a sense of the text's own intentionality.[1]

As this sense develops and the patterns emerge, one begins to allow the text a relative autonomy. It is not that the text does not 'refer' to the world outside it. The overlap, complex as it is, between its world and 'the' world is too obvious for this to be the case; indeed, were this the case, the text could not communicate at all. Rather, the more comprehensive a system of internal relationships, references, and allusions the text becomes, the more it regulates the *way* it refers and the *terms* of its referentiality. It was finally the textual system that precluded Wolff's physiologically referential reading of the heart metaphor in 4.19. The context made it clear that the operative language game was one of emotion-expression and moral agency, not physical malady, the sole occurrence of which (in the first person) is 37.20. Similarly, it was the textual system which proved Bright's historically referential reading of ch. 14 inappropriate. The apparent shift in focus from drought to war was not a matter of two separate historical events' occasioning separate poems; it was a matter of a *matrix* of metaphors common to a blessing-curse formulary being adapted to a drama of judgment-proclamation and communal lamentation. That is to say, genre and context governed the nature of

6. Summary & Hermeneutical Reflections

the material's referentiality. Again, in ch. 20 it was the textual system which overrode the typical muteness of lamentations about their specific occasions and gave the Confession of vv. 7-18 at least a partial referentiality to the Pashhur incident of vv. 1-6.

Perhaps the place where the issues of poetic autonomy, textual intentionality, and mode of reference most frequently intersected was in the repeated distinction between the 'Jeremiah of history' and the 'Jeremiah of the text'. I have not wished to deny a significant conformity between the historical figure and the literary persona. Certainly, it would be rash to argue that what is said by or predicated of the latter never applies with historical veracity to the former. Nevertheless, the point has been to prevent the diachronic question of authorship and historical reference from insinuating itself into and displacing the synchronic question of the text's subject matter. In the Confessions, for instance, the text's intention—what through its grammar, syntax, tone, thematic structure, etc. it aims to do—is the delineation of a prophet who in circumstances of extreme conflict enacts in his speech the meaning of his life and message. The circumstances are, for theological purposes and from the perspective of the text's intentions, adequately specified in the Confessions themselves and in their immediate literary contexts. It is hermeneutically irrelevant if the 'original' circumstances were other than what the text describes. Similarly, it matters not whether the compositions are the product of the historical Jeremiah himself or later redactors. In my opinion, it violates the integrity of the text, *qua* poetry, to replace the given literary context with the conjectured historical occasion of the writing process and so to construe the text as referring to authorial circumstances rather than to the subject as it is literarily defined.

Next, because the texts are poetic and metaphoric, they also exhibit a high degree of what can be called a functional, or deliberate, ambiguity. Obviously, what is meant by 'ambiguity' is not hopeless obscurity or the absence of sense but rather a superfluity of sense, multiplicity of meaning, polysemousness. And by 'functional' it is meant that the polysemous condition fits into a larger pattern; the multiple meanings are related, and there is a point to their relatedness.

The ambiguities observed have been of at least two sorts. There were verbal ambiguities, such as the *zō't rā'ātēk* of 4.18, which sustained the double reading 'calamitous doom' and 'ethical wickedness', and the *yôm rā'â* of 17.17, which referred both to Jeremiah's present, personal distress and to the imminent divine judgment upon the nation. On the other hand, there were the speaker ambiguities of chs 8-10 and 14 where a poetic blurring of distinctions between personae invited us to hear certain material as spoken by a composite voice. Both kinds of ambiguity, however, were fundamentally related to the prophet's identity as mediator between God and people. They served in each case to emphasize that identity and suggest its implications. Ultimately, the literary ambiguities contributed to the book's depiction of the prophet as a theological paradigm.

Any scandal created by talk of 'personae' and 'ambiguities' needs to be addressed. The poetic, metaphoric qualities of our material are clear evidence that the book of Jeremiah is a work of the imagination. This is not to say that it is fanciful, unreal, or untrue. Nor is it even to say that it is dominated by an aesthetic interest. Quite to the contrary, the aesthetic labors in the service of the religious, and the book is clearly engaged in making truth-claims—about the world, about the prophet, and about God—though scarcely in propositional form. The point is that the kind of truth claimed (for instance by addressing God as 'the fountain of living waters' or by affirming that 'the Lord is with me as a dread warrior, therefore my persecutors will stumble') is of a special sort, one that cannot be expressed apart from the imaginatively charged language it employs.

Such truth has to do with matters of the deepest import which a purely discursive language (as in the brute reportage of the 'naked facts') can scarcely hope to express. The rule of thumb is that the more denotative (discursive) the language becomes, the less it is capable of conveying that sense of import. Trying to tell the deep truth of Jeremiah's life, to communicate his significance as an expression of the purpose and pathos of God and at the same time as an expression of the predicament and dread and hope of his people, required an imaginative re-presentation of the highest order. That is why a criticism concerned with elucidating the text's theological significance should not be misled into thinking it must first reduce the text to a historically assured minimum, or restrict the 'authentic' Jeremiah to the *ipsissima verba*, or regard the text primarily as a source for fuller historical reconstructions. This can only result in missing precisely what the text wants to say, and replacing that with something else.

6. Summary & Hermeneutical Reflections

Hence we have regarded the text as an effort of literary and religious imagination. Now, if one concedes that imagination was required in the writing of the text, one must concede that it is also essential to its reading. But before addressing that crucial fact, we need to review the phenomenon of the persona-in-speech.

Self-Constitution and the Language of the Heart

The language of religious faith is the language of emotion. This much is a commonplace. Among believers it is often said that the language of faith is the 'language of the heart'. This is no accident; for surely one of the most basic metaphors in Scripture and in religious literature is the human heart. By it, biblical faith refers to the very essence of a human being, to the inmost center of personal experience.

When religious faith speaks in prayer and worship, we often say that its language gives expression to the deepest aspirations, hopes, desires, and experiences of the human heart... The emotions, attitudes, and feelings which are part of the structure of religious beliefs are found in such language: praise, sorrow, contrition, anguish, hope, and joy. There is nothing so obvious, yet so difficult to make clear to the skeptic.[2]

Our study of Jeremiah's first-person language has ranged from the single metaphor of the heart to the poem-prayers known as the Confessions. As the quotation would suggest, the logic of the single metaphor pervades the full-blown prayers, and all the instances in-between. Consequently, the material as a whole well warrants description as a 'language of the heart', though only if the phrase is not dismissed as a signal for mere sentimentality.

The logic connecting our material goes well beyond similarities in surface grammar, also beyond the fact that aesthetic features are used in the service of religious interests. More important is the language's status as *primary* religious discourse. It is first-order language, concrete and non-theoretical. Jeremiah talks not so much *about* God as *to* him. He does not so much discuss attitudes, feelings, and the like as express them. Relatedly, the language is performative in character. That is, it is an action language. So we saw, even as the prophet made an *assertion*, 'thou art my praise', he was in fact *performing* praise. So also, through the language of the heart, in various ways and in complex combinations, he sorrowed and anguished, repented, hoped, and rejoiced: 'I writhe in pain—Oh, the walls of my heart', 'My grief is beyond healing', 'Is there no balm in Gilead?', 'Correct me, O Lord', 'Our iniquities testify against us', 'We acknowledge our wickedness', 'We set our hope in thee', 'Be not a terror', 'Thou art my refuge', 'Sing to the Lord, for he has delivered the life of the needy'.

The use of such language, it has been argued, entails powers and capacities that are constitutive of human being. Further, using the language appropriately (i.e. when it fits the circumstances) exercises the capacities and develops the powers so that, in turn, one knows the circumstances better. It is as if by being skilled in grief through the hostility incurred by his message, Jeremiah has a clearer view of the tragic dimensions of the coming judgment; or by being able to hope and rejoice in Yhwh's being for him a 'dread warrior' against his persecutors, he is better able to perceive the even greater joy and hope-worthiness of Yhwh's promise to restore the nation's fortunes.

Thus, a responsible language of the heart, and the exercise of the capacities entailed therein, give the self form and definition, depth and breadth. So it is with the prophetic persona's primary religious discourse. In it, we have seen, Jeremiah is engaged in the process of self-constitution. Through it he also manifests a profound concept of himself, though it is a working, not a theoretical, concept. Further, it has been shown that his *differentiated* command of both the first-person singular and plural in such language instantiates a self not immediately and automatically reducible to the community of selves, yet a self which is capable of enacting an identification with that community. Finally, it was repeatedly maintained that the conventional or stereotypic quality of the language of the heart does not in itself negate the language's self-constituting character. It was in this context that we so often insisted upon respecting the normative logic of Jeremiah's prayers in both their intercessory and individual forms.

These thoughts lead to some broader generic considerations. It may seem curious how with all its first-person language the book draws attention to the phenomenon of the self only in the final analysis to look away from it, to subordinate the self to another subject matter, or, from the book's perspective, to a being of more solid and constant reality.[3] Jeremiah's comment is to the point: 'I know, O Lord, that the way of man is not in himself, that it is not in man who walks to direct his steps'. However, it is in the nature of the primary religious discourse, of the emotion language, that this should be so; for while

6. Summary & Hermeneutical Reflections

exercising the self, the language targets something outside the self, namely the particular object and/or grounds of the emotion. Here is where the logic of Jeremiah's language, the overall shape of the book, and a certain mode of (auto)biographical writing converge. This mode is one in which the primary interest is not in the self *per se*, the person for his own sake, but in what he or she represents, signifies, and points to. The self in this sort of writing is a medium for a message.

In this connection, Sallie TeSelle has distinguished between a Petrarchan-Rousseauvian pattern of autobiography, which is marked by self-absorption, and another pattern, one akin to Baltzer's 'ideal biography', whose interest in the self is vocational. Of the latter, the journal, letter, and prayer have been the principal genres. These tend to be more parabolic (as well as less chronological) than the stricter life-story; their presentation of a self takes place in the service of a larger task. 'Yet', TeSelle writes, collecting these genres under the rubric 'confession':

> the interesting feature of the Christian confession that avoids concentration on the self is a self-portrait more compelling than the self-exalting variety. Surely one reason for this apparent contradiction is that the mystery of the self, like all mystery, is visible only indirectly, through the encounters of the self with the world. It is the vocationally-oriented autobiographies, those that point away from a direct, inward perception of the self to what drives the self, drives it concretely in the world, which are most revealing of the self.[4]

While referring specifically to Christian confessions (those of Paul, Augustine, and John Woolman), TeSelle's remarks seem equally descriptive of the book of Jeremiah. Where she says 'Christian', we can read 'Jeremianic' and recognize the Hebrew parentage:

> The peculiarity of the Christian confession is the denial of the self, its hiddenness in and for the vocation, the calling to allow the story of the self to be used as an indirect route of insight for others. It eventuates, however, in a vivid self-portrayal, in an individuality that is not that of an 'interesting Personality' but of someone molded by God...[5]

I want to say of the book of Jeremiah that it too intends its representation of the prophetic self 'be used as an indirect route of insight for others' and that it eventuates in the rendering of a persona 'molded by God'. Indeed, this is precisely what is implied by the concept 'paradigm'.

The Portrait of a Paradigm: Jeremiah and the Reader

It inevitably diminishes the book's identity description to try to abstract from it the persona's salient features. Yet that is what we need to do if only to show what the description sees as paradigmatic. As already noted, the prophet's speech deals with matters 'at the inmost center of personal existence'. Through it he expresses and performs 'praise, sorrow, contrition, anguish, hope, and joy'. But the matter is more complex, for we have seen that his praise can also include, and qualify, reproach, that his joy can exist side-by-side with a near-despair, and that his anguish consists of grief, fear, and anger compounded. Moreover, these smaller elements proved complex also: Jeremiah grieves, for example, for himself over against both God and people; he grieves for and with his people over against God; and he grieves with God over his people. Similarly, he fears for himself and for and with the people—and this while sharing God's anger toward the people, or even while being angry at God. Such emotional complexity is of course profoundly realistic, and typically human. And by being oriented at every point to God and his action it can be theologically paradigmatic.

Beyond these first-order emotion traits, the book characterizes the prophet as wise, obedient, trusting, if also at times faint-hearted and in need of admonishment. Indeed, and what may be more important than any catalogue of qualities, it shows him in the process of embodying extraordinary tensions: Jeremiah is depicted in, and defined by, struggle. This reflects a larger strategy of the text, for the process of self-constitution always involves antagonists, human and divine. And the nature of the struggle counts. Through the conflict with his antagonists, Jeremiah is depicted struggling to obey and to persist obediently in the struggle. Finally, and by no means unrelated to the struggle, Jeremiah is also depicted as the recipient of divine blessing and promise.

It is this larger strategy of the text that results in the rendering of the prophet as a paradigm. That is, in the final shape of the book, by virtue of the arrangement of its materials, of the contexts created for his words, the struggling Jeremiah is shown as the particular instantiation of a type, and in such a way as to be revelatory. He becomes who he is by word, deed, and what he suffers, and both the process of the becoming and the product at given points along the way signify and interpret things beyond himself. It was said that Jeremiah's life interprets his message. He is a metaphor for God's

6. Summary & Hermeneutical Reflections 171

word. Through him we see into God's pathos and purpose and into the plight and destiny of the people. Jeremiah becomes the data board on which is played out the economy of judgment and salvation.

What more might it mean to speak of Jeremiah as a paradigm, or of the book's intention to render him so? Recent work in the philosophy of science suggests some rough analogies.[6] Paradigms in science are *standard* cases of scientific practice, e.g. Newton's *Principia* or Einstein's *General Theory*, through which the student learns the prevailing theories and methods of the field. In their fact-finding and theorizing capacities, these standard cases also seek to describe reality. By studying them, the student hopes to learn what in some measure the world is like. In this respect the Jeremianic paradigm is similar: like the scientific paradigm, it serves as a metaphor for how things are.

In addition, the scientific paradigm, as a model of methods, serves as a norm for how science is done, for what constitutes good procedure. Similarly, Jeremiah functions as an example, a model for imitation by believers who follow him. This suggests a third connection: in science a shared paradigm creates a professional community with common assumptions, interests, and channels of communication; so the Jeremianic paradigm, while itself partly the product of a community of faith, can reshape that community and become a means for its sustenance and perpetuation.

There are of course differences between my use of 'paradigm' and the more technical use in the philosophy of science. Yet one thing the analogies show is that a didactic or pedagogical (or again, revelatory) intent is analytic in the concept. Something is presented as a paradigm for the purpose of instructing students and inducing insight. This might be put more strongly for religious, biblical paradigms: they instruct and induce insight in order to transform.

A literature that puts forward a paradigm with such intent is an especially reader-oriented sort. This fact accentuates a variety of reader-related issues significant for hermeneutics, and here some of the considerations concerning the book of Jeremiah as imaginative and (auto)-biographical literature begin to converge. TeSelle spoke of autobiography functioning as 'an indirect route of insight for others'. This corresponds with her observation that just as 'the very process of writing the [autobiographical] work changes the author—Montaigne says, "I have not made my book more than my book has made me"—

[so] the reader of a good autobiography might also say that it has, in some sense, "made" him or her also'.[7] Similarly, one can say of imaginative literature that it 'allows an intimacy with another point of view, another way of construing the world',[8] or that, in Henry James's words, it gives the reader 'the sense of having lived another life'[9]—although a purely fictive work makes no demands on the reader's beliefs and allows him a certain distance from the ideas expressed in it. In an imaginative *religious* work, however, which either assumes or seeks to create a context of faith, the paradigm is presented in a drama within which the believer is requested to see him/herself as a participant. Hence, the truth-telling of scripture, in the words of one scholar,

> occurs not by a 'willing suspension of disbelief', but by an imaginative engagement with the structure, patterns, imagery, and characters of the literature. In this way the believer is educated to new attitudes, beliefs, emotions, and even desires ... By seeing sin magnified and focussed in particular characters, or by beholding faithfulness and obedience in the extreme the Christian [and/or Jewish] reader is instructed, by imaginative entertainment of the stories, to imagine for himself new desires, to find an order for his existence, 'the opposite of chaos in chaos'.[10]

The concern here is not with reader effects that are only idiosyncratically related to the text. Rather, it is with the reading process and the responses that belong to the logic of the literature *qua* work, i.e. as something written *and read*;[11] the responses are part of, and help establish, the work's meaning. This agrees not only with the Wittgensteinians who argue that meaning is use, but with scholars in the phenomenology of reading.[12] The working hypothesis here has been that meaning does not in any definitive fashion reside *in* the text itself, but issues from the dynamic interaction of text and reader and belongs to the realm of reader experience.

This is why I have so often spoken of charting the reading process (and have laid out my own reading in such detail), because that is where meaning takes place. This is to acknowledge that reader subjectivity is fundamental to meaning-making. It is not to say, however, that interpretation is arbitrary and *purely* subjective, for it must be governed by intersubjective norms and guided and regulated by the textual signs and sequences rooted in those norms. In the words of a leading critic of the field, Wolfgang Iser, 'The text mobilizes the subjective knowledge present in all kinds of readers and

6. Summary & Hermeneutical Reflections 173

directs it to one particular end. However varied this knowledge may be, the reader's subjective contribution is controlled by the given framework.'[13] One may think of the text as a blueprint from which the reader constructs the edifice of meaning, or of the reader as a processing agent who must re-assemble the data of the text to get its sense. In any case the text cannot simply hand over raw meaning to its readers, nor can its readers make of the text anything they want.

By Iser's view the very rudiments of reading involve the imagination, for every text is filled, even at the level of syntax, with gaps that must be bridged if we are to make sense of it. As we read we must forge equivalences across the blanks so as to achieve at least a modicum of consistency. Meanwhile we are constantly seeking to establish criteria of significance. Even with the simplest texts we engage in a *Gestalt*-forming process; as the blanks impede textual coherence, they actually transform themselves into stimuli for complex and varied acts of image-building and ideation. It follows that the more difficult the text, the greater the degree of requisite imagination, or reader participation. And the greater our input, the more we are 'caught up in the very thing we are producing'. The result is inevitable: 'Through the experience of the text, something happens to our own store of experience'.[17] We are affected, and, in some measure, we are changed.

Now, in the book of Jeremiah the idea of the paradigm is a *Gestalt* whose formation was stimulated, and regulated, by the blanks in the text, namely the ambiguities, sudden shifts in perspective, and striking juxtapositions which we so often observed in and around the prophet's speech. Depending on how well the blanks work, we might reasonably expect the book's potential for reader-transformation to be high, since both the reading process itself and its product (the *Gestalt* of the paradigm) move toward that end. The process, for instance, exercises and trains the imagination: By assembling the persona one may become conversant with a theater of experience hitherto unknown, perhaps having to imagine a kind of suffering and hope never imagined before. At the same time, the paradigm instructs, not of course by laying out a set of rules as dogma and doctrine, but by presenting a ruled and ordered life that summons the reader to assemble him or herself analogously. Thus, reconstituting the picture of a self-in-progress, the reader may find how it is he constitutes himself—and how he might. In learning how Jeremiah uses the language of the heart, one learns what prayer is—and perhaps how to pray. And in identifying the dimensions of the prophet's struggle, one gains a new command of the concept 'obedience'—and maybe begins a struggle to obey. All this is well within the book's logic as a literary work.

What happens when the literary work is seen as scripture? Clearly, the logic, the grammar, of the reading shifts. When the *Gestalt* is formed in the context of faith and the paradigm is taken as word of God, then the subjunctive mood and the adverbs of possibility above shift toward the indicative and imperative. This of course means that the quality of the reader's involvement also shifts. Now the paradigm, what as metaphor it reveals and what as model it summons one to imitate, is acknowledged at the outset as in some deep sense true. The text, instead of merely proposing possible ways of construing world and self and beyond simply entertaining the reader with a sense of 'having lived another life', is now viewed as having a claim upon oneself. Its ultimate meaning, what it finally intends, is something that is only completed in the reader's living. How s/he responds to the summons and pursues the intended transformation become part of the work's scope. In fact, that response becomes one criterion for evaluating what the text is and does, what it ultimately means. The transformed life of a competent reader becomes a guide to interpretation.

There is of course much more to be said about reading Jeremiah. Indeed, it is an obvious implication of the hermeneutic sketched in these pages that no reading is final. This one, like any other, is at best only partial, shaped (and misshaped) by the dialogue with earlier readings and limited by the restricted perspective and competences of this particular reader. All the more reason, then, that the reading process itself be further explored. For this study will be a success if it has shown that, in biblical studies as in the religious life, there are two relevant questions: 'What is written in the Law? How do you read?'

NOTES

Notes to Chapter One

1. E.g. Brevard S. Childs, *Introduction to the Old Testament as Scripture* (Philadelphia: Fortress, 1979), p. 348; Otto Eissfeldt, *The Old Testament: An Introduction*, trans. Peter R. Ackroyd (New York: Harper and Row, 1965), pp. 346-47; J. Alberto Soggin, *Introduction to the Old Testament*, trans. John Bowden (Philadelphia: Westminster, 1976), p. 282.
2. Gerhard von Rad, *Old Testament Theology* (hereafter *OTT*), trans. D.M.G. Stalker, II (New York: Harper and Row, 1965), pp. 197, 201.
3. Walther Eichrodt, *Theology of the Old Testament*, trans. J.A. Baker, II (Philadelphia: Westminster, 1967), p. 248.
4. Hans Frei, *The Eclipse of Biblical Narrative* (New Haven: Yale University Press, 1974), pp. 1-50. On 'explicative sense' vs. meaning as reference, see especially pp. 18, 24, 41 and 87.
5. Besides the examples discussed below, see also T.C. Gordon, *The Rebel Prophet: Studies in the Personality of Jeremiah* (New York: Harper & Brothers, 1932); J.P. Hyatt, *Jeremiah, Prophet of Courage and Hope* (New York: Abingdon, 1958); W.F. Lofthouse, *Jeremiah and the New Covenant* (London: SCM, 1925); H.W. Robinson, *The Cross of Jeremiah* (London: SCM, 1925); George Adam Smith, *The Book of Jeremiah*, 4th edn (New York: Harper & Brothers, 1929); Paul Volz, *Der Prophet Jeremia* (Tübingen: J.C.B. Mohr [Paul Siebeck], 1918); and A.C. Welch, *Jeremiah: His Time and Work* (London: OUP, 1928)—among many others.
6. Joseph W. Reed, Jr, *English Biography in the Early Nineteenth Century* (New Haven: Yale University Press, 1966), p. vii.
7. Rudolf Kittel, *Great Men and Movements in Israel*, trans. Charlotte A. Knoch and C.D. Wright (New York: MacMillan, 1929), p. 349.
8. Kittel, p. 350.
9. Julius A. Bewer, Foreword, *Personalities of the Old Testament*, by Fleming James (New York: Charles Scribner's Sons, 1939), pp. vii-viii.
10. Bewer, p. viii.
11. James, *Personalities*, pp. 300-301.
12. See, for instance, Burke O. Long, 'Prophetic Authority as Social Reality' in *Canon and Authority*, ed. Burke O. Long and George W. Coats (Philadelphia: Fortress, 1977), p. 11.
13. John Skinner, *Prophecy and Religion* (Cambridge: CUP, 1930), p. 30.

14. Long, p. 11.
15. Skinner, pp. 33-34.
16. For example, the text says nothing of Jeremiah's familiarity with Hosea, does not even hint at this in ch. 1. And it is not the call of the 'times' to which Jeremiah awakens; it is the call of God. Further, the text does not portray Jeremiah as having a 'foreboding' of doom, or a 'conviction that all is not well between Israel and Yahweh', as if this knowledge were a matter of the man's sensitive theo-political intuition or had come to him through a process of inference and deduction. Rather, according to the *text*, the knowledge comes immediately from God who tells Jeremiah directly of the nation's wickedness and coming doom. Finally, nowhere, in my opinion, is the text concerned to show Jeremiah as 'a great exponent of individual and universal religion'.
17. Skinner, p. 8.
18. Skinner, pp. 14-15.
19. Skinner, pp. 15-16.
20. Jonathan Culler, *Structuralist Poetics* (Ithaca: Cornell University Press, 1975), p. 11.
21. Culler, p. 12. For more on the diachronic-synchronic distinction in linguistics, see Culler, *Ferdinand de Saussure* (New York: Penguin Books, 1976), pp. 29-42; John Lyons, *Introduction to Theoretical Linguistics* (Cambridge: CUP, 1968), pp. 45-50; and Robert Scholes, *Structuralism in Literature* (New Haven: Yale University Press, 1974), p. 17.
22. James Barr, *Comparative Philology and the Text of the Old Testament* (Oxford: Clarendon, 1968), p. 90.
23. See Culler, *Structuralist Poetics*, Chapter 5 'Linguistic Metaphors in Criticism', pp. 96-109.
24. It is by no means implied here that the world of the text has no connections or areas of overlap with the real world, however 'real' is to be conceived. The trick is in recognizing how the text itself regulates the way the connections occur, function, and are to be interpreted.
25. Perhaps not everyone would agree that the Bible should be viewed as a literary work and a functional whole. I do not say that it *must* be, only that, particularly for the purposes of doing theology for Synagogue or Church, it is appropriate to so view it, and in any case that it *can* be so viewed and is a fit object of study as such. Moreover, I feel it can be so viewed without sacrificing intellect, lapsing into dogmatic biblicism, or bracketing off meaning.
26. The scholarly output is too vast to cite *in toto*. The journal *Semeia*, devoted mainly to structural analysis, is certainly evidence of the recent trend. T.R. Henn's *The Bible as Literature* (New York: OUP, 1970) gave the movement, at least in one of its forms, its name. Such scholars as James Ackerman, Robert Alter, J.P. Fokkelman, Edwin Good, David Gunn, Michael Fishbane, David Robertson, and many others continue to make

significant contributions to this approach. For this writer, a particularly formative influence was Luis Alonso Schökel's *The Inspired Word: Scripture in the Light of Language and Literature* (New York: Herder and Herder, 1965) which articulated a theological hermeneutic on the basis of the New Criticism.

27. The reading process, or phenomenology of reading, is a subject of intense inquiry in the fields of aesthetics and literary theory. Witness the following, all within the past decade: David Bleich, *Subjective Criticism* (Baltimore: John Hopkins University Press, 1978); Umberto Eco, *The Role of the Reader* (Bloomington: Indiana University Press, 1979); Stanley Fish, *Is There a Text in This Class? The Authority of Interpretive Communities* (Cambridge: Harvard University Press, 1980); Roman Ingarden, *The Cognition of the Literary Work of Art*, trans. Ruth Ann Crowley and Kenneth R. Olson (Evanston: Northwestern University Press, 1973); and Barbara Jordan, *The Critical Difference: Essays in the Contemporary Rhetoric of Reading* (Baltimore: John Hopkins University Press, 1980). For a comprehensive, annotated bibliography, see Jonathan Culler's *On Deconstruction: Theory and Criticism after Structuralism* (Ithaca, New York: Cornell University Press, 1982), pp. 281-302.

Especially useful in the preparation of this essay have been Culler's *Structuralist Poetics*, Chapter 6 'Literary Competence', pp. 113-30; Wolfgang Iser's *The Implied Reader* (Baltimore: John Hopkins University Press, 1974); and finally Iser's *The Act of Reading* (Baltimore: John Hopkins University Press, 1978), which will come into play in the last chapter.

28. Sean E. McEvenue's recent essay, 'The Old Testament, Scripture or Theology?', in *Interpretation* 35 (1981), pp. 229-42, offers a quite different view from the one taken here, although, as the first sentence of the following quotation would indicate, our differences are not absolute:

> If one says that the literary work has its own meaning apart from authorial intention, and if this means that the Bible should be interpreted on the basis of textual data rather than on the basis of hypotheses about an author's intention as known from independent sources, then I will agree. If it means that the text may have resonances which go beyond what the author himself fully grasped, then I will assent to that view cautiously, particularly in the case of poetic writing where an author chooses intuitively between expressions without being able to specify the exact grounds of many of his choices. (p. 238)

It is the second sentence where the problem emerges, for it frequently happens that a text has resonances that go beyond not only what the author fully grasped but what he ever imagined. For what is at least as significant in poetry as the intuitive choice-making by the author is the sheer fecundity of language, its capacity to keep on meaning, i.e. to keep on revealing new aspects of reality, to continue generating fresh meanings as competent readers bring to the text distinctive contexts into which the text, lo and behold, still speaks. This is a fact about language that always seems to surface when people try to describe what is great about great literature. Here also is where the New-Critical emphasis on the autonomy of the poem and the Heideggerian motto that 'language speaks' were on the mark.

But McEvenue continues:

> If it means that a published text becomes community property and may be given new meanings by the community as it is read in different contexts, I will agree only on the understanding that the new meanings will not be meanings of the text but rather meanings of the community...
>
> If, through the centuries, theologians have concluded to truths which go beyond the New Testament understanding by arguing on the basis of both New Testament and Old Testament texts, such truths are not a meaning of Scripture or a meaning *in* Scripture, but truely [sic] a meaning *beyond* Scripture. (pp. 238-39)

The linguistic and psychological fact is that *all* meanings are 'given' to the text by its readers, for 'meaning' is a reader-dependent concept. The text itself has no meaning; in a very important sense, meaning is *always* 'beyond' it. (Now, the concept 'Scripture', unlike 'text', already includes analytically the notion of a readership, of having been and being read, namely by the communities who regard the biblical text as somehow normative for faith and practice. Thus, to speak of 'meaning in Scripture' is to refer to the meaning(s) that take(s) place in the process of a special kind of reading.)

If one contests that texts *do* have meanings *in* them on the evidence of cases whose meaning is so obvious and self-evident that all competent readers would have to agree upon it, I would respond that indeed such cases exist, and in vast quantity. But what makes their meaning seem self-evident is not that it is *in* the text but that the language is sufficiently denotative to so channel the reading process as to preclude competent language users' formulating different meanings (see Iser, *The Act of Reading*, p. 185), or that the interests and uses attendant upon the readers' reading of the text and the conventions and norms employed are shared among these readers so as to define (and delimit) in advance what the terms 'all' and 'competent' mean (Fish, *Is There a Text in this Class?, passim*).

If one takes recourse to E.D. Hirsch (*Validity in Interpretation* [New Haven: Yale University Press, 1967], p. 8) by insisting that what I call 'meaning' is really 'significance', I respond by saying that that is a highly artificial distinction with little connection to the way its terms work in ordinary discourse. It seems to be in fact a purely theoretical construction, for more often than not the terms are actually used synonymously, even in literary criticism. For instance, when the teacher asks the student what *significance* there is in the repetition of a certain motif, it would be obvious to all that the student has missed the point if he begins to describe his life-relationship with the text, say, by telling how the motif has changed his attitude toward his mother. At an advanced stage of discussing the text's 'significance', such an answer might well be appropriate, depending on the text, but then again one can just as easily say that it is the text's performative 'meaning' that is here being more fully probed. (On 'performative language', a concept that will play an important role in Chapters 4 and 5, see J.L. Austin, *How To Do Things with Words*, 2nd edn [Cambridge: Harvard University Press, 1975] and Donald Evans, *The Logic of Self-Involvement* [London: SCM, 1963], pp. 27-78.)

29. See William K. Wimsatt and Monroe C. Beardsley, 'The Intentional Fallacy', in Wimsatt's *The Verbal Icon* (University Press of Kentucky, 1954), pp. 3-18.

30. See above, n. 28.

31. Again, not everyone believes that the parts of a composite text, or an anthology, are mutually conditioning. E.g. McEvenue: 'But still, for the most part, the canon is no more than an anthology of inspired books, linked for the most part without altering the meaning of the individual books' (p. 239). In this matter the wisdom of T.S. Eliot, one of the more competent readers of our era, seems too compelling to ignore:

> ... [W]hat happens when a new work of art is created is something that happens simultaneously to all the works of art which preceded it. The existing monuments form an ideal order among themselves, which is modified by the introduction of the new ... work of art among them. The existing order is complete before the new work arrives; for order to persist after the supervention of novelty, the *whole* existing order must be, if ever so slightly, altered; and so the relations, proportions, values of each work of art toward the whole are adjusted; and this is conformity between the old and the new. ('Tradition and Individual Talent' in *Selected Essays, 1917-1932* [New York: Harcourt, Brace and Company, 1932], p. 5.)

If this can be so for the whole corpus of Western literature, it must hold all the more for the biblical canon.

32. On these and other issues related to the concept 'intention', see G.E.M. Anscombe, *Intentions* (Ithaca: Cornell University Press, 1963) and Stanley Cavell, 'A Matter of Meaning It', in his *Must We Mean What We Say?* (Cambridge: CUP, 1969), pp. 213-37.

33. Amelie O. Rorty ('A Literary Postscript: Characters, Persons, Selves, Individuals', in *The Identities of Persons* [Berkeley: University of California Press, 1976], pp. 301-23) has shown that the concept 'self' pertains to just one aspect of personhood and coexists in some tension with others. Some care must be taken in its use.

34. Sigmund Mowinckel, *Zur Komposition des Buches Jeremia* (Kristiania: Jacob Dybwad, 1914), pp. 25-26.

35. Baltzer, *Die Biographie der Propheten* (Neukirchen-Vluyn: Neukirchener Verlag, 1975). For the summary and discussion that follows, cf. pp. 19-38, except where otherwise noted.

Martin Kessler's *A Prophetic Biography: A Form Critical Study of*

Jeremiah (Diss. Brandeis 1965 [Ann Arbor: University Microfilms, Inc., 1967]) does not analyze the concept 'biography', but only uses the word 'for the sake of convenience' (p. 94, n. 1).

36. See Robert R. Wilson, 'Form-Critical Investigation of the Prophetic Literature: The Present Situation', in *SBL Seminar Papers*, I (1973), pp. 100-27. By Wilson's analysis, the quest for a basic speech form has made little progress and must not be allowed to 'prevent us from seeing the diversity of the literature' (p. 120). While Baltzer's effort is not precisely that of identifying the basic prophetic *speech* form (in the sense of an oracular pattern), in my opinion Wilson's reflections still apply.

37. Baltzer, pp. 29-71.

38. Baltzer, p. 194.

39. Some of the objections to the thesis should be stated. First, the proposed model of the prophet as vizier seems inadequate. It is questionable whether the place of the vizier in the Egyptian state was at all analogous to that of the prophet(s) in Israel, since the unanimity with which the institution was honored, or at least the authority and formality by which it was sanctioned, in the former were scarcely paralleled in the latter. Accordingly, the model is not an especially apt one by which to evaluate the opposition to the prophets that is so richly attested by the biblical literature. Relatedly, Baltzer treats Israel's prophetic tradition as if it were singular and monolithic—a uniform pattern of ideas, language, behavior, and expectations shared by one and all throughout the society. It might have helped if he had asked about the tradition's tradents, for this could have led to a more precise picture of the variety of traditions, their scope and place in the society and their course down through Israel's history. It would certainly have made a change in the odd picture Baltzer permits of an Institution of One, the lone prophet without visible support group and with hardly ever a rival.

Second, there is a systematic vagueness built into the use of 'genre'. Baltzer appears to proceed with an implicit reliance on the form-critical method to guarantee a consistent standard of what a genre is, something the method does not, probably cannot, do. Just what *does* constitute genre? Is it fixity of form? formulaic language? a bundle of motifs? If the last, must the motifs occur regularly in an ordered configuration, or are they simply building blocks that can be arranged in any order at all? And in this case, how many are required from one instance to the next to maintain the genre's identity? Or is genre constituted by a connection (original or otherwise) to a particular socio-historical setting, to a particular group, or to a recurrent and universal human situation? Or may it be constituted by a particular concern (occupation of mind) or dominant purpose? And if any several or all of these are or can be constitutive factors, then what is the hierarchy of their relations? To the extent that Baltzer actually addresses the point—as in the conclusion when he says, 'In spite of changes in content, the form like the themes of the biographies remains astonishingly constant from the early period beyond the OT canon itself' (p. 194)—the facts belie him. By my reading nothing appeared more fluid than the form. Not only did the texts show numerous omissions and rearrangements of the *Gattung*'s parts, often the parts had virtually to be fabricated, so far removed was the actual material of the texts from the categories in which it was expected to fit. (See, for example, his treatment of Elijah's theophany at Horeb as an 'installation report', in particular the identification of the *Zuständigkeitsbereich* [p. 96]; or his handling of the 'audience' part of the *Gattung* in the Elisha-Elijah story of 2 Kgs 2.9-12 [pp. 99-102]; or his reading of 1 Kgs 3.11-12 as an adaptation of the *Einsetzungswort* [p. 89]; etc.) Generally speaking, I feel that the variety of ways in which the term 'genre' is used in both form-critical and ordinary discourse does not permit the technical precision with which we often seek to invest it.

Finally, Baltzer leaves it unclear by whom the ideal biographies were to be heard and read. If one were to go by what the *Gattung* is supposedly *about*, which is more an office than a man, i.e. prophecy itself, one would be inclined to think that the biographies were originally intended for prophets themselves and their apprentices. This is a far more restricted audience than would seem to be intended for the materials in their present form. The position to be argued in this essay is that Jeremiah's life—i.e. his words spoken and deeds done in the performance of the function for which he was specifically commissioned by God—was felt by the makers of his book to be significant for all Yhwh worshippers, present and future, and not simply for a small professional caste.

40. For his analysis of Jeremiah, see Baltzer, pp. 112-28.

41. Baltzer, p. 20.

42. See for example Marston Balch, *Modern Short Biographies and Autobiographies* (New York: Harcourt, Brace and Company, 1935), p. 3; and Harold Nicolson, *The Development of English Biography* (New York: Harcourt, Brace and Company, 1928), p. 36. As the dates might suggest, there is a noticeable overlap between the 'man-in-himself' school of biography and the 'life and times' genre of Jeremiah scholarship.

Far more chaste in claim and prescription than the examples above are the essays in *Telling Lives: The Biographer's Art*, ed. Marc Pachter (Washington, D.C.: New Republic Books, 1979).

43. In the contemporary situation biographies and autobiographies are recognized as works of literary and aesthetic conception and design as much as they are works of history. Accordingly, they are often expected to answer to the standards of both. See Reed, pp. 154-66; and Pachter, *passim*.

44. Moses Hadas and Morton Smith, *Heroes and Gods: Spiritual Biographies in Antiquity* (Freeport, N.Y.: Books for Libraries Press, 1965), p. 4.

45. The inextricable relation between character and action is the point of Henry James's famous remark, 'What is character but the determination of incident? What is incident but the illustration of character?' ('The Art of

Fiction', in *The Art of Fiction and Other Essays* [New York: OUP, 1948], p. 13; originally in *Partial Portraits* [New York: MacMillan, 1888].)

In certain circumstances this relation could be stated more strongly by saying that incident not only illustrates character but *forms* it. Thus, E.M. Forster hit the mark exactly: 'Incident springs out of character, and having occurred it alters that character. People and events are closely connected...' (*Aspects of the Novel* [New York: Harcourt, Brace, and World, 1927], p. 90). See also Hans Frei, *The Identity of Jesus Christ* (Philadelphia: Fortress, 1975), p. 88. The point is extremely important in assessing the depictive force of Jeremiah's speech, as our Chapters 3-5 will attempt to demonstrate.

46. See Wittgenstein, *Tractatus Logico-Philosophicus*, trans. D.F. Pears and B.F. McGuinness (London: Routledge & Kegan Paul, 1961), pp. 57-58.

47. Kessler, p. 391.

48. Modern biographers are sometimes loath to admit as much. Geoffrey Wolff, for example, writes that in composing a recent biography he 'never calculated Crosby's confessions... to incline toward the aphoristic, to build toward some generalizing trope, some "thesis"... It has been my experience as a reader that a strategy of connection and generalization is bound to fail' ('Minor Lives', in *Telling Lives*, p. 62). However, there is a difference between explicit attempts to state a subject's typicality (i.e. a 'strategy of connection and generalization') and the fact that one's interest in the subject and motivation for writing his life is grounded in his typicality, his connectedness in all his particularity with other human experience. Ultimately, Wolff seems to agree:

> So... one hopes that one's case will touch others. But how to connect? Not by calculation, I think, not by the assumption that in the pain of my toothache, or my father's, or Harry Crosby's, I have discovered a 'universal condition of consciousness'. One may merely know that no one is alone and hope that a singular story, as every true story is singular, will resonate, touch a major chord. (p. 72)

49. See Erik Erikson, *Young Man Luther* (New York: W.W. Norton & Company, 1958). Here a psycho-biography, which one may expect to probe the subject's interiority, his essential or nuclear self, can only do so by looking at the subject in a complex web of social roles and interrelationships.

50. Hermann Gunkel, 'Fundamental Problems of Hebrew Literary History', in *What Remains of the Old Testament? and Other Essays*, trans. A.K. Dallas (New York: MacMillan, 1928), pp. 59-60. On the next page Gunkel accentuates the dichotomy with an inappropriate application of the term 'primitive' to early Israel's thought world. By contrast, see W.F. Albright's 'The Nature and Evolution of Primitive Religion', in *From the Stone Age to Christianity*, 2nd edn (Garden City, N.Y.: Doubleday, 1957), pp. 168-78. (The use of 'primitive' on p. 23 below is of a quite different order from Gunkel's.)

51. Klaus Koch, *The Growth of the Biblical Tradition*, trans. S.M. Cupitt from the 2nd German edn (New York: Charles Scribner's Sons, 1969), p. 11.

52. Von Rad, *OTT*, II, p. 77.
53. On the different uses of 'I', see the discussion in n. 12 of Chapter 2 below, as well as the sections in Wittgenstein's *Philosophical Investigations* cited in that same note.
54. It becomes less clear the more form-critical research continues to reveal a lack of fixity among genres and a high degree of complexity, variability, and mixture in biblical literary types. On some specific problems with the form-critical analysis of genres in Jeremiah, see Jack R. Lundbom, *Jeremiah: A Study in Ancient Hebrew Rhetoric* (SBLDS 18; Missoula, Montana: Scholars Press, 1975), pp. 9-13.

For a more comprehensive (and radically pessimistic) assessment of form-criticism's treatment of genre, see Rolf Knierim, 'Old Testament Form Criticism Reconsidered', *Interpretation* 27 (1973), pp. 435-68.

Notes to Chapter Two

1. Hans Walter Wolff, *Anthropology of the Old Testament*, trans. Margaret Kohl (Philadelphia: Fortress, 1974), p. 40.
2. James Barr, *The Semantics of Biblical Language* (London: OUP, 1961), p. 22.
3. Barr, p. 23.
4. Johannes Pedersen, *Israel: Its Life and Culture*, trans. Aslang Moller, I (London: OUP, 1926), p. 110.
5. Pedersen, p. 102.
6. This is the way Paul Holmer chooses to speak of metaphor in his unpublished essay 'The Human Heart—the Logic of a Metaphor', pp. 10-18. The advantage of this sort of definition is that it generates great insight into the workings of metaphor without the sort of theorizing about the relation between literal and metaphorical senses that too often results in a distortion and flattens out the inscrutability of that relation in particular cases. 'Heart' is one such case.
7. H. Wheeler Robinson, *The Christian Doctrine of Man* (Edinburgh: T. & T. Clark, 1911); *Inspiration and Revelation in the Old Testament* (Oxford: Clarendon, 1946); *Corporate Personality in Ancient Israel* (Philadelphia: Fortress, 1964).
8. L.H. Brockington, 'The Hebrew Conception of Personality in Relation to the Knowledge of God', *JTS* 47 (1946), pp. 1-11.
9. Robinson, *Inspiration*, p. 70.
10. Robinson, *Inspiration*, p. 71.
11. Robinson, *Inspiration*, pp. 71, 82. See especially Brockington, p. 3. In addition to the critique given here, see the criticisms by J.W. Rogerson in

Anthropology and the Old Testament (Atlanta: John Knox, 1978), pp. 55-56, 58-59.

12. Discussion and illustrations of such language are offered by Paul Holmer in his essay 'Wittgenstein and the Self' in *Essays on Kierkegaard and Wittgenstein: On Understanding the Self*, ed. Richard H. Bell and Ronald E. Hustwit (Wooster, Ohio: The College of Wooster, 1978), pp. 10-31. One such illustration is the expression 'I am overjoyed' (p. 25). (An example to be considered subsequently is Jeremiah's cry in 4.19, 'My anguish, my anguish! I writhe in pain!')

Actually, my term 'referential' can be misleading here, since the 'I' in these examples does not refer to, name, or identify something, such as a 'something without a body, the real and immaterial ego, within my body' (Holmer, p. 20), or identify someone in order to avoid a mistaken association of the predicate with someone else (p. 21). The 'I' in 'I am overjoyed' thus has a different logic from that of a genuinely referential 'I' as in 'I have twelve toes' (p. 25). The meaning of the former is not disclosed by uncovering a thing to which it refers but rather resides in (one could even say 'is'—see Wittgenstein, *Philosophical Investigations* [New York: MacMillan, 1968], section 138) its responsible use, resides in the speaker's proper command of it. Such command comes in and with the speaker's *having* joy, his *being* joyful, his exercise of this particular and uniquely human capacity. (For the notion that 'being' states, like sensations and emotions, and their natural expression are an ingredient or constitutive part of the human organism, see John Cook, 'Human Beings', in *Studies in the Philosophy of Wittgenstein*, ed. Peter Winch [London: Routledge & Kegan Paul, 1969], pp. 117-51.) Since this command can come only in *one's own* having, being, and exercising—and not by inference from another's experience or even by inference from an experience to its as yet unidentified owner (Holmer, p. 23)—the use of this sort of 'I' is non-derivative. It cannot be reasoned 'to', i.e. established and justified philosophically, for that is a different language game, one with different rules. Rather, this use of 'I' has a primitive or primary status, attaining its intelligibility from the standard practices and everyday activities that make up one's life (p. 26).

The same point is registered by Norman Malcolm ('Wittgenstein's *Philosophical Investigations*', in *Wittgenstein: The Philosophical Investigations*, ed. George Pitcher [Notre Dame/London: University of Notre Dame Press, 1966], p. 89) when he says, 'The use of first-person sensation-sentences is governed by *no* paradigm'. If the point holds, then the picture of the concept 'self' as emerging in the history of various peoples is out of place. The significant 'history' that takes place is the particular life-history of the individual language user. It might be added that the biological axiom 'ontogeny recapitulates philogeny' does not automatically hold true in linguistics.

13. Aubrey R. Johnson, *The Vitality of the Individual in the Thought of*

Ancient Israel (Cardiff: University of Wales Press, 1964), pp. 81-82, n. 5.
14. Brockington, p. 3.
15. Brockington, p. 1. See also Robinson, *Inspiration*, pp. 71-72, and *Doctrine*, pp. 11-12, 23-24.
16. Robinson, *Doctrine*, pp. 3-7 (*et passim*).
17. Robinson, *Doctrine*, pp. 23-24.
18. Johnson, pp. 37, 39-40, 42, 44n., 45, 49-52, 60-61, 63-67, 71-74, 80-82. Johnson specifically directs many of these observations on the use of synecdoche toward refuting the diffusion-of-consciousness theory.
19. Johnson, p. 50 (emphasis added). It should be noted that if what was said about metaphor in n. 6 is correct, then such use of 'heart' may be unavoidable, not just picturesque and graphic. On the general issue of the cognitive indispensability of metaphor, see Philip Wheelwright, *Metaphor and Reality* (Bloomington: Indiana University Press, 1962), and Sallie TeSelle, *Speaking in Parables: A Study in Metaphor and Theology* (Philadelphia: Fortress, 1975), especially Chapter 3, 'Metaphor: The Heart of the Matter', pp. 43-65.
20. Johnson, p. 81. One should qualify Johnson's identification of the use of *'ănî* or *'ănōkî* with the 'ego or unit of consciousness' in light of the remarks in n. 12 on the non-referential employment of 'I'.
21. Robinson, *Doctrine*, pp. 21-22.
22. Ian G. Barbour, *Myths, Models, and Paradigms: A Comparative Study in Science and Religion* (New York: Harper & Row, 1974). See especially Chapter 3, 'Models in Science', pp. 29-48.
23. See Frederick Ferré, *Language, Logic and God* (London: Harper Torchbooks, 1969), Chapter 3, 'The Limits of Verificational Analysis', pp. 42-57, where he attacks a tendentious delimitation of the term 'fact'.
24. Wheelwright, pp. 41-42.
25. Holmer, 'The Human Heart', pp. 21-22.
26. The lack of any such requirement is established quite explicitly in the Holmer quotation referred to above. The case of 'heart' is thus analogous to that of the non-referential use of 'I', which cannot be justified philosophically but only in the context (the language game) of people exercising various capacities. (See above, n. 12.)

For additional elucidation of the point, consider the following remark, also by Holmer:

> Furthermore, there is no way to project what such a science would look like, when the very facts we wish to generalize about are not open to that disinterested and non-contextual study [one might] propose. On the contrary, like the judgment of color depending upon those who are normal to make the judgment (who are the makers of the game, whereby the rules are set up), so the judgment of who is contrite, glad, angry, and dishonest [i.e. the judgment of the nature of people's hearts] involves, also, criteria that are only available to those who know in virtue of capacities... The

metaphor 'heart', as a name for personality qualification, covers a lot of interlocking capacities. ('The Human Heart', p. 23.)

27. Owen Barfield, 'The Meaning of the Word "Literal"', in *Metaphor and Symbol* (Proceedings of the Twelfth Symposium of the Colston Research Society), ed. L.C. Knights and Basil Cottle (London: Butterworths, 1960), pp. 48-63.

28. I.A. Richards, *The Philosophy of Rhetoric* (London/Oxford/New York: OUP, 1936), p. 96.

29. Barfield, p. 49.

30. Barfield, p. 51.

31. Barfield, p. 52.

32. See above, n. 12.

33. Barfield, p. 54.

34. Barfield, p. 55.

35. Barfield, p. 56.

36. Barfield, p. 55.

37. See above, n. 7.

38. E.g. Richards, pp. 96-100; Wheelwright, p. 91; TeSelle, pp. 45-46. Barfield himself violates Richards' stern prohibition against identifying the literal sense with the vehicle and the metaphorical sense with the tenor. I do not however think that the force of his argument, for my purposes, is thereby significantly undermined.

39. Wolff, pp. 7-8. Wolff's conception of the work, and the procedure it entails, is one of the factors that lead to the 'literalizing' exegesis discussed on pp. 31-34. It is a non-contextual conception (and procedure) in which the role of particular expressions in their standard, everyday uses is frequently disregarded and in which the literary setting of these expressions is given scant attention.

My own use of 'literalizing' above and on pp. 27, 31, and 32 provides occasion to demonstrate a counter-procedure to the one for which Wolff is here censured. The language game to which 'literalizing' belongs in these instances is that of a certain sort of condemnation, one in which people criticize each other's understanding of spoken or written expressions as being superficial, reductionistic, incomplete, and therefore inadequate. It is, in short, a thoroughly pejorative use and, I expect, is easily recognizable as such. It is also by our day a thoroughly ordinary use, which of course is what gives me confidence that it is easily recognizable as pejorative.

Now it might at first seem odd if I should later chide Wolff that his conception and execution of his *Anthropology* lead to a mistaken appraisal of a passage's 'literal sense' (see p. 34). On the one hand I say his interpretations are literalizing, on the other that they misconstrue the literal sense. The oddness disappears, however, when it is observed that the latter term belongs to a different, much more technical and theoretically oriented language game. Specifically, my use of 'literal sense' comes out of recent reflection in the fields of biblical hermeneutics and literary theory on the relation between meaning and context in literary texts. Because of its technicality, which quality may well not be readily recognizable, one must clarify this usage with definitions and explanations, a process that would not ordinarily be required for one's use of 'literalizing'.

Accordingly, by 'literal sense' I have in mind the meaning that arises from a reading 'at the level of the whole biblical story' (Hans Frei, *The Eclipse of Biblical Narrative: A Study in Eighteenth and Nineteenth Century Hermeneutics* [New Haven: Yale University Press, 1974], p. 2). While this definition has been formulated mainly with respect to narrative, a correlative formulation geared to poetry is provided by Northrop Frye (*Anatomy of Criticism* [Princeton: Princeton University Press, 1957], p. 77) when he writes, 'Understanding a poem literally means understanding the whole of it, as a poem, and as it stands. Such understanding begins in a complete surrender of the mind and senses to the impact of the work as a whole, and proceeds through the effort to unite the symbols toward a simultaneous perception of the unity of the structure.' Both statements logically follow from the observation that what seems the obvious meaning of a passage when taken out of context is obviously *not* the meaning when viewed *in* context. From the latter perspective another meaning becomes plain.

It may be added that this notion of literal sense does not necessarily represent a complete departure from an ordinary understanding of it as, in Barfield's words, 'the surface meaning of an expression'. Rather, it represents an extended concept of 'surface', wherein the 'surface' from which meaning arises is that of the text in its entirety.

40. Wolff, p. 8.
41. Johnson, p. 2 (*et passim*).
42. Wolff, p. 40.
43. Wolff, pp. 41-42.
44. Wolff, p. 43.
45. Wolff, pp. 42-43.
46. Part of the burden of Wittgenstein's *Philosophical Investigations* is to point out the dangers and distortions that arise from this sort of transposition. Wittgenstein wants to show that such transposing activity often implies, intentionally or otherwise, the notion that there is a single logic for all of language corresponding to a single, fundamental order of reality. Against this monistic impulse he argues that different uses of language have different logics and that reality has many different orders (e.g. see p. 51, paragraphs 131-32.) What Wittgenstein says of philosophers and his remedy for the problems they create for themselves might profitably be applied to Wolff in his concern with the physical referentiality of Jeremiah's use of 'heart':

> When philosophers use a word—'knowledge', 'being', 'object', 'I', 'proposition', 'name'—and try to grasp the *essence* of the thing, one must always ask

oneself: is the word ever actually used in this way in the language-game which is its original home?

What *we* do is to bring words back from their metaphysical to their everyday use (p. 48, para. 116).

47. On the subject of emotion concepts, see J.C. Gosling, 'Emotion and Object', *Philosophical Review* 74 (1965), pp. 486-503; Anthony Kenny, *Action, Emotion, and Will* (New York: Humanities Press, 1963); G.D. Marshall, 'On Being Affected', *Mind* 77 (1968), pp. 243-59; Moreland Perkins, 'Emotion and Feeling', *Philosophical Review* 75 (1966), pp. 139-60; Gilbert Ryle, 'Feelings', in *Aesthetics and Language*, ed. W. Elton (Oxford: Blackwell, 1954), pp. 56-72: Irving Thalberg, 'Emotion and Thought', in *Philosophy of Mind*, ed. S. Hampshire (New York: Harper & Row, 1966), pp. 201-25; B.A.O. Williams, 'Pleasure and Belief', in *Philosophy of Mind*, pp. 225-42.

48. See Thalberg, p. 213: 'I assume that only actual events, states of affairs, and things can cause other events, states of affairs, and things'. Thalberg's discussion of objects, grounds, and causes of emotions (pp. 212-16) provides a persuasive argument for this assumption.

49. Thalberg, pp. 208-12.

Notes to Chapter Three

1. See, for example, the following commentaries: G.H.A. Ewald, *Prophets of the Old Testament*, trans. J. Frederick Smith, III (Edinburgh and London: Williams and Norgate, 1878), pp. 59-302; Bernhard Duhm, *Das Buch Jeremia* (Tübingen and Leipzig: J.C.B. Mohr [Paul Siebeck], 1901); C.H. Cornill, *Das Buch Jeremia* (Leipzig: Tauchnitz, 1905); P. Volz, *Der Prophet Jeremia*, 2nd edn (Leipzig and Erlangen: Deichert, 1928); W. Rudolph, *Jeremia*, 3rd edn (Tübingen: J.C.B. Mohr [Paul Siebeck], 1968); J. Bright, *Jeremiah* (Garden City, N.Y.: Doubleday, 1965).

2. Of the diachronic studies, see for example Duhm, pp. 47-48; Cornill, pp. 44-46; Volz, pp. 33-42, 49-59; Rudolph, pp. 28-33; Bright, pp. 25-27, 33-34. Ewald identifies 4.3-31 as the contextual unit (pp. 85, 112). He is followed by F. Giesebrecht, *Das Buch Jeremia* (Göttingen: Vandenhoeck & Ruprecht, 1907), p. 23, and A. Weiser, *Das Buch Jeremia*, 6th edn (Göttingen: Vandenhoeck & Ruprecht, 1969), pp. 40-41. For Holladay's rhetorical analysis, see *The Architecture of Jeremiah 1-20* (Lewisburg, Pa.: Bucknell University Press, 1976), pp. 30-101.

It should be observed that rhetorical criticism in general, Holladay's in particular, is a diachronic approach. Like the other branches of historical criticism, its point is to provide a picture of the composition and compilation of the material under investigation. While this aspect of Holladay's work is not of direct relevance to our task, the valid literary insights he registers along the way are. For example, Holladay is able to demonstrate significant connections among the prelude (4.1-4) and the postlude (8.4-10a, 13) of the 'foe cycle' and the 'foe cycle' proper. First is a parallelism in the double use of verbal forms of *šwb* in 4.1 and 8.4, resulting in an envelope structure:

'im-tāšûb yiśrā'ēl... 'ēlay tāšûb   (4.1)
'im-yāšûb we'lō' yāšûb   (8.4)

Second, there are parallels between 4.2 and 5.2 and between 8.5 and 5.3, which tie the envelope structure into the center of the foe material. Holladay explains:

> Specifically, following the double occurrence of *šwb* in 4.1 we have, in v. 2: *we'nišba'tā hay-yhwh be'ĕmet*, 'and (if) you swear "as Yahweh lives" in truth', a parallel to *we'im hay-yhwh yō'mērû, lākēn laššeqer yiššābē'û*, 'and if they say "as Yahweh lives", then they swear falsely', in 5.2. And following the double occurrence of *šwb* in 8.4 we have, in v. 5: *heḥĕzîqû battarmît mē'ānû lāšûb*, a parallel to *ḥizzeqû penêhem missela' mē'ānû lāšûb* in 5.3. This is the only occurrence of *šwb* in the foe cycle proper (4.5–6.30). That is to say, 4.1-2 and 8.4-5 not only point to each other, but both point toward 5.2-3. (*Architecture*, p. 56.)

3. Holladay does acknowledge the connections to Jer 3 (*Architecture*, p. 56).

4. Unless otherwise indicated, translations from the Hebrew are my own, though often representing only minor variations from the RSV.

5. Holladay, *The Root Šûbh in the Old Testament* (Leiden: Brill, 1958), pp. 1-2, 116-20, 128-39, 146, 152-54, 156-57. Holladay discusses the peculiar double ambiguity of *šûb*, noting that it can be used to mean, first, either 'turn back (to)' or 'turn away (from)' in the sense of spatial motion, and second, either 'repent' or 'be apostate', which are religious in sense. The religious sense Holladay calls 'covenantal', by which he means 'expressing a change of loyalty on the part of Israel or God, each for the other' (pp. 2, 116). Holladay argues that it was Jeremiah who most fully developed the latter usage while most fully exploiting the potential for word-play between the physico-spatial and the religious senses of the root as well as the ambiguities respective to each. Statistically, of the 164 instances of the covenantal *šûb* that Holladay finds in the OT, a disproportionate 30% (48) occur in Jeremiah (pp. 117-18).

There are relatively few occurrences of *šwb* in the book that are not evocative of the covenantal usage as Holladay has defined it. Even such an ostensibly mundane case as 28.6 ('May Yhwh... bring back [*lehāšîb*] ... from Babylon the vessels...') when read in its proximity to 31.16-22— which speaks in rapid succession of Israel's apostate turning away, penitent turning back, subsequent returning from exile and Yhwh's restoring their fortunes—even this passage can then resonate with overtones of the covenantal theme. And as it resonates, it becomes part of the theme.

Our warrant for speaking of *šwb* as a leitmotif is not diminished by the historical observation that at a certain point in his ministry Jeremiah gave up hope in the possibility of repentance and so quit preaching it. Even if the book were shaped to reflect that information, the case would not be altered. For *šwb*'s function as a leitmotif is broader than its usage in direct calls to repentance. The important synchronic fact is that there is *no* major section of Jeremiah (MT) in its present arrangement where *šwb* is not used in such a way as to play upon and contribute to the broad web of 'covenantal' connotations with which it has been invested (e.g. by such paradigmatic instances as 2.19, 3.1ff., 4.1, 8.4-5). Observe the distribution of the following examples: 11.10; 15.7, 19; 18.8, 11; 23.14, 22; 24.6-7; 25.5; 26.3; 29.10, 14; 30.3; 31.16-22; 33.26; 34.11, 15-16, 22; 35.15; 36.3, 7; 44.5, 14; 46.27; 48.47; 49.39.

6. H.W. Wolff has demonstrated the important role of *šwb* in Deuteronomy and the Deuteronomic History while also noting the part it plays in the relation of these works to Jeremiah. See 'The Kerygma of the Deuteronomic Historical Work', trans. Frederick Prussner, in *The Vitality of Old Testament Traditions*, ed. Walter Brueggemann and H.W. Wolff (Atlanta: John Knox, 1976), pp. 83-100, especially 90-97.

The term 'voice' points to the fact of a felt human presence and determinate intelligence at work in the selecting, ordering, and rendering of the materials of a literary work. This presence is felt to be within the work, as an integral part of it, yet apart from and behind the personae of the text, in the present case behind even the first-person prophetic figure of Jeremiah. (At the least, equating the work's voice with the persona of Jeremiah is not a *logical* requirement.) The concept, as I intend it, by no means precludes the notions of multiple authorship, various redactional layers, and the like. Yet it *is* meant to suggest, and to offer a conceptual tool for recognizing, the measure of unity and coherence among whatever diverse authorial and editorial strata the historian posits. In the terms of tradition criticism, we might say that a 'school' or 'tradition circle' is recognizable as such to the extent that it speaks with one voice. In short, 'voice' is a way of speaking of the work's authorship while keeping attention fixed upon the surface of the text and maintaining the synchronic orientation that chooses to view the work as a coherent whole. See M.H. Abrams, 'Persona, Tone, and Voice', *A Glossary of Literary Terms*, 3rd edn (New York: Holt, Rinehart and Winston, 1957), pp. 123-126, 148.

7. See above, n. 4.

8. See Holladay, *The Root Šûbh*, p. 2.

9. See Hans Frei's use of the category 'intention-action' in his discussion of personal identity in *The Identity of Jesus Christ* (Philadelphia: Fortress, 1975), pp. 42-44, 91-94.

10. Ronald Hustwit, 'Two Views of the Soul: *Investigations*, Part II, iv', in *Essays on Kierkegaard and Wittgenstein*, ed. Richard Bell and Ronald

Hustwit (Wooster, Ohio: The College of Wooster, 1978), p. 65. Emphasis added.

11. Holladay, *The Root Šûbh*, p. 130.

12. Duhm, p. 45. See also Bright, p. 24.

13. The persistence into our own day of oath-taking in various non-Semitic cultures would be evidence in favor of the temporally and culturally *un*bound quality of this conception of the self, i.e. the conception that 'having a self entails having a telos'.

14. *'emet*: 'Faith, Faithfulness', *IDB*, II (1962), pp. 222-27. *Mišpāṭ*: Abraham Heschel, *The Prophets*, I (New York: Harper & Row, 1962), pp. 195-220. *Ṣ^edāqâ*: 'Righteousness in the OT', *IDB*, IV (1962), pp. 80-85; also Gerhard von Rad, *OTT*, I (New York: Harper & Row, 1962), pp. 370-83.

15. The intelligibility of the text as it stands is either not evident to or not the concern of most of the diachronic commentaries cited above in n. 1. Their tendency, again, is to describe the process of composition and compilation rather than to explicate the text. See, for example, Weiser, p. 40.

16. Granted that the messenger formula may indicate a historical disjunction, i.e. in the sense that vv. 3-4 were originally independent (again, see Weiser, p. 40), this genetic account of the text must not be thought to be automatically determinative for the way the material functions in its present shape.

17. See H.W. Wolff's brief discussion, 'The Deictic Function of *Kî*', in *Hosea*, trans. Gary Stansell (Philadelphia: Fortress, 1965), p. 135.

18. The effect of the present shape of the text is to begin to shift the status of 'Israel', 'Judah', and 'Jerusalem' from differentiated geopolitical concepts to coterminal theological concepts. This is not to say that every mention of Israel in the book is a reference to the 'theological' Israel that includes both North and South. Clearly, the terms 'Israel' and 'Judah' do work in a geopolitically referential way in 2.6-10. Yet the fact that in that passage Judah is said to have committed the same sin as Israel was perhaps one factor leading to the more general, theological redeployment of the terms in other passages where the distinctions between them have been blurred or relativized by the redactors. For example, the editorial introduction (30.1-4) to the Book of Consolation makes it clear that all the material in this section, much of which was undoubtedly addressed to the North at first, is to be read with reference to Israel *and* Judah, conceived singly as 'my people'.

19. Dodd, *According to the Scriptures* (London: Nisbet, 1952), pp. 57-61, 126.

20. This is a remark about reading conventions and reader competences. By 'associative process' is meant first the reader's recognition that the passage at hand *is* similar or identical to another. With this recognition there normally comes both the expectation that the passages are more than just formally related and the inclination to discern that relation. To the extent that some form of this process is fundamental to the very task of language-

learning, it may be supposed to be a competence common to readers of any time and culture. At the same time we should not imagine that all readers have the competence in equal measure. It ranges in degree of acuity and in different cases presupposes different degrees of familiarity with the corpus. Further, it is by no means implied that the relation between associated passages is in every case the same. One text may quote another for the sake of parody, hence to discredit rather than affirm it. Determining the nature of the relation in specific cases can be a very complex task. From making even rather gross assessments of contexts to perceiving the subtlest ironies, readers rely upon a plethora of highly nuanced competences.

Some of the more fundamental of these competences might not normally be thought of as linguistic/literary but rather as attitudinal/emotional in character. However, there would appear to be an important area of overlap between them. Imagine the case of the thoroughgoing cynic who regards with jaundiced eye such concepts as 'covenant love', 'righteousness', 'God'. Would he or she be able to see the logical congruity between those concepts and that of 'blessed life'—which, we propose, is what Jer 4.3 implies and Hos 10.12 directly affirms? Might the cynic not be disposed to miss any connection entirely, or perhaps to regard it as a cruel joke by the authors? The power to imagine or outright believe that such concepts fit together and have a basis in reality is a competence or expectation upon which one's reading of the texts *can* turn. Adjudicating between rival interpretations that arise from the different degrees to which readers do or do not have this competence would be extremely difficult. In fact it would entail analysis not just of reading techniques but of the readers' lives. The fact that human subjectivity is an invariable, and indispensable, component in sense-making, both of texts and other forms of verbal communication, must not be ignored in literary criticism.

21. Wolff, *Hosea*, p. 186. Emphasis added.

22. E.g. Helmut Lamparter, *Prophet wider Willen: der Prophet Jeremia* (Stuttgart: Calwer Verlag, 1964), p. 65. See also Cornill, p. 45, and Weiser, p. 41.

23. Wolff, *Anthropology*, p. 47.

24. Wolff, *Anthropology*, p. 51.

25. Lamparter, pp. 65-71.

26. Samuel Berridge (*Prophet, People, and the Word of Yahweh* [Zurich: EVZ Verlag, 1970], pp. 101-102) observes that the inclusion of the speaker in the OT 'call to lamentation' *Gattung* is found only here and in 6.26. He writes, 'These first person plural readings... are not to be considered as being merely accidental, nor are they to be explained by the conjecture that Jeremiah speaks here as the holder of a liturgical office. These texts may rather be considered as holding a further indication of the bond which united Jeremiah with his people. Because he was a sinful member of a sinful nation, Jeremiah knew that his own sin would be punished at that time when

Yahweh would bring judgment upon all Judah.'

For an alternative but less persuasive interpretation (namely, that the phrase is a hypothetical quotation of the people's lament), see Holladay, *Architecture*, pp. 79-80.

Berridge's comment moves toward an adequate explication of the logic of the first-person plural usage: when someone speaks in that mode he is identifying himself with others; when a text employs that mode, it intends the reader to have the same model in mind, that of the individual speaker identifying himself with a group. Normally, the pronoun 'we' presupposes an 'I'. However, Berridge wants to explain the passage further, and he does so in a way that illustrates again a diachronic, versus a synchronic, approach. He explains the passage by reference to its 'historical background', specifically to 'the failure of Josiah's reform to achieve a lasting peace for Judah' (p. 102). That Jeremiah originally spoke the words of v. 8 into the situation of failed reform might well be the case, but that situation is no longer the context which the text supplies. Berridge cites 2 Chr 29.10, 30.8, and 2 Kgs 23.26 as evidence that 'this terminology was commonly used in connection with reform' (p. 102, n. 165), but again, even if such were the original *Sitz-im-Leben*, it was not determinative in every case for the expression's *Sitz-im-Text*, as Num 25.4 and Ps 85.3 clearly demonstrate. Neither the expression in 4.8b nor the literary fact of Jeremiah's speaking it depends upon the reconstructed historical reference for their intelligibility. The important point is this, that Berridge looks to the text to provide data on a 'Jeremiah of history'; in the literary persona of Jeremiah, Jeremiah as rendered in the text, he has no direct interest. He regards the text as a source for historical reconstruction, not as an arena in which the depicted Jeremiah, as literary-theological construct, assumes a shape and takes on a life of independent reality.

27. It should be noted that while all Israelite prophets were intermediaries (i.e. channels of communication between the divine and human worlds), not all were intercessors. The function of soliciting Yahweh at the request and on behalf of their clientele was characteristic of prophets of the Ephraimite tradition and along with other traits distinguished them from their Judean counterparts. See Robert R. Wilson, *Prophecy and Society in Ancient Israel* (Philadelphia: Fortress, 1980), pp. 150-51, 155-56, 160-66, 238-41 (with regard to Jeremiah), and 301. For the older view that regards intercession as characteristic of Hebrew prophecy in general, see Berridge, p. 13, and von Rad, *OTT*, II, pp. 51-52.

The relation between prophet and people is explored in depth from the sociological perspective in Wilson's book, although the sort of identification manifest in the pathos of Jeremiah's speech is of a different order from that which exists in the relation between a prophet and his 'support group' (Wilson, pp. 51, 241-48).

28. The special empowerment of the prophet is implicit in such texts as

Exod 20.18-20 and Deut 5.23-28, and it is variously described in terms of Yahweh's being with the prophet, putting his words in the prophet's mouth, and taking away his guilt (e.g. Exod 4.10-12; Deut 18.18; Isa 6.6-7; Jer 1.7-9). Hence it is necessary to qualify any notion of a simple equality between Jeremiah and his people, such as seen in the work of V. Herntrich (*Jeremia, der Prophet und sein Volk* [Gütersloh: C. Bertelsmann, 1938], pp. 15, 22, 31, 35-36) and H.J. Stoebe ('Jeremia, Prophet und Seelsorger', *TZ* 20 [1964], pp. 385-409).

29. The correctness of this proposal would be unassailable if 4.19 had the unmistakable earmarks of a lamentation, e.g. such stereotypic terminology as the particle *hôy* or *'ăhāh*, or if it displayed the form of the 'lamentation of the individual' *Gattung* as outlined by Baumgartner (*Die Klagegedichte des Jeremia* [Giessen: Alfred Töpelmann, 1917], pp. 6-7) and others. However, there is evidence to indicate that for ancient Israel the concept 'lamentation' was not confined to our critical categories or so technical as a strict form criticism might have us think. Rather, the concept covers a wide range of expressions of grief, and, in that many of the expressions do adhere to particular linguistic conventions, then both expressions and conventions are best explicated by analysis of the logic of the emotion expressed (e.g. the treatment of *mē'îm*, pp. 53-54).

A crucial passage is 2 Sam 19.1-2 (Eng. 18.33–19.1). David has been given the news of Absalom's death. His response is one of immense pathos; it is also perfectly ordinary, i.e. informal and non-technical: 'O my son Absalom, my son, my son Absalom! Would I had died instead of you, O Absalom, my son, my son!' It is the fully individualized expression of personal grief in a singularly personal, essentially private situation—as opposed to the public, presumably more formal mourning which takes place, v. 3 suggests, in response to the king's spontaneous reaction. The full force and meaning of David's cry, if not absolutely self-evident, are given by the language used to describe the accompanying behavior: David is said to weep (*bky*) and to be shaken (*rgz*). The latter term, while not typically associated with grief behavior, is not necessarily alien to it, as shown by Amos 8.8 where *rgz* occurs parallel to 'mourn' (*'bl*). More significantly, 2 Sam 19.2 has 'It was told to Joab, "Behold, the king is weeping and mourning (*wayyit'abbēl*) for Absalom"', a statement which assuredly refers to David's behavior in the previous verse. The verb *'bl* and its noun form *'ēbel* directly pertain to the idea of lamentation. In fact, as evidenced by such passages as 2 Sam 11.26-27, Esth 4.3, Joel 1.8-13, Amos 5.16, Jer 16.4-7, and especially Jer 6.26, they are used synonymously with *spd/mispād*, *spd* being the verb used in Jeremiah's call to 'lament' in 4.8.

It might be argued that whereas the lexicographical evidence shows *'bl* tolerant of both formal and informal usage, *spd* is used *only* formally, that is, as a technical term referring to regularized or ritual lamentation that employs a set speech pattern. However, of the 46 instances of *spd/mispād* in the OT, only five or six occur with examples of the lamentation itself (e.g. *hôy 'āḥî wᵉhôy 'āḥôt* in Jer 22.18; see also 34.5; 1 Kgs 13.30; Joel 1.13, 15; Amos 5.16 and perhaps v. 18). While all of these employ the stereotypic *hôy* or *'āhāh*, it is questionable whether this sample constitutes a sufficient basis for generalization or, even if it does, whether it significantly qualifies the argument from parallelism and synonymy registered above. Further, it may be that the five examples represent only stylized quotations or abbreviated summary versions of what in the actual case would have been more individualized expressions of sorrow. In any case it seems likely that if a term were needed in Jer 4.8 that corresponded univocally to a specific *Gattung*, it would be not *spd* but *qnn*, the denominative of *qînâ*, meaning 'chant a funeral song', 'sing a dirge'. It appears that no such specialized form was intended.

There is good reason to believe, therefore, that the people of Israel had at their disposal an indefinite variety of linguistic and non-linguistic behavior that could count as 'lamentation'—as is the case in our own day. As Ezek 24.16-17 suggests ('... yet you shall not mourn [*spd*] or weep nor shall your tears run down. Sigh [*'nq*], but not aloud; make no mourning [*'ēbel*] for the dead'), even an inaudible sigh could *in the right surroundings* be understood as lamentation.

The implications for an exegesis of the reading process are profound. In cases where more or less explicit, unambiguous, stereotypic, formal linguistic features are absent that could mark an expression as a lamentation, the recognizability of the expression as such depends on one's knowledge of the sort of circumstances in which people usually grieve, of the typical occasions of sadness, and of the kinds of behavior that typically accompany the language of grief. In the yet more difficult cases it depends on a knowledge of the *specific* circumstances, occasions, and behavior and of the way those ingredients come together in the particular person who is grieving. This means a knowledge of the griever herself, her characteristic speech, the tones and gestures attending her speech, the unique configuration of her emotional emotional life, and more. (Hence the importance of characterization in literary texts as a means of access to such knowledge, although characterization cannot deliver the knowledge independently of reader sensitivity and sensibility.) Such knowledge can hardly be of an abstract, impersonal, and generalizable sort. In short, a lament's recognizability depends upon one's own well-developed subjectivity, a depth and breadth of personal experience and personality qualification which transcends any objective method's ability to impart it as much as Israel's many ways of lamenting transcend form-critical categories.

30. That Jeremiah understands his office in this way is presupposed by 7.16, 11.14, 14.11, and 15.1, all of which are specific injunctions by Yahweh against intercession. Such directives would only be necessary if intercession were in fact deemed normative. 15.1 is of special significance, tying the

intercessory function into the tradition of Moses and Samuel. As further evidence, note 14.17ff. and 27.18.

31. In this respect the prophet, Jeremiah's self as instantiated in his words, becomes an exemplar and model for imitation by the believing reader. Chapters 5 and 6 of this study will treat this feature in some detail.

32. My explication of this formula employs much of the same evidence that Berridge cites in his argument against Reventlow's position on the cultic and non-individualistic character of the expression. While I accept Berridge's conclusions, my orientation is different. For the exegete to locate an expression in its language game, in this case perplexity, is to allow for the possibility that it might be used in any number of sociological settings without significant alteration of its force and meaning. It is to suggest that the logic of perplexity cuts across the boundaries not only of tradition circles but larger cultural groupings as well and is a decisive factor that must be taken into account in any attempt at assessing the thrust of the concept's particular expressions. (Consider in this regard the remarks made in n. 29 about 'lamentation' and the explication of that concept's expressions.) The difference in orientation between the exegesis I attempt and Berridge's follows essentially from the difference between the concept 'language game' and the form-critical category '*Gattung*'.

Relatedly, it bears repeating that the present explication is a synchronic one and does not insist, as Berridge's does, on interpreting the words of the text in reference to a supra-text of an 'actual', but actually hypothetical, history. An example of this characteristic of Berridge's work was discussed in n. 26. Here, observe his effort to ground the saying of v. 10, 'It shall be well with you', once again in the expectations fostered by Josiah's reforms. This grounding is not totally implausible as a piece of historical speculation, but it is one in which the text shows no concern (cf. Berridge, pp. 107-10).

33. See Norman Habel, 'The Form and Significance of the Call Narratives', *ZAW* 77 (1965), pp. 297-323.

34. Berridge comments helpfully on this verse:

> Faced with contradictory prophetic words, Jeremiah calls Yahweh's attention to the state of tension and confusion which exists for his people, and, undoubtedly also for himself. 14:13 may thus be said to have arisen out of a feeling of acute helplessness, and is perhaps to be considered as constituting both a plea for clarity as well as for clemency (p. 111, n. 210).

This statement is no doubt intended as a description of the emotional state of the 'Jeremiah of history'. As such, it is a very reasonable conjecture. As an analysis of the emotion content of the words of the literary persona of Jeremiah, it is nearly incontestable.

The formula 'Then I said, "Alas Lord Yhwh"' also occurs in Ezek 4.14, 9.18, 11.13, and 21.5—in each of which the language game is perplexity.

35. Berridge, p. 108.

36. On translating *kî* as 'how', see W.F. Albright, 'The Refrain "And God saw *KI TOBH*" in Genesis', *Mélanges bibliques rédigés en l'honneur de André Robert* (Paris: Bloud & Gay, 1956), pp. 22-26. See also James Muilenburg, 'The Linguistic and Rhetorical Usages of the Particle *kî* in the Old Testament', *HUCA* 32 (1961), p. 143.

37. Holladay, *Architecture*, pp. 82-84.

38. Note also Jer 5.25 ('Your iniquities have turned these away, and your sins have kept good from you'), which speaks of the same self-attenuation by sin.

39. See above, n. 36. Given the context, it makes better sense to render this sentence as an exclamation than as an explanation, for it is not at all clear what the statement would explain. Jeremiah's vision of disaster and his exclamation of its effect upon him in the previous verses certainly entail the notion of judgment, but they are not an announcement of judgment *per se* such that v. 22 could be construed as the judgment's grounds. There is a certain appropriateness to Yhwh's answering Jeremiah's anguished exclamations and exclamatory questions of vv. 19-21 with an anguished exclamation of his own.

40. Wolff, *Anthropology*, p. 42. The KJV, NEB, and JB all have 'throbbing' for *hmy*, in the same vein as Wolff and the RSV.

41. Bright, p. 30; Wolff, *Anthropology*, p. 42.

42. The point to be registered here is similar to that made in nn. 29 and 32 where we spoke of the need to explicate the expressions of grief and perplexity in terms of their specific language games rather than form-critical *Gattungen*. The language game of grief that governs Jeremiah's 'I cannot keep silent' cuts across the divisions between social settings, groups, and institutions and their indigenous speech genres. It is not as if Jeremiah were borrowing a convention in the way that the prophets make use of, say, a Torah liturgy or dirge. The language game is not a *Gattung*.

43. Abraham Heschel (*The Prophets*, II) takes God's pathos as the key for understanding the prophetic consciousness and activity. The present exegesis of Jer 4.19 can be viewed as a specific illustration and partial confirmation of Heschel's comprehensive thesis.

Notes to Chapter Four

* While the term 'paradigm' had been used of Jeremiah by von Rad (*OTT*, II, p. 216) and Gerstenberger (see below, p. 78), a thematic application was first made by Sheldon Blank in the essay 'The Prophet as Paradigm' (*Essays in Old Testament Ethics*, J.L. Crenshaw and J.T. Willis, eds. [New York: KTAV, 1974], pp. 111-30). Blank's use, however, was in conjunction with an argument for the authenticity of the Confessions. The present study seeks to extend the application both exegetically in the present chapter and theoretically in the final one (see especially pp. 170-74)—but in a different direction from that taken by Blank and independently of the issue of authenticity.

1. Martin Buber, *The Prophetic Faith*, trans. Carlyle Witton-Davies (New York: Harper and Row, 1949), p. 181.
2. Holladay, *Architecture*, p. 75. Emphasis added.
3. Duhm, pp. 104-105.
4. Volz, p. 56.
5. Duhm, p. 105. As an intransitive verb with an objective suffix, the odd $y^e ṣā'unî$ has an analogue in $ya'abrûm$ of 8.13.
6. Walter Baumgartner, *Die Klagegedichte des Jeremia* (Giessen: Alfred Töpelmann, 1917), p. 74.
7. Hans Wildberger, *Jahwewort und prophetische Rede bei Jeremia* (Zürich: Zwingli-Verlag, 1942), p. 85.
8. Lamparter, p. 118.
9. Lamparter, p. 118.
10. E.g. Rudolph, p. 69, and Bright, p. 70.
11. Again, Rudolph, p. 69, and Bright, p. 70.
12. Heschel, I, p. 138. See also Berridge, p. 176, who says that in speaking of 'my tent' and 'my curtains', Jeremiah 'discloses the oneness which he knows with his people'.
13. See above, Chapter 3, n. 43.
14. Weiser, p. 97.
15. H. Graf von Reventlow, *Liturgie und prophetische Ich bei Jeremia* (Gütersloh: Gerd Mohn, 1963), pp. 196-205.
16. Stanley Romaine Hopper, 'Exposition of the Book of Jeremiah', *IB*, ed. George Arthur Buttrick, *et al.* (New York: Abingdon, 1952), V, 901-902.
17. Hopper, p. 838.
18. Skinner, p. 50, n. 1.
19. Berridge, p. 176; Bright, p. 70; Holladay, *Architecture*, p. 117; Hyatt, 'The Book of Jeremiah: Exegesis and Introduction', *IB* V, 901; Lamparter, p. 117; Rudolph, p. 69; Volz, p. 126; and Weiser, p. 96.
20. Reventlow (p. 196) argues that the unit begins only with v. 19, since in the basic pattern of the complaint liturgy, as he construes it, the divine word comes in response to the people's lament, not in introduction to it. I would take issue with the guiding principle behind this assessment. Reventlow consistently makes the structure and function of the material in its original *Sitz-im-Leben* determinative for its shape and function in its textual setting. It does not seem to occur to him as a possibility that, once included in a larger literary context, the material may operate differently from the way it did before its inclusion. I contend that in its present setting 10.19 presupposes and requires what comes before it—much as 4.19 requires, and is poetically

coordinated with, 4.18.

21. The final *yodh* may represent either a gentilic or an archaic case ending, not an uncommon stylistic feature in poetry. Cf. Exod 15.6 *ne'dārî*; Deut 33.16 *šōkᵉnî*. See Gesenius–Kautzsch, *Hebrew Grammar*, ed. A.E. Cowley (Oxford: Clarendon, 1910), § 90n, pp. 253-54.

22. The variation between *'ôy lî* and *'ôy lānû* is a function of the varying strictness in the personification's construction.

23. To be sure, this is spoken by Jeremiah in the corporate solidarity he has with his people by virtue of his prophetic commission. But this observation does not vitiate the literary facts: 1. that we hear his voice as Jerusalem's and 2. that the personified Jerusalem is a persona of the text. The metaphorical depiction of the city as speaker and the more literal representation of Jeremiah as speaking for the city are simultaneous features of the text highlighting different aspects of the text's meaning.

24. Bright (p. 43) treats all three statements of vv. 4-5 as an exchange solely among the enemy forces. While this cannot be dismissed as a possibility, *'ôy lānû* seems a bit too strong simply to express the one party's disappointment over having to postpone the attack on account of darkness. Holladay (*Architecture*, p. 90) attributes v. 4b to the people.

25. Cited by Hopper, p. 838.

26. See Jer 6.7; 14.17; 19.8; 30.12, 14, 17; Isa 1.6; 10.26; 14.6; 30.26; Mic 1.9; Nah 3.19.

27. *yᵉrî'â*: Exod 26.1ff.; 36.8ff.; Num 4.25. [*mêtār*]: Exod 35.18; 39.40; Num 3.26, 37; 4.26, 32.

28. See Jer 3.21; 6.1; 7.30; 16.14-15; 23.7; 32.30, 32; 49.6; 50.4, 33.

29. It is important to note that this blending is the effect of a specific literary configuration and is not to be generalized to every first-person text as Buber's remarks would recommend.

30. E.g. Pss 30.7; 31.23; 39.2; 41.5; 94.18; 116.11. See also Isa 38.10, 11; Jon 2.5; Jer 20.9.

31. So Lamparter, p. 118; Bright, p. 70; and others.

32. Jer 3.22b-25 might appear to be an anomaly. However, its present juxtaposition with 4.1ff. may well function to place the genuineness of the repentance in question or to suggest that the verdict is still out, though shortly to come in. Cf. Berridge, p. 168.

As will be argued later, the confession in 14.7-9 is rejected as insincere in 14.10. The case of 31.18-19 is substantially different, coming as it does after the turn from judgment to salvation. Finally, see the discussion on the sarcasm in 8.14 on p. 107 below.

33. The fact that this 'grieving over' has in Jer 10.19b become a 'grieving with' may well reflect a development within prophecy itself. If so, it may well be related to the substantially heightened concern with the prophetic office and the suffering it entails, a concern attested in various strata of the book of Jeremiah and in Ezekiel as well. And if *this* is so, we might speculate as

belonging to the same concern, the fact that the self-quotation formula is increasingly used in those books to introduce expressions of perplexity and/or anguish by the prophet in response to oracles he has been entrusted to deliver or visions of judgment to which he has been made privy. See Jer 4.10; 14.13; Ezek 4.14; 9.8; 11.13; 21.5. Cf. Isa 49.4.

34. The essentially *narrative* character of 'I said' is obvious. Any discussion of 'point of view' presupposes and elaborates upon this basic fact. (See 'Point of View' in Abrams, *Glossary*, pp. 133-36.)

35. This is also the procedure by which we would identify the 'I' of Jer 6.2 as Yhwh's.

36. In Ps 75.5 the mention of 'God' in the immediate context (v. 2) and the content of the 'I said' statement lead us to recognize Yhwh as the speaker there, rather than the psalmist.

37. The qualification 'first-person *perspective*' permits us to distinguish between the prophetic books and name-titled books in which the point of view is primarily, or exclusively, third-person, e.g. Joshua and Samuel.

38. This point will be elaborated in depth in the following sections.

39. This of course is not to suggest that Jeremiah attributes these qualities to himself, only that he enacts them in his speech.

40. *Prophecy and Society in Ancient Israel*. On Ephraimite tradition as it relates to intercession, see especially pp. 151, 156, 162-66. On Jer 14.1–15.4, see pp. 238-40.

41. Wilson, p. 239.

42. Wilson, p. 240.

43. It is interesting that the only time the book reports a challenge on the basis of intercession, it is *Jeremiah* who lodges it against his prophetic opponents. See 27.16-17, a passage also cited by Wilson (p. 238).

44. Wilson, p. 238.

45. Gerstenberger, 'Jeremiah's Complaints: Observations on Jer 15.10-21', *JBL* 82 (1963), p. 404. Cf. Mowinckel, *Komposition*, p. 22; Gunkel–Begrich, *Einleitung in die Psalmen: Die Gattungen der religiösen Lyrik Israels* (Göttingen: Vandenhoeck & Ruprecht, 1933), pp. 236-38.

46. Gerstenberger, p. 405.

47. Gerstenberger, p. 401.

48. Gerstenberger, p. 406.

47. Gerstenberger, pp. 406-407. Emphasis added. Gerstenberger's reference to the 'deuteronomist' reflects the essentially diachronic orientation of his study, for he is interested in reconstructing the growth and compilation of the text, and the motivations behind its various stages, as the means of establishing its theological meaning. However tendentious the reconstruction may be, and however dubious the implied hermeneutic, his sense of the *effect* of the final shape of the text is quite astute. Even what might be considered his more dubious methodological and interpretive moves, namely his handling of 15.13-14 (pp. 394-96), do not undermine either the parallelism

he perceives between chs. 14 and 15 or the overall conclusions he draws with respect to the depiction of the prophet. In other words, the results of his diachronic analysis are not incommensurate with a synchronic reading (and certainly not so in principle).

I would venture a minor qualification of his basic position. In the final shape of the text, 15.5-9 may belong more with 15.10ff. than with 14.7ff. (cf. pp. 404-405). I would view these five verses in analogy with 14.2-6, thus as a form of prophetic announcement that elicits the following complaint. As such, they complete the parallelism between 14.1-15.4 and 15.10ff. and accord with the pattern throughout the book (e.g. 3.22-23; 4.18-19, 30-31; 8.13ff.; 10.17ff.). Incidentally, this is an instance where the difference in readings *is* a function of the difference between the diachronic and synchronic orientations.

50. See Reventlow, pp. 149-87.

51. E.g. John Bright, 'Jeremiah's Complaints: Liturgy, or Expressions of Personal Distress?', in *Proclamation and Presence: Old Testament Essays in Honor of Gwynne Henton Davies*, ed. John I. Durham and J.R. Porter (London: SCM, 1970), pp. 189-214. Berridge's *Prophet, People, and the Word of Yahweh* is perhaps the most comprehensive effort at refuting Reventlow's thesis. However, Berridge devotes but two short paragraphs to the communal laments without addressing Reventlow specifically.

52. Reventlow's most explicit statement to this effect is made in reference to 10.19ff. (pp. 204-205), but is clearly intended for our passage as well.

53. Bright, 'Complaints', p. 193.

54. This is not to attack a straw man, and the criticism is not as trifling as it might appear. Reventlow went to pains to distinguish his, and Weiser's, position from that of Gunkel and Mowinckel (and, by extension, Gerstenberger), who each saw our passage as the 'imitation' of a liturgical style. Reventlow explicitly *equates* the passage with, says that it *is*, the liturgy (p. 152). What was an analogical use of the term in others becomes a univocal use with him. The interpretive ramifications of this move are serious and will be illustrated in the exegesis to follow.

55. Specifically, see Bright, 'Complaints', p. 190, and *Jeremiah*, pp. 111-12; Berridge, pp. 24-25; and von Rad, *OTT*, II, pp. 201-204.

56. Paul Tillich, *Systematic Theology*, II (Chicago: University of Chicago Press, 1957), p. 9.

57. The fact that the murder of a mere messenger, an arbitrarily chosen and purely neutral, sign-like representative, would typically evoke a special sense of outrage is an indication that among people such representative phenomena normally have a trivial status. The execution is felt to be utterly incongruous with the messenger's involvement in and responsibility for the message.

58. See E.M. Forster's discussion of 'round' and 'flat' characters in *Aspects of the Novel* (New York: Harcourt, Brace & World, Inc., Harvest Books,

1927), pp. 67-78; the discussion of 'mimetic' vs. 'illustrative' characters in Robert Scholes and Robert Kellogg, *The Nature of Narrative* (New York: OUP, 1966), pp. 89-105; finally, the treatment of Abraham as a character 'fraught with background' in Auerbach's *Mimesis* (Princeton: Princeton University Press, 1953), pp. 3-23.

59. Von Rad, *OTT*, II, pp. 95-98; and Walther Zimmerli, *Ezekiel I*, trans. R.E. Clements (Philadelphia: Fortress, 1979), pp. 29, 156-57.

60. See von Rad, *OTT*, II, pp. 232-33.

61. On Abraham, Moses, and Samuel as prophetic intercessors, see Wilson, pp. 150-51, 157-66, and 169-84 respectively. It may be added that the deuteronomic interpretation of Moses' death in the Trans-Jordan as a vicarious punishment for the people's sin at Meribah (Deut 1.37; 3.26; 4.21-22; cf. Num 20.10-13; 27.12-23) reinforces the picture of the concept 'representative' which we see at work in the prophetic office.

62. On the revelation formula, see Gerstenberger, p. 403, nn. 41, 42; and Wildberger, pp. 11-13, 19-24. Wildberger's interest in distinguishing between the prophet's own speech and that of Yhwh in the earliest stratum of the book leads him to preclude from further consideration instances of the formula that he judges to be secondary. The result is that his study fails to do justice to the full theological force and function of the formula at the level of the finished text.

63. Wolff, *Hosea*, p. 4.

64. Hyatt, p. 794.

65. Further evidence for our case is provided by the peculiar use of the revelation formula in 40.1. In every other instance the formula is followed by speech that can be taken in some literalness as a 'word' of Yhwh. Here, however, no such literal word follows, rather, a speech by the Babylonian captain-of-the-guard announcing Jeremiah's release from captivity. Thus, a specific event in Jeremiah's life, and not even something that he does but rather that is done to him, has been counted by the editors as a 'word of Yhwh'. Jeremiah's life is itself made a part of the divine communication with Judah/Israel.

66. See above, p. 62 and Chapter 4 n. 20; and Reventlow, p. 200. In this understanding of the liturgy's form, Reventlow is following Mowinckel (*Komposition*, pp. 22-23).

67. Reventlow, p. 154.

68. See Reventlow, pp. 154-58.

69. As we have seen before in this essay, an expression need not be taken as always *either* literal *or* metaphorical. The expression 'word of Yhwh' works more literally in some contexts, less so in others.

70. Translation Bright's, *Jeremiah*, p. 97.

71. Reventlow, p. 159; Skinner, p. 130.

72. Pss 23.3; 25.11; 31.4; 79.9; 109.21; 115.1; 143.11.

73. Weiser identifies the covenant cult as the *Sitz-im-Leben* of the

expression 'act for thy name's sake' (*Die Psalmen* [Göttingen: Vandenhoeck & Ruprecht, 1955], pp. 19, 27; and *Jeremia*, p. 129). Similarly, the formula for the proclamation of the divine name, quoted above from Exod 34.6-7, may also have originated in a covenant-renewal ceremony in the cult. Further, at an early stage in the formation of Exod 34 the formula appears to have been used by J to preface his version of the covenant. The covenantal context was obviously not completely dissolved when the formula was later given a penitential orientation in the final shaping of the chapter. See B.S. Childs, *The Book of Exodus: A Critical, Theological Commentary* (Philadelphia: Westminster, 1974), pp. 607-609.

74. *Miqweh*: Jer 14.8; 17.13; 50.7; Ezr 10.2; 1 Chr 29.15.

75. R.E. Clements, *God and Temple* (Philadelphia: Fortress, 1965), p. 80.

76. Kurt Galling, 'Die Ausrufung des Namens als Rechtsakt in Israel', *TZ* 81 (1956), cols. 65-70.

77. Gerstenberger, p. 401.

78. *Contra* Gerstenberger (p. 401 and n. 34), Deut 28.10 attests a theological use of the formula in the *pre-exilic* period. It also seems possible that P's use of the formula to state the significance of the ancient Aaronic blessing (Num 6.27) points to the formula's currency in the pre-exilic cult. For P, to give the blessing was to 'set Yhwh's name over the people of Israel'.

79. Galling, col. 65.

80. Reventlow, p. 159, citing Gunkel–Begrich, p. 131. Skinner, *passim*.

81. Translation Bright's, *Jeremiah*, p. 98, with minor modifications.

82. See Reventlow (pp. 168-71), on the triadic formula in Jeremiah. On the addition of $š^eb\hat{\imath}$ to the list, see Reventlow, pp. 176-77, and Delbert Hillers, *Treaty Curses and the Old Testament Prophets* (Rome: Pontifical Biblical Institute, 1964), pp. 33-34. On Lev 26 and Deut 28 in general, see Hillers, pp. 30-42.

83. Weiser, *Jeremia*, p. 130. Reventlow, p. 162. See also below, n. 119.

84. On the relation (at least in the deuteronomic tradition-stream) between the genuineness of prayer and God's 'knowing the heart' of those who pray, see also 1 Kgs 8.39.

85. Reventlow, p. 165.

86. Cf. Ezekiel's dumbness (Ezek 3.22-27; 33.21-22), which represents a development of the prohibition beyond what we have in Jeremiah. See Robert Wilson, 'An Interpretation of Ezekiel's Dumbness', *VT* 22 (1972), pp. 91-104.

87. The first chapter of Isaiah would suggest that the Davidic covenant and the Zion traditions associated with it (i.e. the tradition-complex to which some of Jeremiah's prophetic opponents undoubtedly adhered) were substantially the same in structure as the Mosaic covenant with regard to the obligations of the people. That is to say, in both, the promise of blessing was normatively conditional upon obedience.

88. Bright, *Jeremiah*, p. 103.

89. Hillers, *Treaty-Curses*, pp. 12-79.
90. Reventlow, pp. 172-73.
91. Reventlow, p. 171. Also see Hillers: 'The existence of a tradition of curses over a thousand years old renders any attempt to relate individual curses to particular historical periods highly suspect' (*Treaty-Curses*, p. 35).
92. Weiser, *Jeremia*, p. 132.
93. Reventlow, p. 170.
94. Cf. Jer 23.13-15. The particularly pernicious quality of the prophets' sinfulness (and note that the priests are included in 23.11) is that they have 'led my people Israel astray', 'they strengthen the hands of evildoers', and from them 'ungodliness has gone forth into all the land'. In addition, note that the motif of giving them 'poisoned water to drink' in v. 15 was applied to the people as a whole in 8.14 and 9.14.
95. Reventlow, pp. 153, 174-75.
96. Reventlow, p. 174, citing Volz and Stoebe.
97. Reventlow, p. 153. Emphasis added. Again, Reventlow follows Mowinckel (p. 23).
98. By attempting to recover the original distinctions form critically, some commentators are led to conclude that *bat-'ammi* is a mark of Jeremiah's voice. Apart from questioning the soundness of the method, I would point to 9.6 where the term occurs in a judgment speech of *Yhwh*. See Berridge, p. 112, nn. 217, 218; Holladay, *Architecture*, pp. 79, 180, n. 38. On 8.18-23, see Section III below, pp. 108-13.
99. E.g. Holladay, *Architecture*, p. 99; and Weiser, *Jeremia*, p. 79.
100. E.g. Bright, *Jeremiah*, pp. 60-75.
101. While it is not the case that the reflexive stem of a verb necessarily shares or reflects the usage of the verb in the base stem, it seems likely that the hithpo'lel of *byn* was comfortably at home in wisdom thought and literature. Of the twenty instances of the stem, our verse excepted, eight occur within Job. Two of the four instances in Isaiah are clearly of a wisdom character (1.3 involves a nature-analogy while 14.16 occurs within the *māšāl* of vv. 4-20). Within the psalter, all four occurrences are in wisdom-stamped material (Pss 37.10; 107.43; 119.95, 100, and 104). In Jer 9.9 the conjunction of *hitbōnⁿnû* and *haḥăkāmôt* does not *prove* the presence of a wisdom concern. On the other hand, the possibility that it represents a poetic allusion, that it is meant to make the point by indirection, can by no means be dismissed.
102. Jer 8.8b ('the false pen of the scribe...') is not to be seen as a polemic against either the commitment to writing of sacred tradition or redactional tampering with the tradition as already recorded. The repeated references in the passage to faithless conduct indicate that the issue here is obedience. (So Lamparter, p. 100.) Neither should any antithesis be drawn between 'law' (v. 8) and 'word of Yhwh' (v. 9), as Bright attempts (*Jeremiah*, p. 63). The terms occur in synonymous parallelism in 6.19.

103. Holladay, *Architecture*, pp. 99, 106, 110.
104. E.g. Duhm, p. 90; Cornill, pp. 118-19; Rudolph, p. 56; Bright, *Jeremiah*, p. 61; Gesenius-Kautzsch, p. 344, sect. 113w.
105. See the discussion of 'voice' in Chapter 3, n. 6.
106. See above, pp. 48-49, 91-92.
107. E.g. Duhm, p. 91; Skinner, p. 126; Rudolph, pp. 56, 59; Lamparter, p. 104; Bright, *Jeremiah*, p. 65.
108. Holladay, *Architecture*, p. 110.
109. Wildberger treats all the so-called Scythian songs as words of Jeremiah solely. He grounds this conclusion on their lack of the messenger formula. How the conclusion follows from that evidence he does not say, although he does show us something of his method when he makes 6.22 conform to the rest of the 'evidence' by deleting the messenger formula there, without textual evidence for doing so. And 5.15-17, which shares the same tone and images as the other songs but which is clearly in Yhwh's voice, he completely ignores. (This passage *is* included in Hyatt's list of the Scythian songs, p. 779.)
110. The translation assumes the typical emendation *mablîgîtî mibb^{e}lî g^{e}hōt*. However, the Jewish Publication Society's translation makes a good case for the MT: 'Though I would take comfort against sorrow, / My heart is faint within me'.
111. Noted by Cornill (p. 260), Volz (p. 230), and Berridge (pp. 162-63, n. 257), this rhetorical device has been best described by Holladay in his essay 'The So-Called "Deuteronomic Gloss" in Jer. VIII 19b', *VT* 12 (1962), pp. 494-98. Nevertheless, the present analysis differs from Holladay's at several points.
112. *Contra* Berridge, pp. 162-63, n. 257.
113. See above, pp. 56, 77-78.
114. For the comparison with 1 Kgs 19, see Rudolph, p. 61. On the connection with Ps 55, see Weiser, *Jeremia*, p. 85; and Berridge, p. 174.
115. Holladay, *Architecture*, pp. 111-12.
116. E.g. Volz, p. 112; Bright, *Jeremiah*, pp. 67, 71, 73; Rudolph, p. 58.
117. E.g. Skinner, p. 132; Wildberger, p. 84; Berridge, p. 173.
118. Only the deletion of *n^e'um-Yhwh* is warranted by the LXX, which agrees with the MT on the first-singular objective pronoun. The commentators are not applying the text-critical evidence consistently.

On several occasions Wildberger takes recourse to the theory that abbreviations of the Tetragrammaton led to confusion with the first-singular suffix. On this basis he freely emends in both directions (pp. 16, 54, 55); but without better substantiation for the general case, indeed without evidence that the abbreviations were current in the specific texts in question, his emendations can only be highly subjective and, given his intent to make objective discriminations between speakers, misleading.

119. In Wolff's own words: 'Prophetenrede ist ihrem Wesen nach in

willigem oder erzwungenem Gehorsam weitergegebene Jahwerede... Aber Zitat ist ein Eingeschaltetes. Jahwewort ist jedoch nicht zwischeneingekommen in die prophetische Verkündigung, sondern so sehr Anfang und Ende, dass gar das eigene Propheten-wort, wenn es auftaucht, eingesprengt erscheint' ('Das Zitat im Prophetenspruch', in *Gesammelte Studien zum Alten Testament* [Munich: Chr. Kaiser Verlag, 1964], pp. 38-39).

Wolff's observation cuts to the heart of the problem with Wildberger's study, which at times appears to want to penetrate into the very phenomenon of the reception of the divine word. It is no less hopeless to try simply to discriminate between Yhwh's and the prophet's speech on formal grounds. As indicated above, the effort leaves him in the position of making extremely subjective evaluations under the guise of objective ones. Consider the way he uses two of his criteria. The first is genre. The *Gattung* of a unit of speech is useful if it can be *shown*, not just presumed, always to work in one fashion or another, i.e. as human speech or divine, not both. But when at the *outset* Wildberger defines individual and communal laments as genres that do *not* carry the word of Yhwh, he is presupposing precisely what needs to be proved, begging the very question that the book of Jeremiah raises (see Wildberger, pp. 14-16).

The second of the two criteria is mode of address ('*Stilform*'). Wildberger lists five possible forms a speech of Yhwh can take; among these is one in which Yhwh refers to both himself and Israel in the third-person. Yet Wildberger ends up invalidating the authenticity of all the cases of this form that he finds, Jer 2.3 and 4.4 on the basis of the argument discussed above in n. 118, 14.10, 22.8-9, and 23.7 without specific explanation (Wildberger, pp. 60, 62). (Indeed, we are led to believe that 14.10 is dismissed as a borrowing upon Hos 8.12-14, but this leaves unexplained the authenticity of the *Stilform* in *that* passage. On the third-person reference to Israel in Jer 14.10, see above, p. 90.) We can only conclude that Wildberger's own preconceptions of the forms Yhwh's speech can and cannot take have determined his handling of the evidence.

Is it in fact the case that Yhwh would not refer to himself in the third-person? Apart from the high dubiety of ever being able to factor the human intermediary out of the divine word, one can cite any number of other texts from various genres which have Yhwh referring to himself just so. Whether one sees in these a breakdown of the fiction of divine speech or regards them as providing direct evidence of how Yhwh actually spoke, at the very least the texts prove that the third-person form of the self-references did not prevent their being *heard* as divine speech (e.g. Exod 15.26; 34.10, 14; Exod 20.7ff.; Ezek 13.5-6).

It might be added, with respect to the issue of citations, that Wildberger is no more willing or able than anyone else to specify how much of a given context is governed by the formula n^e'um-Yhwh and what criteria are to be employed for making judgments in this matter (Wildberger, pp. 80, 84).

120. The translation of vv. 2a-c follows Holladay's (*Architecture*, p. 182, n. 4), which makes good sense of the MT. However, his interpretation that 'the tongue is an arrow shot out by the bow of falsehood' is less compelling. While 9.7 may indeed call the tongue an arrow, that image does not work here. One treads/bends (*drk*) not the arrow but the bow.

The translation of the last colon is a minor variation on Berridge's, p. 174, which also stands apart from most of the commentators and the RSV by according well with the MT.

121. Cf. Berridge, p. 173; the MT; and the JPS.
122. So Bright, *Jeremiah*, pp. 67, 72.
123. Berridge, pp. 173-74. One wonders if underlying this proposed structure there is not the invective/threat model of prophetic speech whereby the prophet shapes the invective while the threat represents Yhwh's own words, marked by the messenger formula (see, for example, von Rad, *OTT*, II, pp. 72-73, 132). However accurate this model may be for Amos, it is surely inadequate for the book of Jeremiah. 9.6-8 itself contains elements of both invective (v. 7) and threat (vv. 6, 8).
124. We might speculate that the parallel with Ps 55.12, in particular the final words *tōk ûmirmâ*, induced the Greek translators of Jeremiah to render 9.5 as they did.
125. Berridge, p. 174.
126. Cf. JPS.
127. Bright, *Jeremiah*, p. 72. The tendency to confuse the text's historical-compositional dimension with the way it works literarily is epitomized by Bright's remark, 'the speaker is Jeremiah (vss. 9 and 10 are separate fragments)'. The assumption is that because two verses were originally separate (if indeed they were), they cannot now function together as the connected words of a single speaker.
128. See Chapter 3, n. 6, and p. 107.
129. Note that v. 18 has the same grammatically ambiguous *nišma'* that was seen in 8.16. Here as there it may be heard as '*We* hear'.
130. Wildberger deletes the messenger formula here without textual grounds and without comment (as also he deletes the conflated form *kōh n^e'um-Yhwh*, which is lacking in the Greek). The fact that it can only be a matter of speculation to say that the passage was not originally Yhwh's speech deserves at least to be acknowledged.
131. Walther Zimmerli, 'Ich bin Yhwh', in *Geschichte und Altes Testament* (Tübingen: J.C.B. Mohr [Paul Siebeck], 1956), pp. 179-209.
132. Zimmerli, 'Ich', p. 200.
133. Note in this context, and especially the next (dealing with the depiction of Jeremiah as the true prophet), the essay of Thomas W. Overholt, 'Remarks on the Continuity of the Jeremiah Tradition', *JBL* 91 (1972), pp. 457-62. Overholt deals specifically with the concept *šeqer* 'falsehood' and the way it functions in the different strata of the book. He

concludes, 'Within the Book of Jeremiah the term displays the same patterns of usage and connotations in all three of the main 'sources'... Continuity rather than diversity in matters of theological content becomes the main impression left by the material' (p. 462).

Notes to Chapter Five

1. The title 'Confessions' has a time-honored place in the history of interpretation and will be maintained here. Although it may not be the most precise generic description ('complaints', 'petitionary laments', or simply 'prayers' might be better), it is at least useful for suggesting comparisons with later, similarly titled classics of undisputedly autobiographical character. It leads us to recognize the self-constituting quality such prayer normatively has. In the effort to gather one's life and present it before God, the self is being explored, expressed, shaped and reshaped.

There are other titles that would help to draw attention to significant features in the material. For instance, to view it under the rubric 'dramatic monologue' could indicate the reader's role in filling in the situation behind and around the speech itself. When the material is set in a larger literary context (as with the soliloquies in Shakespeare's plays, unlike the poems of Browning), the reader performs this convention of 'filling in' with respect to that context. My effort at this fits in with the synchronic orientation of the whole study.

Because the orientation remains synchronic, the Confessions will not be divided and rearranged internally according to reconstructions of their original form, occasion, and order of delivery. While, for example, Baumgartner identifies ten units (*Klagegedichte*, pp. 28-67), we shall follow the biblical ordering of five basic blocks: 11.18–12.6, 15.10-21, 17.(12-13)14-18, 18.19-23, and 20.7-18. Verses 14-18 of ch. 20 were no doubt originally an independent unit, being a self-curse rather than direct address to God. However, in their present location they function as part of, and as the conclusion to, the preceding lament of vv. 7-13. (See below, pp. 152, 158ff.)

2. Baumgartner, p. 86.

3. Von Rad, 'Die Konfessionen Jeremias', *EvT* 13 (1936), pp. 265-76. Among others to develop von Rad's insight, Berridge has written concerning Jer 20.7-9: 'Here Jeremiah bitterly laments the nature of his prophetic ministry, drawing attention to the full control which Yahweh exercises over his life. The prophet's words undoubtedly contain a reflection of the fact that his life in its entirety has been claimed by Yahweh. As we have noted earlier, Yahweh's coming judgment was not only verbally proclaimed by Jeremiah, but it was also necessary that this judgment be symbolically portrayed in his own life' (*Prophet, People, and the Word of Yahweh*, p. 155). Much of the

present chapter will be concerned to analyze closely this symbolic portrayal, along with another way in which the prophet's person is part of his proclamation (i.e. as exemplar).

4. 'Jeremiah's Complaints', discussed previously in this study, pp. 77-79.

5. If Reventlow's very distinctive approach is ignored here, it is only because it has been treated at some length previously in this study (pp. 79ff.). Suffice it to add that the problems afflicting his interpretation of Jeremiah's intercessory communal prayers (Jer 14) are only exacerbated when that interpretation is applied to the Confessions. See the well-put criticisms of A.H.J. Gunneweg on p. 399 of the article noted immediately below.

6. Gunneweg, 'Konfession oder Interpretation im Jeremiabuch', *ZTK* 67 (1970), pp. 395-416. Welten, 'Leiden und Leidenserfahrung im Buch Jeremia', *ZTK* 74 (1977), pp. 123-50.

7. D.J.A. Clines and D.M. Gunn, 'Form, Occasion and Redaction in Jeremiah 20', *ZAW* 88 (1976), p. 400.

8. Gunneweg, pp. 397-98.

9. Gunneweg, p. 416. Gunneweg does not say precisely what he means by these terms. The one constant feature in their current usage (at least among some circles) is that 'piety' bears a pejorative connotation and 'kerygma' a positive one. A more neutral stance is preferable. Therefore, 'piety' will be taken to mean the behavior of faith, where 'behavior' can include feeling, thinking, believing, speaking, and acting. 'Kerygma' will be understood as referring to both the act and content of proclamation. Broadly defined, kerygma is scripture's attestation of God's self-revelation and self-disposition to humanity.

10. Even less is the concern with substituting psychoanalytic categories for theological ones.

11. Welten, pp. 145-48.

12. See above, pp. 111-12. Both the Elijah and Psalmist analogies suggest the idea of isolation (cf. Welten, p. 146.)

13. Welten, p. 149. On the whole it is impressive both how cogently the different elements of Jeremiah's suffering fit together and how logically they follow from such Source A passages as 4.19-21; 5.12-13; 5.10; 8.19, 21, 23; 9.1; and 10.19-21. Furthermore, the fact that these elements have antecedents among Jeremiah's predecessors makes their emergence here if not predictable, at least hardly surprising. The theme of persecution (with the implication of righteous suffering) is attested in the book of Amos (2.11-12; 7.10-13) and in the Elijah traditions (1 Kgs 18-19). Also, the picture in Jer 16 of a symbolic action that draws the prophet's person into his proclamation and assigns his consequent suffering a representative status has its analogy in Hosea's marriage (Hos 1-3). In sum, and aided by hindsight, we might say that the crystallization and convergence of the various elements of suffering are by Jeremiah's time virtually given by the nature of the prophetic vocation itself.

14. See Welten, pp. 146, 148, 150.

15. To say that the strata have different theologies would make better sense if: 1. the features emphasized or developed in each stratum were shown to be mutually incompatible and to entail fundamentally different views of the nature of suffering *per se* (i.e. views in which the reasons or causes of suffering were unrelated, in which suffering is constituted by different configurations of beliefs and emotions, and in which suffering has significantly different consequences, such as violence on the one hand and paralysis on the other, or rejection of one's belief structure vs. recommitment to it); and 2. such features were shown to represent the central and controlling interests of the stratum in which they appear. In my opinion Welten's analysis satisfies neither of these criteria.

16. Baumgartner, p. 43.
17. Baumgartner, p. 40; Berridge, pp. 149-50.
18. So Bright, *Jeremiah*, p. 119.
19. Baumgartner, p. 41.
20. See above, Chapter 4, n. 73.
21. See above, pp. 86 and 100.
22. Bright (*Jeremiah*, p. 119) sees a 'contrast' with the Temple Sermon here, if not an outright contradiction. My position is more in line with that of Berridge, pp. 150-51.
23. Whether to render the colon in the imperfect indicative or in the jussive ('Let all...') is a difficult decision since the mood of *yēbōšû* is perfectly ambiguous. If the jussive is chosen, then the expression appears as a request for vindication or vengeance, and the psalmic parallels are many (Pss 25.3; 31.18; 35.4, 26; 40.14; 70.3, 4; 71.13). If the indicative is chosen, as here, and the expression is read as a confidence motif, the close parallels are fewer (Pss 6.11; 71.24; and the communal lament 44.8). It may prove upon further research that the grammatical distinction is spurious, in which case so would be a rigorous form-critical distinction between the confidence and vengeance motifs.
24. In hymns and communal laments the enemies are either Yhwh's or Yhwh's and Israel's indistinguishably. See Pss 14.6 (= 53.6); 83.18; and 129.5.
25. Baumgartner, p. 42.
26. See above, pp. 76, 97-98, 107-108.
27. The root *rp'* is also attested in Jer 3.22; 6.14; 8.11; 19.11; 30.17; 33.6; 46.11; 51.8, 9.
28. Berridge, p. 148. The phrase 'to whom this word was spoken' signals Berridge's two-part thesis: that the Confessions (1) were the prophet's own compositions and (2) functioned from the outset as part of his public proclamation. This thesis also underlies the citation next below. As repeatedly emphasized, our interest is not in this thesis but in the 'paradigmatic significance' of the prophetic words and persona.
29. Berridge, pp. 147-48. (See note above.)

30. Such would be the normative logic of the situation. Any prayer of course, however exalted in form and content, can be trivialized by one's shallow use of it. But that would be an aberrant, not a normative use. Incidentally, the character qualifications most relevant to the normative/aberrant distinction are moral, not intellectual.

31. See the discussion of praise and gratitude in prayer in Don E. Saliers' *The Soul in Paraphrase: Prayer and the Religious Affections* (New York: Seabury, 1980), pp. 50-59.

32. Elsewhere in the book $t^ehillâ$ occurs only three times, all within the oracles against the nations (48.2; 49.25; and 51.41), and without reference to either Jeremiah or Israel.

33. See Berridge, p. 141.

34. Baumgartner, pp. 42-43. Cf. Bright, 'Jeremiah's Complaints', pp. 205-207, who agrees. By contrast, Reventlow places the whole Confession in the cult where it is spoken by Jeremiah *qua* cultic intercessor. The 'word' refers to an out-standing priestly salvation oracle (*Liturgie und prophetische Ich bei Jeremia*, pp. 229-40). Cf. Gunneweg and Welten below.

35. Gunneweg, pp. 406-407; Welten, p. 141.

36. Baumgartner, pp. 42-43.

37. Berridge, p. 138. So also Bright, 'Jeremiah's Complaints', pp. 206-207.

38. Berridge, p. 138.

39. Berridge, p. 146.

40. Berridge, p. 146.

41. Berridge, pp. 146, 160.

42. Pss 18.19; 20.2; 37.19, 39; 41.2; 50.15; 59.17; 77.3; 86.7; 102.3. In five of these ten passages the *nomen rectum* bears the first-singular suffix. This is indicative of the individual quality of the distress. Only in two royal psalms, 21.10 and 110.5, is it likely that the *'ēt/yôm* expressions refer to Yhwh's judgment and have the eschatological component that they bear in prophetic speech.

43. Berridge, pp. 141-43.

44. Berridge (p. 141) renders *yôm 'ānûš* as 'the day from which there is no recovery' to underscore the contrast with the complaint-psalm oriented '*Krankheitstag*' of Reventlow (p. 238).

45. Berridge, pp. 139-41.

46. Berridge, pp. 144-45.

47. Berridge, pp. 145-46.

48. Baumgartner, p. 43.

49. Baumgartner, p. 43. The same movement is evident in several of the other Confessions: 11.19-20, 18.19-23, and 20.7-12.

50. Berridge, p. 149.

51. Berridge, pp. 146-48.

52. On both the linguistic and thematic levels the connections between the Confession and vv. 19-27 are almost nil, certainly fewer than those between

the Confession and vv. 1-11.
53. See above, p. 218.
54. For *brk* in parallel with *'rr* (or *qbb* or *qll*), see Prov 3.33; 11.26; 20.21; 28.20; and 30.11. See also the wisdom psalm 37.22 (*mebōrākāyw/mequllālāyw*).
55. On 'trust', see G. von Rad, *Wisdom in Israel*, trans. James D. Martin (Nashville: Abingdon, 1972), pp. 190-206.
56. See above, pp. 74-75, 123.
57. Gunneweg reflected on Jeremiah's depiction here and in 20.14-18 and characterized it as that of a 'suffering sage' (p. 412). Clines and Gunn found this improbable (p. 407, n. 82). I would hope that the more extended reflection offered here might alter their opinion and reinforce Gunneweg's.
58. Ps 1.1 is a notable example, given its other connections with our passage. See also Pss 2.12; 32.1-2; 33.12; 41.2; 65.5; 84.5-6, 13; 89.16; 106.3; 112.1; 119.1-2; 128.1; 137.8-9; 144.15; 146.5.
59. See above, p. 141.
60. On *'ănî Yhwh*, see above, pp. 121-23.
61. For this dimension of *bḥn*, see Pss 66.10; 81.8; Job 7.18; 23.10; 34.36. For *ḥqr*, note the use in Ps 139.1 which begins an extended reflection upon Yhwh's knowledge of the complainant. Verse 5 has 'Thou dost beset (*ṣartānî*) me behind and before and layest thy hand upon me', which sounds like a lament yet is followed by 'Such knowledge is too wonderful for me'. The clear implication is that Yhwh's searching and besetting the psalmist are the same, or at least are both a function of Yhwh's knowing him. See also Job 13.9 where Job retorts to his friends, 'Will it be well with you when he searches (*yaḥqōr*) you out?', i.e. will they speak so glibly when God does to them what he has done to Job? God's searching, in other words, refers to an ordeal of suffering.
62. To be sure, a balancing statement, or symmetry, is not form-critically required. Nevertheless, it is a reasonable expectation based on the cursed-blessed polarity and the structure of vv. 5-8.
63. Baumgartner, p. 43.
64. Clines and Gunn, 'Form, Occasion and Redaction in Jeremiah 20', *ZAW* 88 (1976), pp. 390-409.
65. Clines and Gunn, pp. 392-93.
66. Clines and Gunn, pp. 394-95. Cf. Baumgartner, pp. 65-66; and Berridge, p. 114, n. 1.
67. Clines and Gunn, 'Form', p. 395.
68. Clines and Gunn, '"You Tried to Persuade Me"', p. 24.
69. Cf. Clines and Gunn, '"You Tried to Persuade Me"', p. 26.
70. Clines and Gunn, 'Form', p. 396. Cf. Baumgartner, p. 49.
71. Clines and Gunn, 'Form', pp. 396-97.
72. Cf. Jer 12.1; 15.18.
73. The turn from protest to assurance is strongly marked in v. 11 by the rhetorical assonance among the five verbs that describe the enemies'

retribution (*yikkāšᵉlû*, *yukālû*, *bōšû*, *hiśkîlû*, *tiśśākēah*).
74. Clines and Gunn, 'Form', p. 399.
75. Clines and Gunn, 'Form', p. 399.
76. Clines and Gunn, 'Form', p. 400.
77. Clines and Gunn, 'Form', p. 402. Again, their position is that 20.7-13 was originally spoken in the course of Jeremiah's public ministry in order to affirm in the face of mockery that the word he spoke was Yhwh's, not his own, that he delivered it under divine compulsion, and that it would ultimately triumph over its opposition (pp. 401-402). Read synchronically, this part of the Confession can retain its proclamatory function and continue to speak its original message.
78. Clines and Gunn, 'Form', p. 404, citing W. Thiel, *Die deuteronomistische Redaktion von Jeremia 1-25* (Neukirchen-Vluyn: Neukirchener Verlag, 1973), pp. 219-29.
79. Cf. Clines and Gunn, 'Form', pp. 402-404.
80. Cf. Clines and Gunn, 'Form', pp. 404-405.
81. Clines and Gunn, 'Form', p. 405.
82. Clines and Gunn, 'Form', pp. 405-406.
83. Clines and Gunn, 'Form', p. 406.
84. Clines and Gunn, 'Form', pp. 406-407, citing D.H. Hillers' study, 'A Convention in Hebrew Literature: The Reaction to Bad News', *ZAW* 77 (1965), pp. 86-90.
85. Clines and Gunn, 'Form', p. 407. Emphasis added.
86. Hillers, 'A Convention', p. 89. Emphasis added.
87. Clines and Gunn, 'Form', p. 407. Hillers, 'A Convention', p. 89, n. 11.
88. I would allow *'āmāl*, *yāgôn*, and *bōšet* their objective quality while maintaining that they may simultaneously carry a subjective significance. One noteworthy implication is that once again there is a metaphoric linkage between the person of the prophet and the people as a whole.
89. Cf. Jer 11.21-23; 12.5-13; 15.19-21; 17.1-4, 5-11.
90. Clines and Gunn observe that vv. 14-18 are 'not only the sequel to vv. 7-13, but are also the preface to ch. 21-24, a collection of judgment speeches against Judah' ('Form', p. 408), and it is worth noting that at several places this material evokes elements of Jeremiah's paradigmatic status. For example, in the oracles against the kings, especially in 22.16-17, 21-22, 26, there is a series of motifs that were central in the Confessions and by their use here (in application to the king who is also a figure representative of the nation as a whole) allow us to see Jeremiah as a metaphor of the divine-human relationship (e.g. the motifs of violence against vs. justice for the needy, innocent suffering, obeying and knowing Yhwh, shame and confusion, mother and son). On the other hand, the oracles against the prophets in 23.9ff. have the effect of recommending Jeremiah as an exemplary figure of obedience (see the discussion of 9.11 and its relation to 23.9ff. on p. 124 above). It may not be possible to separate these two aspects,

the metaphoric and the exemplary, in ch. 21 and its development in the B material.

91. Reacting against Kremers' position ('Leidensgemeinschaft mit Gott im Alten Testament: Eine Untersuchung der "biographischen" Berichte im Jeremiabuch', *EvT* 13 [1953], pp. 122-40), both Martin Kessler ('Jeremiah Chapters 26-45 Reconsidered', *JNES* 27 [1968], pp. 81-88) and E.W. Nicholson (*Preaching to the Exiles* [New York: Schocken Books, 1970], pp. 104-13) have argued that the subject of the B material is not so much Jeremiah's suffering as it is the history of the word of Yhwh. Welten shows, quite successfully in my opinion, that these two subjects are intimately related: the nation's response to the word mirrors its response to the prophet and vice-versa, the rejection of the one entails the rejection of the other, and the narratives are designed to reflect this (Welten, pp. 135-36). It is interesting to note that by this analysis the personal fate of Jeremiah should not be seen as tragic (because of the text's final silence), for the ultimate triumph of the word is his triumph as well.

92. In support of Welten's thesis described above, we should note the tone of the narrative at this point. While for the most part quite neutral and detached, with the reportage of Jeremiah's descent and rescue from the cistern it conveys a strong sense of pathos. Partly by its very starkness and partly by the repetition of *ṭîṭ*, 'mire', 38.6b exudes a sense of dread: *ûbabbôr 'ên-mayim kî 'im-ṭîṭ wayyiṭba' yirmᵉyāhû baṭṭîṭ* ('And there was no water in the cistern but only mire, and Jeremiah sank into the mire'). And note the understated compassion shown Jeremiah by Ebed-melek as he instructs him to 'put the rags and clothes between your armpits and the ropes' (38.12).

93. The difference in the formulation of the promise does not in my opinion represent a difference in content. It may be noted that accompanying the formula in the oracle to Ebed-melek there is language very similar to that used in the promises to Jeremiah, e.g. 'But I will deliver (*wᵉhiṣṣaltîka*) you on that day, . . . and you shall not be given into the hand of the men of whom you are afraid. For I will surely save you . . . '

94. The verb *swt*, 'incite', is an extraordinarily good parallel to *pth* which is interpreted by Clines and Gunn as 'urge strongly', 'persuade' ('"You Tried to Persuade Me"', pp. 20-23).

Notes to Chapter Six

1. See above, pp. 16-18.
2. Saliers, pp. 21-22.
3. In this context we may recall the observations of Kessler and Nicholson that the B stratum, for example, is not so much the story of Jeremiah as it is the story of God's word. (See Chapter 5, n. 91.) By the

model proposed here, and described by Sallie TeSelle below, it is the story of both. The prophet's life and God's word are mutually illuminating.

4. TeSelle, pp. 165-66.
5. TeSelle, p. 169.
6. See Thomas S. Kuhn, *The Structure of Scientific Revolutions*, 2nd edn (Chicago: University of Chicago Press, 1970). The implications of Kuhn's work for religion have been explored by Ian G. Barbour in his *Myths, Models, and Paradigms*. For the discussion that follows, see Barbour, pp. 8-11, 92-118.
7. TeSelle, p. 156.
8. David J. Gouwens, 'Some Aspects of Imagination and Truth-Telling in Christian Discourse', S.T.M. Thesis Yale University Divinity School, 1974, p. 45.
9. Henry James, *Theory of Fiction*, ed. James E. Miller, Jr (Lincoln: n.p., 1972), p. 93.
10. Gouwens, pp. 68-69.
11. See Alonso Schökel, pp. 274-75.
12. Of the latter, see especially Wolfgang Iser, *The Act of Reading*, discussed below. See also Chapter 1, n. 27.
13. Iser, *Reading*, p. 143.
14. Iser, *Reading*, p. 126.
15. Iser, *Reading*, p. 194.
16. Typical examples cited by Iser are the novels of Ivy Compton-Burnett and James Joyce.
17. Iser, *Reading*, pp. 126, 132.

BIBLIOGRAPHY

Abrams, M.H. *A Glossary of Literary Terms*. 3rd edn. New York: Holt, Rinehart and Winston, 1957.
Achtemeier, E.F. 'Righteousness in the OT'. *IDB*. Ed. G.A. Buttrick, *et al.* Nashville: Abingdon, 1962, IV, 80-85.
Adams, James Truslow. *The Tempo of Modern Life*. New York: Albert & Charles Boni, 1931.
Albright, William Foxwell. 'The Refrain "And God Saw *KI TOBH*" in Genesis'. In *Mélanges bibliques rédigés en l'honneur de André Robert*. Paris: Bloud & Gay, 1956, pp. 22-26.
—*From the Stone Age to Christianity*. 2nd edn. Garden City, N.Y.: Doubleday, 1957.
Alonso Schökel, Luis, S.J. *The Inspired Word: Scripture in the Light of Language and Literature*. Trans. Francis Martin, O.C.S.O. New York: Herder and Herder, 1972.
Anscombe, C.E.M. *Intentions*. Ithaca: Cornell University Press, 1963.
Auerbach, Erich. *Mimesis: The Representation of Reality in Western Literature*. Trans. Willard R. Trask. Princeton: Princeton University Press, 1953.
Austin, J.L. *How To Do Things with Words*. 2nd edn. Cambridge: Harvard University Press, 1975.
—'Performative Utterances'. In *Philosophical Papers*. Oxford: Clarendon Press, 1961, pp. 220-39.
Balch, Marston, ed. *Modern Short Biographies and Autobiographies*. New York: Harcourt, Brace and Company, 1935.
Baltzer, Klaus. *Die Biographie der Propheten*. Neukirchen-Vluyn: Neukirchener Verlag, 1975.
Barbour, Ian G. *Myths, Models, and Paradigms: A Comparative Study in Science and Religion*. New York: Harper & Row, 1974.
Barfield, Owen. 'The Meaning of the Word "Literal"'. In *Metaphor and Symbol*. Proceedings of the Twelfth Symposium of the Colston Research Society. Ed. L.C. Knights and Basil Cottle. London: Butterworths, 1960, pp. 48-63.
Barr, James. *Comparative Philology and the Text of the Old Testament*. Oxford: Clarendon Press, 1968.
—*The Semantics of Biblical Language*. London: OUP, 1961.
Baumgartner, Walter. *Die Klagegedichte des Jeremia*. Giessen: Alfred Töpelmann, 1917.
Bell, Richard H. and Ronald E. Hustwit, eds. *Essays on Kierkegaard & Wittgenstein: On Understanding the Self*. Wooster, Ohio: The College of Wooster, 1978.

Berridge, John MacLennan. *Prophet, People, and the Word of Yahweh: An Examination of Form and Content in the Proclamation of the Prophet Jeremiah*. Zurich: EVZ-Verlag, 1970.

Blackman, E.C. 'Faith, Faithfulness'. *IDB*. Ed. G.A. Buttrick, *et al.* Nashville: Abingdon, 1962, II, 222-27.

Blank, S.H. 'The Confessions of Jeremiah, and the Meaning of Prayer'. *HUCA* 21 (1948), pp. 331-54.

—'The Prophet as Paradigm'. In *Essays in Old Testament Ethics*. Ed. J.L. Crenshaw and J.T. Willis. New York: KTAV, 1974, pp. 111-30.

Bleich, David. *Subjective Criticism*. Baltimore: John Hopkins University Press, 1978.

Blenkinsopp, Joseph. 'Biographical Patterns in Biblical Narrative'. *JSOT* 20 (1981), pp. 27-46.

Bradford, Gamaliel. *Biography and the Human Heart*. Boston & New York: Houghton Mifflin Company, 1932.

Bright, John. *Jeremiah*. The Anchor Bible. Garden City, N.Y.: Doubleday, 1965.

—'Jeremiah's Complaints: Liturgy, or Expressions of Personal Distress?' In *Proclamation and Presence: Old Testament Essays in Honor of Gwynne Henton Davies*. Ed. J.I. Durham and J.R. Porter. London: SCM, 1970, pp. 189-214.

—'The Prophetic Reminiscence: Its Place and Function in the Book of Jeremiah'. In *Biblical Essays. Proceedings of the ninth meeting of 'Die Outestamentiese Werkgemeenskap in Suid-Afrika'*. Pretoria: University of Stellenbosch, 1966, pp. 11-30.

Brockington, L.H. 'The Hebrew Conception of Personality in Relation to the Knowledge of God'. *JTS* 47 (1946), pp. 1-11.

Buber, Martin. *The Prophetic Faith*. Trans. Carlyle Witton-Davies. New York: Harper & Row, 1949, repr. New York: Harper Torchbooks, 1960.

Carlyle, Thomas. 'Biography'. In *Critical and Miscellaneous Essays*. Vol. IV. London: Chapman and Hall, 1872, pp. 51-66.

Cavell, Stanley. *Must We Mean What We Say? A Book of Essays*. Cambridge: CUP, 1976.

Childs, Brevard S. *The Book of Exodus: A Critical Theological Commentary*. Philadelphia: Westminster, 1974.

—*Introduction to the Old Testament as Scripture*. Philadelphia: Fortress, 1979.

Clements, R.E. *God and Temple*. Philadelphia: Fortress Press, 1965.

Clines, D.J.A. and D.M. Gunn. 'Form, Occasion and Redaction in Jeremiah 20'. *ZAW* 88 (1976), pp. 390-409.

—'"You Tried to Persuade Me" and "Violence! Outrage!" in Jeremiah 20:7-8'. *VT* 28 (1978), pp. 20-27.

Cornill, C.H. *Das Buch Jeremia*. Leipzig: Tauchnitz, 1905.

Culler, Jonathan. *On Deconstruction: Theory and Criticism After Structuralism.* Ithaca, New York: Cornell University Press, 1982
—*Ferdinand de Saussure.* New York: Penguin Books, 1976.
—*Structuralist Poetics: Structuralism, Linguistics, and the Study of Literature.* Ithaca, N.Y.: Cornell University Press, 1975.
Dodd, C.H. *According to the Scriptures: The Sub-structure of New Testament Theology.* London: Nisbet, 1952.
Duhm, Bernhard. *Das Buch Jeremia.* Tübingen and Leipzig: J.C.B. Mohr [Paul Siebeck], 1901.
Durling, Dwight and William Watt, eds. *Biography: Varieties and Parallels.* New York: The Dryden Press, 1941.
Eco, Umberto. *The Role of the Reader: Explorations in the Semiotics of Texts.* Bloomington: Indiana University Press, 1979.
Eichrodt, Walther. *Man in the Old Testament.* Trans. K. & R. Gregor Smith. Chicago: Henry Regnery, 1951.
—*Theology of the Old Testament.* Trans. J.A. Baker. Vol. II. Philadelphia: Westminster, 1967.
Eissfeldt, Otto. *The Old Testament: An Introduction.* Trans. Peter R. Ackroyd. New York: Harper and Row, 1965.
Eliot, T.S. 'Tradition and Individual Talent'. In *Selected Essays 1917-1932.* New York: Harcourt, Brace and Company, 1932, pp. 3-11.
Erikson, Erik. *Young Man Luther: A Study in Psychoanalysis and History.* New York: W.W. Norton, 1958.
Evans, Donald. *The Logic of Self-Involvement: A Philosophical Study of Everyday Language with Special References to the Christian Use of Language about God as Creator.* London: SCM, 1963.
Ewald, G.H.A. *Prophets of the Old Testament.* Trans. J. Frederick Smith. Edinburgh and London: Williams and Norgate, 1878. Vol. III.
Ferré, Frederick. *Language, Logic and God.* New York: Harper & Row, 1969.
Fish, Stanley. *Is There A Text in This Class? The Authority of Interpretive Communities.* Cambridge: Harvard University Press, 1980.
Forster, E.M. *Aspects of the Novel.* New York: Harcourt, Brace & World, 1927.
Frei, Hans W. *The Eclipse of Biblical Narrative: A Study in Eighteenth Century Hermeneutics.* New Haven: Yale University Press, 1974.
—*The Identity of Jesus Christ: The Hermeneutical Bases of Dogmatic Theology.* Philadelphia: Fortress, 1975.
Frost, S.B. 'Asseveration by Thanksgiving'. *VT* 8 (1958), pp. 380-90.
Frye, Northrop. *Anatomy of Criticism: Four Essays.* Princeton: Princeton University Press, 1957.
Galling, Kurt. 'Die Ausrufung des Namens als Rechtsakt in Israel'. *TLZ* 81 (1956), cols. 65-70.
Gerstenberger, Erhard. 'Jeremiah's Complaints: Observations on Jer. 15:10-21'.

JBL 82 (1963), pp. 393-408.
Gordon, R. Crouther. *The Rebel Prophet: Studies in the Personality of Jeremiah*. New York: Harper & Brothers, 1932.
Gosling, J.C. 'Emotion and Object'. *Philosophical Review* 74 (1965), pp. 486-503.
Gouwens, David J. 'Some Aspects of Imagination and Truth-Telling in Christian Discourse'. S.T.M. Thesis, Yale University Divinity School, 1974.
Gunkel, Hermann and Joachim Begrich. *Einleitung in die Psalmen: Die Gattungen der religiösen Lyrik Israels*. Göttingen: Vandenhoeck & Ruprecht, 1933.
—'Fundamental Problems of Hebrew Literary History'. In *What Remains of the Old Testament? and Other Essays*. Trans. A.J. Dallas. New York: Macmillan, 1928.
Gunneweg, A.H.J. 'Konfession oder Interpretation im Jeremiabuch'. *ZTK* 67 (1970), pp. 395-416.
Habel, Norman. 'The Form and Significance of the Call Narratives'. *ZAW* 77 (1965), pp. 297-323.
Hadas, Moses and Morton Smith. *Heroes and Gods: Spiritual Biographies in Antiquity*. Freeport, N.Y.: Books for Libraries Press, 1965.
Henn, T.R. *The Bible as Literature*. New York: OUP, 1970.
Herntrich, V. *Jeremia, der Prophet und sein Volk*. Gütersloh: Bertelsmann, 1938.
Hermann, Siegfried. 'Die Königsnovelle in Ägypten und in Israel'. In *Wissenschaftliche Zeitschrift der Karl Marx Universität* 8 (1953-54), pp. 51-62.
—'Forschung am Jeremiabuch: Probleme und Tendenzen ihrer neueren Entwicklung'. *TLZ* 102 (1977), cols. 481-90.
Heschel, Abraham. *The Prophets*. 2 vols. New York: Harper & Row, 1962; repr. New York: Harper Torchbooks, 1969 (vol. I), 1971 (vol. II).
Hillers, Delbert. 'A Convention in Hebrew Literature: The Reaction to Bad News'. *ZAW* 77 (1965), pp. 86-90.
—*Treaty Curses and the Old Testament Prophets*. Rome: Pontifical Biblical Institute, 1964.
Hirsch, E.D. *Validity in Interpretation*. New Haven: Yale University Press, 1967.
Hobbs, T.R. 'Some Remarks on the Composition and Structure of the Book of Jeremiah'. *CBQ* 34 (1972), pp. 257-75.
Holladay, W.L. *The Architecture of Jeremiah 1-20*. Lewisburg, Pa.: Bucknell University Press, 1976.
—'A Fresh Look at "Source B" and "Source C" in Jeremiah'. *VT* 25 (1975), pp. 394-412.
—*The Root Šûbh in the Old Testament: With Particular Reference to its*

Usages in Covenantal Contexts. Leiden: Brill, 1958.
—'The So-Called "Deuteronomic Gloss" in Jer. VIII 19b'. *VT* 12 (1962), pp. 494-98.
Holmer, Paul. 'About Being a Person: Kierkegaard's *Fear and Trembling*'. (Unpublished paper, Yale University.)
—'About "Understanding"'. (Unpublished paper, Yale University.)
—'The Case for the Virtues'. (Unpublished paper, Yale University.)
—'The Human Heart—the Logic of a Metaphor'. (Unpublished paper, Yale University.)
—'Saying and Showing: A Religious Consideration'. (Unpublished paper, Yale University.)
Hopper, Stanley Romaine. 'Exposition of the Book of Jeremiah'. In *IB*. Ed. George Arthur Buttrick, *et al.* New York: Abingdon Press, 1952, V, 794-1142.
Hyatt, James P. 'The Book of Jeremiah: Introduction and Exegesis'. In *IB*. Ed. G.A. Buttrick, *et al.* New York: Abingdon Press, 1952, V, 777-1142.
—*Jeremiah, Prophet of Courage and Hope.* New York: Abingdon, 1958.
Ingarden, Roman. *The Cognition of the Literary Work of Art.* Trans. Ruth Ann Crowley and Kenneth R. Olson. Evanston: Northwestern University Press, 1973.
Iser, Wolfgang. *The Act of Reading: A Theory of Aesthetic Response.* Baltimore: Johns Hopkins University Press, 1978.
—*The Implied Reader: Patterns of Communication in Prose Fiction from Bunyan to Beckett.* Baltimore: Johns Hopkins University Press, 1974.
James, Fleming. *Personalities of the Old Testament.* New York: Charles Scribner's Sons, 1939.
James, Henry. 'The Art of Fiction'. In *Partial Portraits.* New York: MacMillan, 1888; repr. in *'The Art of Fiction' and Other Essays.* New York: OUP, 1948, pp. 3-23.
—*Theory of Fiction.* Ed. James E. Miller, Jr. Lincoln: University of Nebraska Press, 1972.
Johnson, Aubrey R. *The Vitality of the Individual in the Thought of Ancient Israel.* 2nd edn. Cardiff: University of Wales Press, 1964.
Jordan, Barbara. *The Critical Difference: Essays on the Contemporary Rhetoric of Reading.* Baltimore: Johns Hopkins University Press, 1980.
Kenny, Anthony. *Fiction, Emotion, and Will.* New York: Humanities Press, 1963.
Kessler, Martin. 'Jeremiah Chapters 26-45 Reconsidered'. *JNES* 27 (1968), pp. 81-88.
—*A Prophetic Biography: A Form-Critical Study of Jeremiah, Chapters 26-29, 32-45.* Diss. Brandeis, 1965. Ann Arbor: University Microfilms, 1967.
Kittel, Rudolph. *Great Men and Movements in Israel.* Trans. Charlotte A. Knoch and C.D. Wright. New York: MacMillan, 1929.
Knierim, Rolf. 'Old Testament Form Criticism Reconsidered'. *Interpretation*

27 (1973), 435-68.
Koch, Klaus. *The Growth of the Biblical Tradition: The Form-Critical Method*. Trans. S.M. Cupitt from 2nd German edn. New York: Charles Scribner's Sons, 1969.
Kremers, Heinz. 'Leidensgemeinschaft mit Gott im Alten Testament: Eine Untersuchung der "biographischen" Berichte im Jeremiabuch'. *EvT* 13 (1953), pp. 122-40.
Kuhn, Thomas S. *The Structure of Scientific Revolutions*. 2nd edn. Chicago: University of Chicago Press, 1970.
Lamparter, Helmut. *Die Botschaft des Alten Testaments. Prophet Wider Willen: der Prophet Jeremia*. Stuttgart: Calwer, 1964.
Lewis, I.M. *Ecstatic Religion: An Anthropological Study of Spirit Possession and Shamanism*. Baltimore: Penguin Books, 1971; repr. 1975.
Lofthouse, William F. *Jeremiah and the New Covenant*. London: SCM, 1925.
Long, Burke O. 'Prophetic Authority as Social Reality'. In *Canon and Authority: Essays in Old Testament Religion and Theology*. Ed. Burke O. Long and George W. Coats. Philadelphia: Fortress, 1977, pp. 3-20.
Lundbom, Jack R. *Jeremiah: A Study in Ancient Hebrew Rhetoric*. SBL Dissertation Series 18. Missoula, Montana: Scholars Press, 1975.
Lyons, John. *Introduction to Theoretical Linguistics*. Cambridge: CUP, 1968.
McEvenue, Sean E. 'The Old Testament, Scripture or Theology?'. *Interpretation* 35 (1981), pp. 229-42.
Malcolm, Norman. 'Wittgenstein's *Philosophical Investigations*'. In *Wittgenstein: The Philosophical Investigations*. Ed. George Pitcher. Notre Dame: University of Notre Dame Press, 1966, pp. 65-103.
Marshall, G.D. 'On Being Affected'. *Mind* 77 (1968), pp. 243-59.
Mihalic, Joseph L. 'Dialogue with God: A Study of Some of Jeremiah's Confessions'. *Interpretation* 14 (1960), pp. 43-50.
Mowinckel, Sigmund. *Zur Komposition des Buches Jeremia*. Kristiania: Dybwald, 1914.
Muilenburg, James. 'Baruch the Scribe'. In *Proclamation and Presence: Old Testament Essays in Honor of Gwynne Henton Davies*. Ed. J.I. Durham and J.R. Porter. London: SCM, 1970, pp. 215-38.
—'The Linguistic and Rhetorical Usages of the Particle *kî* in the Old Testament'. *HUCA* 32 (1961), pp. 135-60.
Nicholson, E.W. *Preaching to the Exiles: A Study of the Prose Tradition in the Book of Jeremiah*. New York: Schocken Books, 1971.
Nicolson, Harold. *The Development of English Biography*. New York: Harcourt, Brace and Company, 1928.
Overholt, Thomas W. 'Jeremiah and the Nature of the Prophetic Process'. In *Scripture in History and Theology: Essays in Honor of J. Coert Rylaarsdam*. Ed. Arthur Merrill and Thomas Overholt. Pittsburgh:

Pickwick, 1977, pp. 129-50.
—'Jeremiah 27-29: The Question of False Prophecy'. *JAAR* 35 (1967), pp. 241-49.
—'Remarks on the Continuity of the Jeremiah Tradition'. *JBL* 91 (1972), pp. 457-62.
Pachter, Marc, ed. *Telling Lives: The Biographer's Art*. Washington, D.C.: New Republic Books, 1979.
Patterson, John. 'Jeremiah'. In *Peake's Commentary on the Bible*. Ed. Matthew Black and H.H. Rowley. London: Nelson, 1962, pp. 537-62.
Pedersen, Johannes. *Israel: Its Life and Culture*. Trans. Aslang Moller. London: OUP, 1926. Vols. I and II.
Perkins, Moreland. 'Emotion and Feeling'. *Philosophical Review* 75 (1966), pp. 139-60.
Price, Martin. 'The Other Self: Thoughts about Character in the Novel'. In *Imagined Worlds: Essays on Some English Novels and Novelists in Honour of John Butt*. London: Methuen, 1968, pp. 279-99.
von Rad, Gerhard. 'Die Konfessionen Jeremias'. *EvT* 13 (1936), pp. 265-76.
—*Old Testament Theology*. Trans. D.M.G. Stalker. Vol. I. New York: Harper & Row, 1962. Vol. II, 1965.
—*Wisdom in Israel*. Trans. James D. Martin. Nashville: Abingdon, 1972.
Reed, Joseph W. Jr. *English Biography in the Early Nineteenth Century, 1801-1838*. New Haven: Yale University Press, 1966.
Rendtorff, Rolf. *Men of the Old Testament*. Trans. Frank Clarke. Philadelphia: Fortress, 1968.
Reventlow, H. Graf. *Liturgie und prophetische Ich bei Jeremia*. Gütersloh: Mohn, 1963.
Richards, I.A. *The Philosophy of Rhetoric*. New York: OUP, 1936.
Robinson, H. Wheeler. *The Christian Doctrine of Man*. Edinburgh: T. & T. Clark, 1911.
—*Corporate Personality in Ancient Israel*. Philadelphia: Fortress, 1964.
—*The Cross of Jeremiah*. London: SCM, 1925.
—*Inspiration and Revelation in the Old Testament*. Oxford: Clarendon Press, 1946.
Rogerson, J.W. *Anthropology and the Old Testament*. Atlanta: John Knox, 1978.
Rorty, Amelie Oksenberg. 'A Literary Postscript: Characters, Persons, Selves, Individuals'. In *The Identities of Persons*. Ed. Amelie O. Rorty. Los Angeles: University of California Press, 1976, pp. 301-24.
Rudolph, Wilhelm. *Jeremia*. 3rd edn. Tübingen: J.C.B. Mohr [Paul Siebeck], 1968.
Ryle, Gilbert. 'Feelings'. In *Aesthetics and Language*. Ed. W. Elton, Oxford: Blackwell, 1954, pp. 56-72.
Saliers, Don E. *The Soul in Paraphrase: Prayer and the Religious Affections*. New York: Seabury, 1980.

Scholes, Robert and Robert Kellogg, *The Nature of Narrative*. New York: OUP, 1966.
Scholes, Robert. *Structuralism in Literature: An Introduction*. New Haven: Yale University Press, 1974.
Shoemaker, Sydney. *Self-Knowledge and Self-Identity*. Ithaca, N.Y.: Cornell University Press, 1974.
Skinner, John. *Prophecy and Religion: Studies in the Life of Jeremiah*. Cambridge: CUP, 1930.
Smith, George Adam. *The Book of Jeremiah*. 4th ed. New York: Harper & Brothers, 1929.
Soggin, J. Alberto. *Introduction to the Old Testament*. Trans. John Bowden. Philadelphia: Westminster, 1976.
Stoebe, H.J. 'Jeremia, Prophet und Seelsorger'. *TZ* 20 (1964), pp. 385-409.
Strawson, P.F. 'On Referring'. *Mind* 59 (1950), pp. 320-44.
Taylor, Richard. *Metaphysics*. 2nd edn. Englewood Cliffs, N.J.: Prentice-Hall, 1974.
TeSelle, Sallie McFague. *Speaking in Parables. A Study in Metaphor and Theology*. Philadelphia: Fortress, 1975.
Thalberg, Irving. 'Emotion and Thought'. In *Philosophy of Mind*. Ed. S. Hampshire. New York: Harper & Row, 1966, pp. 201-25.
Thiel, W. *Die deuteronomistische Redaktion von Jeremia 1-25*. Neukirchen-Vluyn: Neukirchener Verlag, 1973.
Tillich, Paul. *Systematic Theology*. Chicago: University of Chicago Press, 1957. Vol. II.
Torrey, Charles Cutter, ed. *The Lives of the Prophets*. Philadelphia: Society of Biblical Literature and Exegesis, 1946.
Vesey, Godfrey. *Personal Identity: A Philosophical Analysis*. Ithaca, N.Y.: Cornell University Press, 1974.
Volz, D. Paul. *Der Prophet Jeremia*. 2nd edn. Leipzig and Erlangen: Deichert, 1928.
Wanke, Gunther. *Untersuchungen zur sogenannten Baruchschrift*. Berlin: Walter de Gruyter, 1971.
Weippert, H. *Die Prosareden des Jeremiabuches*. Berlin: Walter de Gruyter, 1973.
Weiser, Artur. *Das Buch Jeremia*. 6th edn. Göttingen: Vandenhoeck & Ruprecht, 1969.
—*Die Psalmen*. Göttingen: Vandenhoeck & Ruprecht, 1955.
Welch, A.C. *Jeremiah: His Time and Work*. London: OUP, 1928.
Welten, Peter. 'Leiden und Leidenserfahrung im Buch Jeremia'. *ZTK* 74 (1977), pp. 123-50.
Wheelwright, Philip. *Metaphor and Reality*. Bloomington & London: Indiana University Press, 1962.
Wildberger, Hans. *Jahwewort und prophetische Rede bei Jeremia*. Theologische

Dissertationen Bd. 2. Zürich: Zwingli, 1942.
Williams, B.A.O. 'Pleasure and Belief'. In *Philosophy of Mind*. Ed. S. Hampshire. New York: Harper & Row, 1966, pp. 225-42.
Wilson, Rawdon. 'On Character: A Reply to Martin Price'. *Critical Inquiry* 2 (1975), pp. 791-98.
Wilson, Robert R. 'Form-Critical Investigation of the Prophetic Literature: The Present Situation'. In *SBL Seminar Papers* I (1973), pp. 100-27.
—'The Hardening of Pharaoh's Heart'. *CBQ* 41 (1979), pp. 18-36.
—'An Interpretation of Ezekiel's Dumbness'. *VT* 22 (1972), pp. 91-104.
—*Prophecy and Society in Ancient Israel*. Philadelphia: Fortress, 1980.
Wimsatt, William K. *The Verbal Icon*. Lexington: University Press of Kentucky, 1954.
Wittgenstein, Ludwig. *Philosophical Investigations*. Trans. G.E.M. Anscombe. 3rd ed. New York: Macmillan, 1958.
—*Tractatus Logico-Philosophicus*. Trans. P.F. Pears and B.F. McGuinness. London: Routledge and Kegan Paul, 1961.
Wolff, Hans Walter. *Anthropology of the Old Testament*. Trans. Margaret Kohl. Philadelphia: Fortress, 1974.
—*Hosea: A Commentary on the Book of the Prophet Hosea*. Trans. Gary Stansell. Philadelphia: Fortress, 1974.
—'The Kerygma of the Deuteronomic Historical Work'. Trans. Frederick Prussner. In *The Vitality of Old Testament Traditions*. Ed. Walter Brueggemann and H.W. Wolff. Atlanta: John Knox, 1976, pp. 83-100.
—*Das Zitat im Prophetenspruch: Eine Studie zur prophetische Verkundigungsweise*. München: Kaiser, 1937; repr. in *Gesammelte Studien zum Alten Testament*. München: Kaiser, 1964, pp. 36-129.
Zimmerli, Walther. *Ezekiel I: A Commentary on the Book of the Prophet Ezekiel, Chapters 1-24*. Trans. Ronald E. Clements. Philadelphia: Fortress, 1979.
—'Ich Bin Yhwh'. In *Geschichte und Altes Testament*. Tübingen: J.C.B. Mohr (Paul Siebeck), 1956, pp. 179-209.

INDEXES

INDEX OF AUTHORS

Abrams, M.H., 190, 200
Ackerman, J., 176
Albright, W.F., 182, 197
Alonso Schökel, L., 177, 215
Alter, R., 176
Anscombe, G.E.M., 179
Austin, J.L., 179

Balch, M., 181
Baltzer, K., 19-22, 24, 169, 179-181
Barbour, I., 185, 215
Barfield, O., 29-30, 186-187
Barr, J., 14, 25, 176, 183
Baumgartner, W., 60-61, 65-66, 127-128, 132-133, 135, 137-138, 141, 151, 154, 194, 198, 208, 210-212
Beardsley, M.C., 179
Begrich J., 200, 203
Bentham, J., 29
Berridge, J.M., 115-116, 132, 138-144, 148, 192-193, 196, 198, 201, 204-205, 207-208, 210-212
Blank, S., 197-198
Bleich, D., 177
Bright, J., 55, 79, 93, 117, 165, 188, 191, 197-199, 201-205, 207, 210-211
Brockington, L.H., 26-27, 183, 185
Buber, M., 58-59, 62, 198-199

Carlyle, T., 9
Cavell, S., 179
Childs, B.S., 175, 203
Clements, R.E., 203
Clines, D.J.A., 152-159, 209, 212-214
Cook, J., 184
Cornhill, J.H., 188, 192, 205
Culler, J., 14-15, 176-179

Darwin, C., 23
Dodd, C.H., 41, 191
Duhm, B., 60-61, 188, 191, 198, 205

Eco, U., 177
Eichrodt, W., 7-8, 175
Einstein, A., 23, 171
Eissfeldt, O., 175
Eliot, T.S., 179
Erikson, E., 8
Evans, D., 179
Ewald, G.H.A., 188

Ferré, F., 185
Fish, S., 177-178
Fokkelman, J.P., 176
Forster, E.M., 182, 201
Frei, H., 8, 175, 182, 187, 190
Freud, S., 23, 30
Frye, N., 187

Galling, K., 203
Gerstenberger, E., 77-78, 80, 82, 101-102, 110, 128, 152, 197, 200-203
Gesenius, W., 199, 205
Giesebrecht, F., 188
Good, E., 176
Gordon, T.C., 175
Gosling, J.C., 188
Gouwens, D., 215
Gunkel, H., 22, 24, 88, 182, 200-201, 203
Gunn, D.M., 152-159, 176, 209, 212-214
Gunneweg, A.H.J., 128-129, 131, 137-138, 132, 152, 209, 211-212

Habel, N.C., 196
Hadas, M., 181

Heidegger, M., 178
Henn, T.R., 176
Herntrich, V., 194
Heschel, A., 58, 62, 191, 197-198
Hillers, D., 93, 159, 203-204, 213
Hirsch, E.D., 178
Holladay, W.L., 35-37, 58-59, 105-106, 112, 188-191, 193, 194-195, 204-207
Holmer, P., 183-185
Hopper, S.R., 62-63, 67, 198-199
Hustwit, R., 38, 190
Hyatt, J.P., 175, 198, 202, 205

Ingarden, R., 177
Iser, W., 172-173, 177-178, 215

James, F., 9-10, 18, 175
James, H., 172, 181, 215
Johnson, A., 27, 31, 184-185, 187
Jordon, B., 177

Kautzsch, E., 199, 205
Kellogg, R., 202
Kenny, A., 188
Kessler, M., 22, 179, 182, 214
Kierkegaard, S., 38, 184
Kittel, R., 9-10, 18, 175
Knierim, R., 183
Koch, K., 22, 24, 182
Kremers, H., 214
Kuhn, T., 215

Lamparter, H., 61-62, 192, 196-197
Lofthouse, W.F., 175
Long, B.O., 175-176
Luther, M., 22-23, 182
Lyons, J., 176

McEvenue, S., 177-179

Malcolm, N., 184
Marshall, G.D., 188
Marx, K., 23

Montaigne, M., 171
Mowinckel, S., 19-20, 22, 24, 179, 200-202, 204
Muilenburg, J., 197

Newton, I., 171
Nicholson, E.W., 214
Nicolson, H., 181

Osborne, J., 21
Overholt, T.W., 207

Pachter, M., 181
Pedersen, J., 25-26, 183
Perkins, M., 188

von Rad, G., 7, 23, 127, 175, 183, 191, 193, 197, 201, 202, 207, 208, 212
Reed, J.W. Jr, 175, 181
von Reventlow, H., 62, 79-80, 83-84, 88, 91, 93, 95, 97, 196, 198, 201-202, 209, 211
Richards, I.A., 29, 186
Robinson, H.W., 26-31, 175, 183, 185
Rogerson, J.W., 183
Rorty, A., 179
Rudolph, W., 58, 188, 198, 205
Ryle, G., 188

Saliers, D.E., 211, 214
de Saussure, F., 14
Scholes, R., 176, 202
Skinner, J., 10-13, 18, 62, 84, 88, 175-176, 198, 202-203, 205
Smith, G.A., 175
Smith, M., 181
Soggin, A., 175
Stoebe, H.J., 194, 204

Te Selle, S., 169, 171, 185-186, 215
Thalberg, I., 188
Thiel, W., 213

Index of Authors

Tillich, P., 201
Toynbee, A., 9

Volz, P., 60-61, 175, 188, 198, 204

Weiser, A., 62, 90, 93, 188, 191-192, 198, 201, 203-205.
Welch, A.C., 175
Wellhausen, J., 12
Welten, P., 128-131, 137-138, 209, 211, 214
Wheelwright, P., 28, 185-186

Wildberger, H., 61, 65, 198, 202, 205-207
Williams, B.A.O., 188
Wilson, R.R., 75-77, 180, 193, 200, 202-203
Wimsatt, W.K., 179
Wittgenstein, L., 18, 30, 38, 172, 182-184, 187
Wolff, G., 182
Wolff, H.W., 25, 29, 31-34, 41, 44, 55, 82, 113, 183, 186-187, 190-192, 197, 202, 205-206

Zimmerli, W., 202, 207

INDEX OF HEBREW WORDS

'*bl*, '*ēbel* (to mourn, mourning), 194-195
'*ăhâ* (Ah!) 47, 92, 194-195
'*ôy* (woe!), 59-60, 64-65, 68, 199
'*ôt* (sign, symbol), 81
'*āmartî, wā'ōmar, wa'ănî 'āmartî* (and/then/but I said), 47-48, 59-61, 69-74, 92
'*emet* (faith, -fulness), 36, 39, 114, 122, 191
'*ănî, 'ānōkî* (I), 27, 122, 185
—'*ănî Yhwh* (I am Yhwh), 121, 212
'*sp* (to gather), 64, 105-106, 120, 122
'*ārûr* (cursed), 145, 147, 212
'*ašrê* (happy), 147
bw' (to come), 137, 139
bwš (to be ashamed, H. to shame), 132-134, 141, 210, 213
—*bōšet* (shame), 158, 213
bḥn (to test), 148-150, 212
byn (to understand), 103, 118, 204
bky (to weep), 68, 111, 194
—*bᵉkî* (weeping), 113
bānay (my sons), 60, 64, 67-69
bārûk (blessed), 145, 147, 212
bat 'ammî (daughter of my people), 109, 111, 204
g'l (to loathe), 98-99
dbr, dābār/dibrê (to speak, word/things), 82, 120, 153
—*dᵉbar Yhwh* (word of Yhwh), 82, 137-140
dmm (to be silent, perish), 53, 105-107
ha—'im—maddûa' (triple question pattern), 109-111
hôy (alas! woe!), 194-195
hmy, hāmôn (to moan, moaning/murmuring), 45-55, 197
zkr (to remember), 89, 98, 100
z'q (to cry out), 153
ḥwl (to writhe), 53, 55
ḥay Yhwh (as Yhwh lives!), 36, 39, 189
ḥkm (to be wise), 103, 118, 120, 204
ḥly, ḥolî (to be afflicted, affliction), 59, 61, 65-66, 69
ḥāmās wāšôd (violence and destruction), 66, 77, 153-154, 157
ḥesed (covenant love), 121
ḥqr (to search), 148-149, 212
ḥtt (to dismay), 142
ṭby (to sink), 162, 214
yāgôn (sorrow), 108, 158, 213
yd' (to know/acknowledge), 123, 141, 148-149

Index of Hebrew Words

yôm 'ānûš/rā'â (day of distress/evil), 137, 140-143, 166, 211
ykl (to prevail/succeed), 153-155, 161-163
yš' (to save), 85, 134-135, 163
kōh 'āmar Yhwh (thus says the Lord), 36, 40, 89, 92, 106, 118, 120, 145
kî (for, surely, how!), 36, 40, 50-52, 94, 98-99, 118-121, 191, 197
kissē' (throne), 98, 100, 132
lēb, lēbāb (heart), 14, 26, 31, 36, 47, 50, 53-55, 144-145, 148-149
m's (to reject), 98-99
mwl (to circumcise), 36, 42
makkâ (blow/stroke), 61, 65-66, 68, 94, 154
mē'îm (innards/bowels), 14, 53-55, 194
miqweh (hope), 85-86, 88, 132, 203
mišpāṭ (justice), 36-37, 39, 121, 191
n^e'um Yhwh (utterance of the Lord), 36, 40, 54, 105-106, 113-115, 120, 205-207
nehî (wailing), 117-119
nwd (to be aimless/wander), 36-39, 89
nyr (to till), 36, 41
swr (to turn aside), 36-38, 42, 134, 144-145
swt (to incite/persuade), 162, 214
spd, mispēd (to lament, mourning), 194-195
'zb (to forsake), 68, 94, 112, 132, 134, 144
'āmāl (toil), 158, 213
prr (to violate), 99
pth (to persuade/seduce), 155, 161, 163, 214
ṣ^{e}dāqâ (righteousness), 36-37, 40-41, 121, 191
rgz (to be shaken), 194
rā'â (calamity/evil/doom/wickedness), 50-53, 55-56, 140, 142-143, 154, 165-166
rp' (to heal), 134-135, 163, 210
—*marpē'* (healing), 98, 107, 135
śkl (to discern), 103
šbr, šeber (to destroy, destruction/hurt/wound), 59, 61, 65-68, 72, 94, 109, 141, 154
šwb (to return/repent), 36-38, 66, 189-190
šālôm (peace), 92, 100, 116
šeqer (deceit), 92, 207-208
t^{e}hillâ (praise), 134-137, 211
tôrâ (Torah/Law), 53, 104

INDEX OF SUBJECTS

Abimelech, 81
Abraham, 40, 81, 202
Absalom, 194
afflict(s), -ed, -ing, -ion(s), 52, 59, 63, 70, 73, 84, 131, 143
allegory, 63
ambiguity, ambiguities, ambiguous, 50-52, 58-59, 61, 74, 96-97, 107-108, 111, 113, 138, 154, 160, 165-166, 172, 189, 207, 210
anger, angry, 38, 45, 48, 56, 109-112, 117, 125, 155, 170, 185
anguish, -ed, 32, 56, 71, 74, 129, 158, 160, 167, 170, 184, 197, 200
anthropology, 25, 31
antipathy, 160
Augustine, 169
authentic, -ity, 10, 23, 40, 48-49, 79, 88, 91, 128, 130, 156, 166, 198, 206
autobiographical, autobiography, 8, 10, 21, 24, 27, 68, 73, 169, 171-172, 181, 208

Baruch, 7, 10, 64, 102, 161-162
biographical, biography, 8, 10, 13, 18-22, 24, 27, 75, 127-128, 130-131, 160, 169, 171, (*biographischen*) 179-182, 214
bitter, 50, 52, 71, 142, 160
blessed, 42, 144-147, 150, 192, 202

capacity, capacities, 16, 24, 26, 32, 43-44, 46-47, 49, 57, 83, 85, 147, 156, 168, 184-186
character(s), 12, 19, 21-22, 27, 80, 172, 179, 181-182, 201-202, 211
characterization, characterize, characterizing (see also depiction, description, portrait), 37, 47, 49, 58, 72-73, 75, 86, 89, 107-108, 123, 125, 154, 156-157, 170, 195
communal, community, 7-8, 39, 58-59, 62, 73, 76, 79-80, 83, 86, 88, 90, 95-96, 119, 125, 128, 130, 164, 168, 171, 178, 201, 206, 209-210
compassion (see also love), 54, 214
competence(s), competent, 16, 26, 174, 177-178, 179, 191-192
complaint(s) (see also confession, lamentation), 60-61, 64, 69-74, 76-79, 83, 85-86, 88, 95-96, 98-99, 101, 110, 132, 137-140, 142-143, 150, 152-153, 156, 161, 198, 200-201, 208-209, 211
compulsion (prophetic), compel, -ling, 32, 52-53, 55-56, 153-155, 213

confess, -ion(s), -ional (see also complaint, lamentation), 7-8, 24, 39, 63, 70, 74-76, 78-79, 84-85, 97-99, 102, 107, 121, 123, 126-131, 133-134, 136-150, 152, 156-157, 161-165, 167, 169, 189-199, 208-213
confidence, 85-86, 89, 92-93, 99, 132-134,, 136, 146, 150, 155, 210
conflict, 138-139, 142-143, 147, 154, 170

Index of Subjects 233

confused, confusion (see also consternation, dismay, perplexity, 48, 63, 85, 101, 196, 213
consolation, Book of Consolation, 61, 66, 68, 151, 191
consternation (see also confusion, dismay, perplexity), 52, 63, 109
convention(s), -al, ality, 16, 22, 24, 53-56, 72-73, 155, 157-159, 168, 178, 191, 194, 197, 208, 213
corporate, 13, 24, 66, 73
corporate personality, 26-27, 183, 199
courage, 47, 148
covenant, -al, 40-42, 84-87, 89-90, 92-93, 99-100, 121, 132, 147-148, 179-180, 182, 202-203
cult, -ic, -ically, 20, 42, 62, 79, 82-83, 88, 91, 125, 138, 196, 202-203, 211
curse(s), 87, 90, 93, 99, 101, 132, 150, 152, 164, 204, 208, 212
cursed, 144-147, 150-151, 158

David, -ic, 73, 194, 203
Deborah, 20
deceit, -ful, deception (see also false, falseness), 48, 92-93, 103-104, 114-116, 144, 148
delight, 52, 54, 121-122
depict, -ed, -ing, -ion, -ive (see also characterization, description, portrait), 8-10, 18, 21, 24, 57, 63-64, 66, 74, 77, 80, 90, 97, 107, 117, 124-125, 139, 143, 146, 151, 157, 182, 193, 199, 207, 212
description (re: identity) (see also characterization, depiction, portrait), 13, 47, 124, 170
despair, 159-160, 170
deuteronomic, deuteronomist, 37, 78, 86, 121, 157, 190, 200, 208-209, 211
diachronic, -ically, diachrony, 14-15, 18, 23, 35, 113, 128-129, 144, 165, 176, 188, 191, 193, 200-201
diffusion of consciousness, 26-27, 185
dismay, -ed (see also confusion, consternation), 108-109, 111, 141-142, 158-159
distress, -ed, -ing, 54, 63, 65, 67, 69-70, 73-74, 78, 83, 85, 93, 95, 139-143, 153, 158-159, 166, 201, 211
doom (see also judgment), 11, 50-52, 55, 78, 138, 142, 153, 157, 165, 176
dread, 155, 163, 166, 168, 214

Ebed-melek, 161-162, 214
Elijah, 112, 181, 209
emotion(s), -al, -alism, 12, 24, 26-28, 32-34, 38, 44, 48, 53-56, 95-96, 110, 113, 136, 156, 158-159, 164, 167-170, 172, 184, 188, 192, 194-196, 210
enmity, 109, 111
exemplar, example, exemplify (see also imitate, model, paradigm), 127-129, 143, 145, 150, 153, 160, 196, 209, 213-214

Ezekiel, 203

fact(s), 27-30, 56, 136, 159, 185
faith, -ful, -fulness, -less, 9, 12, 37, 84, 86, 90, 117, 129, 132-133, 140-142, 148, 151, 160-161, 167, 171-172, 174, 178, 191, 204, 209
false, -hood, -ly, -ness (see also deceit, deceitful), 48, 70, 76, 89, 92-94, 99, 104, 106, 114, 116, 122-124, 139, 189, 206-207
fear, 32-34, 44, 56, 142, 146-147, 170
first person, 7-8, 13, 23, 26-27, 45-47, 56, 58, 72-74, 76, 79, 95-97, 102-103, 106-119, 124-125, 127-128, 131, 133, 157, 159, 163-164, 167-168, 184, 190, 192, 199-200, 205, 211
folly, fool(s), foolish, 44, 52, 70, 144-145, 149-150
form critic(s), -al, -ally, -ism, 11, 18-19, 22, 35, 60-61, 66, 69-70, 72, 88, 93, 127, 136, 152, 154, 158-159, 161, 164, 179-181, 183, 194-197, 204, 210, 212
formula(s), -ic, 39, 48, 69, 87, 93, 106, 111-112, 118, 132, 141, 146-147, 158-159, 161, 196, 203, 206, 214
—of divine self-disclosure, 120-122, 148
—of divine word, 108-109, 113, 115
—messenger formula, 115-116, 119, 123, 147, 191, 205, 207
—of revelation, 77, 82-83, 132, 202
—of self-quotation, 69, 71, 73, 200
forsake, 132-134, 150

Gattung, -en, 19-20, 66, 85, 91, 95, 127-128, 133, 152, 157, 181, 192, 194-197, 200, 206
generic, -ally, -genre(s), 10, 15, 18-21, 24, 73, 79, 133, 144-145, 155, 164, 168-169, 180-181, 183, 197, 206, 210
Gestalt, 173-174
Gideon, 20
grace, gracious, 78, 84, 136
gratitude, 136, 211
grief, grieves, grieving, 45-49, 52, 54-56, 69-71, 84, 96-97, 102, 108, 111-113, 118, 120, 123, 125, 168, 170, 194-195, 197, 199

Hananiah, 48
heal, -er, -ing, 38, 66, 98, 100, 104, 107-108, 111, 133-138, 143, 151, 168
heart(s), 9, 12, 14, 25-34, 37, 42-45, 47-57, 64, 69, 74, 90, 100, 108, 144-145, 148-150, 163-164, 167-168, 173, 183, 185, 187, 205
hermeneutic(s), -al, -ally, 11-13, 133, 151-152, 163, 165, 171, 174, 187, 200
historical, historicism, history, 8-24, 26, 29-30, 40, 77, 79, 93, 156-157, 164-167, 180-182, 184, 190-191, 193, 196, 204, 207, 214
historical-critical/criticism, 8, 35, 37, 47, 73, 127, 129, 131, 188, 190

Index of Subjects

historical Jeremiah (also Jeremiah of history), 8-9, 11, 13, 57, 79, 127-128, 152, 165, 193, 196
Hosea, 11, 176, 209
hypocrisy, hypocritical, 74, 89-90, 100-101, 110

I, 7-8, 18, 23-24, 58-59, 62, 72-73, 75, 79-80, 95-97, 113, 117-118, 125, 127, 132-133, 138, 143, 145, 153, 183-185, 187, 193, 200
identification, identifies, identify, 46, 48, 51, 58-59, 69, 72-73, 100-102, 110, 117, 125, 128, 133, 153, 160, 168, 170, 179, 182, 193
identity, 13-14, 16, 20-22, 26, 38, 40, 46-47, 49, 52, 56-57, 62-73, 86-87, 101, 108-109, 113, 117, 124-125, 166, 179, 190
imagination, imaginative, 10, 28-29, 166-167, 171-173, 215
imitate, imitation, imitative (see also example, model, paradigm), 129, 143, 151-152, 156, 160-161, 171, 174, 196
indignation, 56
individual(s), -ism, ity, -ize, individuate, 7, 11-13, 20, 22, 26-27, 39, 58-59, 64, 66-67, 73-74, 80, 86-88, 91, 97, 100, 134, 140, 159, 168-169, 176, 179, 184, 194, 211
individual complaint/lament, 61, 65-66, 79, 86, 88, 127-128, 131-133, 135, 139, 145, 152, 155, 184, 206
innocence, innocent, -ly (see also righteous), 130, 132, 137, 141, 150, 153, 213
intend, intent, -ion, ional, -ionality, 8, 10, 15-18, 26, 33, 38, 57, 77, 118, 151, 157, 160, 164-165, 169, 171, 174, 177, 179, 190, 193
intercession, intercessor, -y, 46, 49, 75-77, 79-83, 87-92, 95, 100-102, 107-108, 119, 125, 133, 135, 138, 168, 193, 195-196, 200, 202
intermediary, intermediaries, intermediation, 46, 94, 193, 206
invective, 89, 96, 207
invocation, 86, 132-134, 150, 152
ironic, -ally, irony, 69-70, 74, 85-87, 89, 99, 104, 147, 154-155, 161, 192

Jacob, 81
Jehoiakim, 161
Joshua, 20
joy, -ful, 71, 133, 137, 167-168, 170, 184
judgment (see also doom), 45-47, 49, 66, 74, 76-77, 84, 87, 90-91, 93-94, 96-97, 100-102, 106, 108, 110, 113, 117-118, 120-121, 124, 130, 134, 137-144, 147, 150-151, 153-154, 162, 164, 168, 171, 193, 197, 199-200, 204, 208, 211, 213
justice, 37, 121, 148, 213

kerygma, 129, 143, 150-151, 209
know(s), -est, -ing, (God), knowledge (of God), 52, 55-56, 72, 90, 94, 103, 107, 113, 115, 120, 122-124, 137, 141, 144, 148-149, 156, 176, 183, 203, 212-213

lament, -ation (see also individual complaint/lament), 45-47, 49, 51-56, 61-62, 65-66, 69-70, 76, 78-79, 83-84, 88, 95-97, 100, 108,, 116-119, 125, 127-128, 131-136, 138-139, 145, 148, 152-153, 155-158, 161, 164-165, 192-196, 198, 201, 206, 208-210, 212
language game(s), 18, 32, 37, 39, 45, 47, 53-56, 64, 164, 184-188, 196-197
literal, 29-31, 34, 42, 49, 65, 68, 83, 106, 183, 186-187, 199, 202
literalizing, 27, 31-32, 186-187
liturgical, liturgy, 62, 77-80, 83, 88-89, 95-96, 184, 197-198, 201-202
love (see also compassion), 9, 41, 84, 121, 192

Manasseh, 101
meaning(s), -ful, -fulness, 9, 11, 13-18, 29-30, 39-40, 43, 52-53, 80, 83-84, 90, 124, 128, 130, 159, 162-165, 172-174, 176-179, 184, 186-187, 194, 196, 199-200
mediate, mediation, mediator, 47, 166
merciful, mercy, 38, 54, 84
messenger formula, See formula
metaphor(s), -ical, -ically, 16-17, 25-31, 34, 37, 41-45, 47, 49-50, 52, 54, 56-58, 62, 64-65, 67-68, 74, 108, 114, 120, 143, 151, 160, 162-164, 166-167, 170-171, 174, 176, 183, 185-186, 199, 202, 213-214
mockery, 55, 138, 153, 157, 213
model, -ing (see also example, imitate, paradigm), 20, 124, 129, 150-151, 156, 160-161, 171, 174, 185, 196
Moses, Mosaic, 20, 76-77, 81, 100-101, 196, 202-203
mourn, -ing, 84, 109, 194-195

norm(s), -ative, -atively, 15, 22, 39, 84-85, 87-90, 92, 95, 99, 125, 133-134, 147, 168, 171-172, 178, 195, 203, 208, 211

oath, 39-40, 191
obedience, obedient, -ial, -ly, 40, 44, 74-75, 90, 100, 104, 123-124, 129, 133, 140-141, 147-151, 156, 160-161, 170, 172, 174, 203-204, 206 (*Gehorsam*), 213
office (prophetic), 20-21, 47, 49, 75, 78, 91, 97, 181, 192, 195, 199, 202
oppression, oppressive, oppressor(s), 61, 130, 132, 151, 153-155

P (Priestly writers), 68, 86, 203
pain(s), -ed, -ful, 32-34, 53, 56, 67, 138, 184
paradigm(s), -atic, -atically (see also example, imitiate, model), 55, 77-78, 86, 88, 102-103, 122, 124-125, 127-128, 135-137, 140, 143, 146, 151-152, 154, 166, 169, 170-174, 185, 197, 210, 213, 215
particularity, particular, -ize, -izing, 20-21, 24, 32, 131, 134-135, 137, 141, 143-144, 147, 150, 152-153, 156, 182
Pashhur, 157-158, 160, 164-165

Index of Subjects

pathos, 38, 52, 56, 62, 70, 77, 96, 102, 117, 120, 151, 161, 171, 193-194, 197, 214
Paul, 169
peace, 48, 92, 94, 98, 104, 106-108, 116, 193
performative, 136, 147, 167, 179
perplexed, perplexity, 47-49, 92, 10o, 121, 124, 196-197, 200
persecute, persecuting, persecution, persecutors, 90, 134, 141-143, 150, 154-157, 160, 166, 168, 209
person, -al, -alism, -ally, -hood, 7-8, 12-13, 18-22, 27, 37-38, 44, 48, 51, 58, 62-63, 65-66, 69, 71-72, 74-75, 78-82, 90, 95, 97, 108, 125, 127-128, 130, 138-140, 142-143, 150, 154, 156-158, 160, 167, 179, 190, 194-195, 201, 209, 213-214
persona(e), 10, 13, 15, 24, 47, 57, 59, 69-70, 72-74, 80, 88, 102, 107, 112-113, 117-118, 122, 124-125, 128-129, 131, 138, 143-144, 151-152, 154-160, 164, 167-170, 173, 190, 193, 196, 199, 210
personification, personify, 60-61, 63-64, 66-69, 73-74, 199
perspective(s) (see also point of view), 70, 72-73, 83, 107-113, 116, 173, 200
petition, -ary, -er (see also request), 70, 85, 87, 90, 99-100, 142, 152, 156, 208
physical, -ly, 28-34, 37, 42-44, 47, 50, 55-56, 65, 164, 187, 189
physiological, -ly, physiologist, physiology, 28, 30-32, 34, 44, 53, 164
piety, 11, 13, 129, 143, 150-151, 160, 209
point of view (see also perspective), 18, 109-110, 200
portrait, portray(s), -al, -ed, -ing (see also characterization, depiction, description), 8-10, 21, 58, 122, 128, 169-170, 176, 208-209
praise, 63, 129, 133, 135-137, 146, 150, 152, 156, 160, 163-164, 167, 170, 211
pray(s), -ed, -er, -ing, 48, 70, 72, 74-76, 81, 83-92, 95-96, 98-101, 121, 123-125, 132-133, 135-137, 143, 156, 167-169, 173, 203, 208, 211
proclaim(s) (prophetically), -ed, proclamation, proclamatory, 83, 129, 134, 139-141, 150-151, 153, 156, 158-159, 164, 206, (*Verkündigung*), 208-210, 213
prohibit, -ion(s), 76-77, 87, 91, 100-101, 203
promise, promissory, 37, 40-42, 78, 86, 91-92, 99, 101-102, 142, 147-148, 151, 158, 161-162, 168, 170, 203, 214
protest, -ed, 12, 48-49, 141, 153, 156, 160, 212
psyche, psychic, -al, psycho-, -logical, -logically, -logy, 11, 25, 27-31, 44, 95, 128-129, 151, 155, 159, 178
psychologizing, 90, 129

Qoheleth, 73

Rachel, 68
read, -er, -ing, 8, 15-18, 35, 37, 41-42, 44, 50-51, 63-64, 70, 72-73, 76, 78, 82-83, 93, 95-96, 113, 115-116, 118, 124-125, 128-130, 144, 147-149, 151-152, 157-160, 163, 165, 167, 171-174, 177-178, 182, 187, 191-193, 195-196, 201, 208, 215

rebelled, rebellion, rebellious, 44, 51-52, 54, 78
redaction, -al, redactors, 11, 57, 60, 79, 82-83, 93, 96, 128-130, 152, 157, 165, 190-191, 204, 209, 212
redaction criticism, 35
refer, -ence, -ential, -entiality, 8, 11, 13, 15, 29, 32-33, 46, 50-51, 55-56, 63, 74, 93, 95, 125, 128, 157, 164-165, 178, 184-185, 187, 191, 193-194, 196, 206
refuge, 141, 143, 146, 155, 163
religion, religious, 9-13, 16, 37, 75-76, 84, 88, 97, 129, 166-168, 171-172, 176, 182, 185, 189, 215
remorse, -ful, 104, 107
repent, -ance, -ed, 7, 37, 70-71, 75, 78, 85, 104, 167, 189-190, 199
represent(s), -ative, -ing, 26, 62, 75, 78-81, 88, 92, 95, 97, 102, 113, 125, 143, 169, 201-202, 209, 213
reproach(es), 55, 75, 85-86, 98-99, 109, 111, 138, 141, 153, 155-156, 163-164, 170
request(s) (see also petition), 74-76, 84-85, 91, 99, 131-137, 142-143, 155, 193, 210
rhetoric, -al, -ally, 50-51, 58-59, 85, 96, 104, 108-109, 111, 140, 156, 163, 183, 186, 197, 205, 212
rhetorical criticism/analysis, 35-36, 58, 188
righteous, -ly, -ness (see also innocence), 37, 41, 75, 121, 128, 139-140, 143, 145, 148, 150, 153, 158, 160, 191-192, 209

salvation, 48, 76-78, 85-86, 89, 91, 101-102, 109, 121, 135, 137, 139, 171, 199, 211
Samson, 26
Samuel, 20, 81, 100-101, 196, 202
sarcasm, sarcastic, -ally, 105-107, 199
Saul, 81
science, scientific, 27-29, 171, 185, 215
scorn, -ed, -ing, 43, 55, 141, 150
scripture, 8, 10, 58, 77, 129, 163, 167, 172, 174, 177-178, 209
self, -hood, selves, 8, 18-22, 24-27, 34, 37-44, 46-50, 52, 56-58, 70, 74, 80-82, 85, 89, 97, 101, 108, 123, 127, 147-149, 152, 156, 168-169, 173-174, 179, 182, 184, 196-197, 206, 208-209
self-constituting/constitution, 22, 24, 44, 48-49, 56-57, 69, 73, 75, 78-79, 86, 88, 108, 117, 123-125, 136, 156, 163, 167-168, 170, 208
self curse, 152, 158-160, 162, 164
self involvement/involving, 81, 92, 100, 125, 136, 174, 179
self-disclosure, see formula,
self-quotation, see formula,
self-referential, 26
shame (also ashamed), 39, 46, 119, 132-134, 141, 144, 155, 158-160, 213

Index of Subjects

sign, 42, 80, 88
Sitz-im-Leben, 62, 83, 138, 158, 193, 198, 202
Sitz-im-Text/Buch, 158, 193
sorrow (see also anguish, grief, sadness), 158-160, 167, 170, 195, 205
stereotype, see type
stubborn, -ly, 44, 74
suffer(s), -er, -ing, 32, 55, 61, 65, 78, 97, 102, 109-110, 119-121, 129-130, 132, 136, 142-143, 145, 150, 153-154, 158, 160, 162, 170, 173, 199, 209-210, 212-213
superscription, 73, 82
symbol(s), -ic, -ically, -ize, 68, 80-81, 130, 151, 156, 161, 186-187, 208-209
sympathetic, sympathy, 47, 56, 58, 75, 97, 110, 112, 160
synchronic, -ally, synchrony, 14-16, 18, 20, 23, 25, 35, 40-41, 60, 129, 131, 138, 144, 164-165, 176, 190, 193, 196, 201, 208, 213
synecdoche, 27, 31, 67-68, 185

tears, 11, 94-96, 112-113, 118-119, 195
teleological, teleology, telos, 38-40, 43, 45, 49, 191
terror, 141, 155, 157
thanksgiving, 69, 71, 131, 138
tradent(s), tradition, -al, 7, 19, 68, 75, 87-88, 93, 118, 128, 131, 179-180, 190, 193, 196, 200 203-204, 207, 209
true, truth(s), truth-telling, 10, 12, 23, 28, 43, 49, 114, 122, 124, 139, 166, 172, 174, 178, 207, 215
trust, -ing, 9, 86, 129, 132-134, 145-148, 150-152, 155-156, 161, 170, 212
type, typify, typical, -ity, stereo-, 20, 24, 26, 79-82, 88, 95, 125, 131-132, 134, 137, 140, 143-145, 150-153, 156-158, 168, 170, 182, 194-195

vehicle (-tenor), 29-30, 186
vengeance, vengful, 74, 142, 151, 210
vocation (prophetic), 12-13, 22, 69, 127, 133, 169, 209
voice(s), 37, 52, 58-60, 62, 68-69, 71-75, 106-114, 116, 118-119, 125, 133, 166, 190, 204-205
vow, 131, 136

wail, -ing, 45, 61, 117, 119
weep(s), -ing, 68, 71, 113, 117-119, 194-195
wise, wisdom, 75, 103-108, 118-120, 112-124, 131, 144-150, 164, 170, 204, 212
woe, 59, 62, 64, 71, 73-74
wound, 59, 61-62, 65-66, 73, 100, 109, 111

Zedekiah, 161-162

LIBRARY OF DAVID